Bullets Not Ballots

A VOLUME IN THE SERIES

Cornell Studies in Security Affairs

Edited by Robert J. Art, Robert Jervis, and Stephen M. Walt

A list of titles in this series is available at cornellpress.cornell.edu.

Bullets Not Ballots

Success in Counterinsurgency Warfare

JACQUELINE L. HAZELTON

Cornell University Press

Ithaca and London

First published 2021 by Cornell University Press

Printed in the United States of America

Library of Congress Cataloging-in-Publication Data
Names: Hazelton, Jacqueline L., author.
Title: Bullets not ballots : success in counterinsurgency warfare / Jacqueline L. Hazelton.
Description: Ithaca, [New York] : Cornell University Press, 2021. | Series: Cornell studies in security affairs | Includes bibliographical references and index.
Identifiers: LCCN 2020029368 (print) | LCCN 2020029369 (ebook) | ISBN 9781501754784 (hardcover) | ISBN 9781501754791 (epub) | ISBN 9781501754807 (pdf)
Subjects: LCSH: Counterinsurgency. | Government, Resistance to.
Classification: LCC U241 .H39 2021 (print) | LCC U241 (ebook) | DDC 355.02/18—dc23
LC record available at https://lccn.loc.gov/2020029368
LC ebook record available at https://lccn.loc.gov/2020029369

For my family

There is nothing more difficult to take in hand, more perilous to conduct, or more uncertain in its success, than to take the lead in the introduction of a new order of things. Because the innovator has for enemies all those who have done well under the old conditions, and lukewarm defenders in those who may do well under the new.

—Niccolo Machiavelli, *The Prince*

Contents

Acknowledgments

Every work of scholarship is a collective enterprise. I am fortunate to have had the support of several communities in writing this book. Above all, I have to thank Robert Art as my adviser, mentor, and guide to the world of international relations. It is a pleasure and a privilege to serve as his apprentice. He very properly recused himself from this project. Along with Bob, Steven Burg provided wise advice and support through his comparativist's eye as this project took shape. I thank Robert Pape for sending me to work with Bob Art; this was a great gift. Bob Pape tutored me in the ways of academia when I was an MA student who had never studied political science but brought a journalist's experience and keen mind to the problems of compellence, terrorism, and Islamic political thought. Other members of my community at the University of Chicago, the Massachusetts Institute of Technology, and the Harvard Kennedy School have also been unfailingly supportive and generous. This community includes Steven Miller and Stephen Walt of the International Security Program at the Belfer Center, my scholarly home for two idyllic years; Barry Posen, who introduced me to Dhofar; and John Mearsheimer and Charles Glaser. I appreciate the welcome I have received at workshops held by the International Security Program at the Kennedy School, the Security Studies Program at MIT, and the Program on International Security Policy at Chicago. They are where I learned my trade.

I appreciate the unfailing interest and generosity of the community of scholars of insurgency and counterinsurgency and practitioners of counterinsurgency who seek theoretically and empirically sound answers to important policy questions, including Dale Andrade, Huw Bennett, Stephen Biddle, Andrew Birtle, Nick Carter, Joe Collins, Conrad Crane, Greg Daddis, William Fallon, Brendan Green, Karl Hack (whose exclamation that the standard story about the Malayan Emergency is just not true heartened me in my exploration of what counterinsurgency involves in real life), Tim Hoyt, Colin Jackson, Chaim Kaufmann, Jen Keister, Austin Long, Michael Parkyn, David Petraeus, Daryl Press, Joshua Rovner, David Strachan-Morris, Christian Tripodi, Benjamin Valentino, the late Vol Warner, Bob Wilson, Isaac Wilson, and Toshi Yoshihara.

Others who read all or part of this manuscript in a rough or abbreviated form, early or late or both, and helped me strengthen it include Fiona Adamson, Alex Downes, Roger Haydon, Jeremy Pressman, Steve Simon, the Cornell series editor responsible for shepherding it through the process, and the anonymous reviewer. I am particularly grateful to Richard Betts, Michael Desch, David Edelstein, Sean Lynn-Jones, Steve Miller, Ken Oye, Roger Petersen, Josh Rovner, and William Wohlforth for reading a full, if rough, draft and spending a day talking about it. I appreciate greatly the support of the International Security Program in this endeavor.

For endless moral and professional support, I can never sufficiently thank guides, philosophers, and friends Teresa Cravo, Susan Lynch, Emily Meierding, and Karthika Sasikumar. Others whose support has kept me going include Deborah Avant, Jon DiCicco, Janina Dill, Rebekka Friedman, Frank Gavin, Anne Harrington, Ron Hassner, the late Joyce Heckman, Helen Kinsella, Nuno Monteiro, Karen Motley, Dipali Mukhopadhyay, the late Aaron Rapport, Norrin Ripsman, Andy Ross, Paul and Alison Schulte (who kindly and repeatedly hosted an iterant scholar in Kilburnistan), Monica Toft, and Leslie Vinjamuri. Ana Steffan showed me the power of thinking like a social scientist. Bob Reid generously provided the cover image. Josh Busby suggested the title. Thank you to *International Security* for allowing me to draw on my article, "The 'Hearts and Minds' Fallacy: Violence, Coercion, and Success in Counterinsurgency Warfare."

On Dhofar specifically, for their help and hospitality, I thank the fellows, students, and staff at the Middle East Centre at St. Antony's, Oxford; Lawrence Freedman; Charles Guthrie; J. E. Peterson; Abdel Razzak Takriti; and especially the members of the Sultan's Armed Forces, the British Army, and others who worked in Dhofar who have spoken and corresponded with me with great generosity and hospitality, including Donal Douglas, Ian Gordon, Peter Isaacs, Tony Jeapes, Nigel Knocker, Ken Perkins, and Martin Robb.

On El Salvador, I thank Dale Andrade, Andrew Bacevich, John Clearwater and Lisa Moore at Fort Bragg, Sarah Zukerman Daly, James Hallums, Peter Kornbluh, Rodrigo Javier Massi, Benjamin Schwarz, Kalev Sepp, Jocelyn Viterna, Timothy Wickham-Crowley, and most of all those who shared with me their experiences in and thoughts on El Salvador, including Cecil Bailey, Ari Bogaard, Charles Briscoe, Alvaro Antonio Calderón Hurtado, Charles Clements, Jeffrey Cole, Edwin Corr, Commandante Ernesto (the nom de guerre of a Salvadoran insurgent leader), John Fishel, Todd Greentree, Mark Hamilton, Kevin Higgins, Max Manwaring, Bob Nealson, Francisco

Pedrozo, Gilberto Perez, the late Rene Emilio Ponce, Henry Ramirez, Leamon Ratterree, Ranger Roach, Luis Orlando Rodriguez, Hy Rothstein, Nina Serafino, Simeon Trombitas, and Mauricio Vargas.

I am most appreciative of support from Brandeis University and its politics department, the Mellon Foundation, the U.S. Army Center of Military History for a Ridgway Research Grant, and the Naval War College Foundation.

Archivists and librarians are fundamental to scholarly work, and I cannot love them enough. Thanks to the archivists at the Imperial War Museum, London, including Simon Innes-Robbins and Paul Cornish for his amazing tour of Dhofar-type small arms in the bowels of the former Bedlam; the Liddell Hart Centre for Military Archives at Kings College London and Cathy Williams; the UK National Archives; the Oman Archive at St. Antony's College, Oxford, and archivist Deborah Usher; the Tameside Local Studies and Archives Centre, Ashton-under-Lyne, Lancashire, and Adam Allen; the U.S. Army Center of Military History, Carlisle, Pennsylvania, including Pam Cheney, Con Crane, Randall Rakers, and Richard Sommer; the National Security Archive, Washington, DC, and Mary Curry; the Bodleian Library, Oxford, and senior archivist Lucy McCann; the U.S. National Archives and Elizabeth Gray; and the librarians at Brandeis, Harvard, Rochester, and the Naval War College, particularly the staff at Newport, including Heidi Garcia, Robin Lima, and Jack Miranda.

Finally, my family raised me to question assumptions and challenge easy answers. It is not always comfortable to do so, for me or anyone in my vicinity, but they set me on the path to living an examined life. I am forever grateful. I could not have done any of it without them and without the comforting companionship of my cats.

All views are my own, not those of any government entity, as are all errors.

Bullets Not Ballots

Counterinsurgency

Eating Soup with a Chainsaw

The United States and its partners destroyed the political order in Afghanistan in 2001 and in Iraq in 2003.[1] They have been trying ever since to create a new political order, one that is more just and thus more stable. The Western military term for what they have been trying to achieve is *success in counterinsurgency*: defeating armed, organized, persistent political challengers to the government. At the time of writing, they have achieved success in neither theater, while political violence and disorder have spread in the region and beyond, making the question motivating this book more relevant than ever to foreign and military policy in Western liberal states.

What explains success in counterinsurgency? I argue that government success against an insurgency is a nonviolent and violent competition among elites that leads to political stability after a single armed actor—the counterinsurgent government—gains dominance over the others within its territory. Fighting insurgents is important in this process. Ruthlessly controlling civilians and taking other measures to prevent the flow of food and other resources to insurgents is also important. Both are made possible by the government's accommodation of domestic elites who provide cooperation, information, and fighting power. One might think of successful counterinsurgency as alliance building among elites within the state for the purpose of reducing the insurgent military threat to little more than an annoyance.

I define success according to the *U.S. Government Counterinsurgency Guide* as the "marginalization of the insurgents to the point at which they are destroyed, co-opted, or reduced to irrelevance in numbers and capability."[2] The guide is intended for the United States, but this definition is reasonable for democratic great powers generally because it recognizes that a small number of insurgents may remain active while unlikely to seriously threaten the counterinsurgent government. The core of this definition is that the counterinsurgent government remains in power.

1

What succeeds in counterinsurgency is uglier, costlier in lives, more remote from moral and ethical considerations, and far less ambitious than what the United States and its partners are attempting in trying to build and reform the political systems in so-called weak states and ungoverned spaces today. Both the accommodation and the violence are necessary for success. Neither is sufficient. The use of compellence (the use or threat of force to change an actor's behavior) and brute force (the power to take and to hold) *together* break the challenger's ability and will to fight.[3]

Successful counterinsurgency is not, contra the conventional wisdom, a process of building a centralized, modern, liberal, democratic state; providing political, economic, and social reforms intended to support such an effort; and providing public goods to the people to gain their support for the government. It is not a competition to govern with the people as the prize. Counterinsurgency is competition for power among armed groups. Successful counterinsurgency is one armed group coming to dominate the rest.

Explaining counterinsurgent success matters because of the dilemma that democratic great powers face when they back a threatened client government in an internal conflict, intervening militarily because they believe that client survival is an important security interest of their own. These powerful states can find themselves paying what can become exceptionally high costs in struggling to defeat a weaker adversary by what are intended to be moral means. The United States has struggled in Iraq and Afghanistan to restore stable governance after shattering the existing political order with a military invasion. The U.S. costs of the so-called Global War on Terror are at $6 trillion and counting, though the adversaries are fragmented, factionalized groups with relatively little financial and military power and even less political appeal to local and global audiences.[4] Similarly, the United States struggled for twelve years and spent more than $4 billion to help the Salvadoran government succeed against the Farabundo Marti National Liberation Front and yet failed to defeat it militarily. It took Great Britain twelve years to defeat the small, isolated, and unpopular Malayan National Liberation Army. The French colonial state fell to Viet Minh insurgents in Indochina despite massive U.S. aid.

Questions about counterinsurgency success are not hypothetical or "academic" questions in the popular sense of the term. These are questions of immediate moment to U.S. and partner governments, their militaries and families, and millions of civilians experiencing the costs of internal conflict every day. These are pressing questions as the states of Europe and the United States grapple with the political effects of receiving refugees from war-splintered states. This book is not a prescription for counterinsurgent success. I do not advocate implementation of my findings. This book is an analysis of government choices with powerful implications for the decisions of great powers considering military intervention to back a threatened client government and considering continuing such interventions. It presents a theory explaining and predicting counterinsurgency success. It is not a plan for action.

Liberal Great Power Military Intervention

My research here focuses on counterinsurgency as a form of liberal great power military intervention with relevance to contemporary Western policy debates and also to better understand how the use of force may—or may not—help threatened governments attain their political objectives. I analyze how Western great powers attempt to create greater security within other states by using and supporting uses of force to shape the political landscape, and under what conditions they achieve their goal. In short, this book is about great power efforts to create greater order through the use of organized violence.

Understanding the processes and outcomes of counterinsurgency matters in scholarly terms because my theory of counterinsurgent success extends our understanding of the functions of force. It identifies a political process involving targeted political concessions among elites, compellence, and brute force that attains the core political goal of survival for the challenged government, if not the more ambitious goals of its liberal great power backer. My theory also contributes to our scholarly understanding of violence because it sheds light on the functions of force in internal conflict. Much excellent research on the uses of force within international relations focuses on the uses of force between states, logically enough as the subdiscipline's focus is interstate relations. My findings increase our understanding of the role of brute force and compellence in internal conflict involving a domestic ruler, a domestic armed challenger, and an intervener.

This book develops a new dimension in the study of counterinsurgency by examining the counterinsurgent's choices and the political outcomes of those choices rather than focusing on patron demands or client promises. It relies on comparative historical case studies to investigate the conduct of these counterinsurgency campaigns, deepening our historiographic understanding of the cases and systematizing what has often been a less than rigorous subject for study. It intervenes in the debate over whether politics or warfighting matters more in counterinsurgency success by tracing the political effects of counterinsurgent uses of force rather than assuming their outcomes.

I examine a specific type of military intervention into internal conflict: when a great power backs a client government facing an insurgency, an armed, organized, persistent, internal political challenge. Great power military intervention is not uncommon. Military intervention may include diplomatic support, weapons sales, military training and advising, and even provision of fighting forces, although this is less common because more costly to the intervening state. Democratic states may intervene to support a threatened government, as the United States has done in Nigeria and Somalia in the post-9/11 era, or to back a challenge to a government, as with the Contras in Nicaragua in the 1980s. It may include regime change, as with the U.S. campaigns in Grenada in 1983 and Panama in 1989. It may focus on peacekeeping, as with the U.S. effort in Lebanon in 1982–1984, or morph from a humanitarian operation into a manhunt, as in Somalia in 1993. Other examples include the British military action to retain the Falkland Islands against Argentine incursions in 1982; its military support for the threatened government of Sierra Leone in 2000; post–World War II Western efforts to support threatened governments in Indonesia, Greece, and Malaya; and current French operations in Mali in support of the government against various rebel groups. Frequently the great power's stake in these conflicts— "small wars" only to those outside the target state—are low, though they may see intervention as necessary to protect their own security.

Military intervention is a broad category; nondemocratic great powers also conduct such campaigns. Often it is studied in isolation to gain understanding of a particular type of intervention, as with work on peacekeeping operations. There is scope for further investigation of military intervention as a larger phenomenon with policy implications in multipolar and unipolar worlds. During the Cold War, amid proxy wars between the United States and the Soviet Union in peripheral areas around the world, international relations scholars argued over whether bipolarity was more secure or more destabilizing as small states had little choice but to align with one or the other superpower.[5] In the current unipolar environment, U.S. military intervention is largely unconstrained, meaning intervention is possible at potentially lower cost for intervening great powers, if not in costs paid by the small states they involve themselves in.[6] Should the international system again become multipolar, rising powers might push back further against democratic great power involvement in their spheres of influence, as Russia and China have begun to do, or they could welcome great power policing efforts as a cost-saving measure supporting their own security needs, as a number of smaller states already have in the Global War on Terror.

Costly Success

Counterinsurgency success is the outcome of a violent process of state building in which elites contest for power, popular interests matter little, and the government benefits politically from uses of force against civilians as well as insurgents. My theory of counterinsurgency success, which I call the compellence theory, differs in two important ways from the conventional wisdom, which I call good governance counterinsurgency for its focus on developing liberal democratic states.[7] First, my theory identifies armed and unarmed elites as the key actors in counterinsurgency, rather than the populace or the great power intervener, along with the need to accommodate the few rather than provide benefits for all. The need for coalition building as part of the state-building process is not a new political insight, but it is not one that has previously been highlighted in the counterinsurgency debate. Second, the compellence theory identifies the government's use of force against civilians as well as insurgents as an important factor in counterinsurgency success rather than a choice likely to damage or doom the government's chance of success.

Counterinsurgency success requires neither good governance reforms that redistribute power and wealth among all citizens nor popular support for the state. Rather, success of a counterinsurgent has three requirements. The first is the government's relatively low-cost accommodation of elite domestic rivals—that is, political actors such as warlords and other armed actors, regional or cultural leaders, and traditional rulers—to gain fighting power and information about the insurgency. The second requirement is the application of brute force to reduce the flow of resources to the insurgency, often but not always and certainly not only by controlling civilian behavior with brute force. The third requirement is the direct application of force to break the insurgency's will and capability to fight on. These three elements represent a phased process in which the counterinsurgent government builds its strength and, as it does so, exerts its capabilities to directly and indirectly weaken the insurgency and remove the threat it poses to government survival.

These findings show that counterinsurgency success as the first step in establishing a relatively stable political order has moral and human costs.[8] These findings also pose an important corrective to assumptions about the positive value of U.S. intervention in support of a counterinsurgent partner. My argument suggests that U.S. efforts to reduce violence in internal conflicts by introducing political reforms are unlikely to flourish, and that such efforts will continue to raise human, moral, and financial costs for the United States, as well as within its partners' borders.

Why It Matters

My findings suggest the need for radical reconsideration of democratic great power intervention policies and efforts, current and future. If the intervention goal is humanitarian, then the great power's interest should be in ending the violence as quickly as possible. If the intervention goal is to retain the government in power, then the great power's focus should be on achieving that goal at the lowest possible cost in human and other resources, rather than a drawn-out effort to induce good governance reforms with the unwarranted assumption that these efforts will flourish and that counterinsurgency success will follow.

It is unlikely that the future will bring successful efforts to use good governance to succeed in counterinsurgency. Governments willing and able to make good governance reforms do so. Those that resist reforms continue to resist, and for logical reasons.[9] Making governance more equitable and just, serving popular interests, institutionalizing and bureaucratizing the state, instituting free and fair elections, liberalizing the media, instituting the rule of law—these are all reforms that directly or indirectly reduce the power and wealth of government-aligned elites. Corrupt, repressive governments persist because corruption and repression serve the interests of those in power. They are not a function of ignorance or error. Any great power interested in forcing a client into making reforms needs leverage. Great powers that commit themselves to client survival, however, yield significant leverage over their client, leaving them with little power to impose reforms.[10] Even when U.S. forces ruled directly in Japan, Germany, Iraq, and Afghanistan, they were forced to accommodate the interests of elites within the occupied state.[11]

The scholarly and policy worlds have seen, see, and will see real-world experiments testing my theory. I expect that further Western efforts to press clients to institute what are expected to be insurgent-defeating reforms will not attain that goal and that counterinsurgency success is likely to continue to require the mistreatment of civilians, the deprivation of their human rights, and bloody-handed governments' bargaining with warlords, killers, and other corrupt political players. Insurgents may be the bad guys, but it is also the bad guys who succeed in counterinsurgency. There are no good guys in this armed elite competition to rule. State building is a nasty business.

"The bad guys win" is not the answer that U.S. forces, policymakers, or civilians want to hear about counterinsurgency success, but the historical record is clear. The problem of insurgency challenging Western democratic states' interests from afar is not a problem with an easy or a normatively palatable solution. Western great powers are, nonetheless, likely to embroil themselves in internal conflicts as long as great power policymakers continue to believe that another state's type of government affects their own state's security. A world of democracies is quite arguably a better world for all, but it is not one that democratic powers can attain through military intervention.

All the successful cases I examine here show surprisingly limited democratizing reforms, a disappointing result but an unsurprising one given the likelihood that elites everywhere prefer to keep what they have rather than to share it. The limits of reform efforts by the counterinsurgent's great power backer are all the more evident given policymaker emphasis on major, systemic political changes within target states. These efforts highlight an underappreciated fact in military intervention and foreign policy: great power control over events and other actors' choices is limited. The counterinsurgent government itself, fighting for survival, is the central actor on the state side.

Outline of the Book

In the next chapter, I analyze the existing literature on counterinsurgency and other approaches to internal conflict to build a foundation for my theory of counterinsurgent success, and I lay out my theory. In the chapters that follow, I analyze six successful counterinsurgency campaigns to ask what the government did and when and where it did it, and what came of their choices. I do not rely on what the government said it would do. Asking what governments actually did in their successful campaigns identifies choices overlooked or downplayed in most work on counterinsurgency. To answer these questions, I examined contemporaneous documents in U.S. and British archives, memoirs, and oral histories. I also studied the secondary literature and interviewed participants in some conflicts.

I selected this set of six cases for the explanatory scope and external validity they provide. These campaigns are the British in Malaya from 1948 to 1957; the U.S.-backed counterinsurgency campaign in Greece from 1947 to 1949; the U.S.-backed campaign against the Huk in the Philippines from 1946 to 1954; the British-backed and British-led campaign in Dhofar, Oman, from 1965 to 1976; the U.S.-backed campaign in El Salvador from 1979 to 1992; and, finally, the U.S.-backed Turkish campaign against the Partiya Karkeren Kurdistan (Kurdistan Workers' Party, PKK) from 1984 to 1999. The first five are frequently claimed as examples of liberal good governance success. They should be difficult cases for my theory to explain. The sixth, Turkey, is widely recognized as one of the more brutal among recent campaigns. The similarities between the first five and the sixth are striking, demonstrating that the compellence theory explains more than just the cases I analyze.

Counterinsurgency

What It Is and Is Not

Today's Western policy prescription for insurgency is based on the good governance approach, which flows from the belief that the counterinsurgent government must do three things to succeed. It must provide political, economic, and social reforms that meet the needs of the population and gain its support; it must make sure that these reforms reduce the grievances fueling the insurgency in order to obtain information about the insurgency from civilians and, ideally, gain their support; and it must use force against the insurgency with great care to avoid civilian harm, again to gain popular support and thus information on the insurgency.

I call this the good governance approach to underscore its causal logic vis-à-vis the populace. *Good governance* typically means "economic growth, political representation, and efficient administration." In this view, good governance is necessary to defeat insurgency because it is bad governance that causes insurgency. Greater representative governance and more public goods will build broad popular support for the government, attract civilian cooperation against the insurgency, and marginalize the insurgents.[1] In a list of requirements to defeat an insurgency, leading counterinsurgents listed their first to-do item as "identify and redress the political, economic, military, and other issues fueling the insurgency."[2] More recently, a leading scholar of counterinsurgency has argued that success requires government reforms to address popular grievances.[3]

The U.S. Army/Marine Corps *Counterinsurgency Field Manual* exemplifies the good governance approach, drawing on sixty years of Western practitioner accounts of successful counterinsurgency campaigns. "Soldiers and Marines are expected to be nation builders as well as warriors," Gen. David Petraeus and Gen. James Amos write. "They must be prepared to help reestablish institutions and basic services. They must be able to facilitate establishing local governance and the rule of law." Successful counterinsurgency is "armed social work."[4] Separately, in a military journal, Gen. Peter Chiarelli and Maj. Patrick R. Michaelis explain the logic based on their experience in Iraq: "A gun on every street corner, although visually appealing, provides only a short-term solution and does not equate to long-term security grounded in a democratic process."[5] Governments must prevent harm to civilians because harm will only increase support for the insurgency. The field manual advises, "Only attack insurgents when they get in the way."[6] Petraeus told troops in Afghanistan, "If we kill civilians or damage their property . . . we will create more enemies than our operations eliminate."[7]

The Good Governance Approach

The good governance approach grows from modernization theory, which identifies insurgency as a problem created by incomplete modernization of government, political system, economic system, and society and the solution as state bureaucratization, economic development, and democratization to resolve popular grievances. Some recent social science research identifying economic, political, and security grievances as causes of internal conflict supports the primary assumption of the good governance approach.[8] There is a long-standing debate in the civil wars literature over whether insurgency is caused by greed or grievance—that is, whether the opportunity to mount an insurgency, such as the presence of funding resources, is a likelier cause of internal conflict or whether political grievances such as a high level of inequality are a likelier cause. The position advocating good governance logically flows from a belief that grievances cause insurgency.

Contemporary empirical investigations into counterinsurgency ask interesting questions and apply more rigor to answering them than many earlier practitioners and students of counterinsurgency have.[9] This work typically breaks down the question of what causes counterinsurgency success into components, often examining a tactic, such as the counterinsurgent's provision of an incentive to civilians in a small geographic area, or the political effects of counterinsurgent harm to civilians within a relatively narrow time frame and geographic space. It often focuses specifically on the role of benefits provision in reducing insurgent violence.[10] There is less consideration of politics more broadly, such as a possible role for nationalism or domestic elite competitive politics, or of the external validity of the findings. Much of this research is driven by the wealth of flawed data available from occupying forces in Iraq and Afghanistan. The use of these data and the implication that it is possible to draw broader conclusions based on these cases are troubling because these cases are outliers. They involved the long-term presence of tens of thousands of U.S. and other foreign troops. There is also no outcome in either case at the time of writing, meaning that conclusions about insurgent defeat and counterinsurgent success must hang in abeyance. Existing work investigating these facets of insurgency and counterinsurgency provides valuable assessment tools to consider in weighing the causes of insurgency and the likelihood of a specific outcome in any particular competition but does not try to answer my question: What causes counterinsurgency success?[11]

Recent work by several scholar-practitioners addresses success in counterinsurgency more broadly. Nadia Schadlow, Paul D. Miller, and the members of the Empirical Studies of Conflict project based at the University of California, San Diego, and at Princeton discuss interesting processes in counterinsurgency that reflect the governance model and its assumptions, while avoiding practical political problems at the heart of such military intervention efforts.

Schadlow writes that the U.S. military must continue to fill ungoverned spaces with "governance operations—those political and military activities undertaken by military forces to establish and institutionalize a desired political order during and following the combat phase of war." She argues that this process is a crucial effort to support U.S. interests and international security. Her prescription includes recognition that "governance tasks are not separate from 'conventional' war," and thus policymakers must recognize that both activities take place concurrently. She also urges unity of command; acceptance that the military rather than civilians conducts governance operations in war zones; recognition that uses of technology and force will not attain U.S. political objectives on their own; and, finally, that the United States must have and retain the capability to achieve "sustainable political outcomes in war."[12]

Schadlow makes strong points about gaps in the U.S. military conceptualization of counterinsurgency. Yet her argument is not a theory of counterinsurgency success but a normative prescription for successful U.S. military intervention in a variety of circumstances. While providing sensible suggestions for U.S. policymakers and military practitioners, Schadlow leaves aside questions about politics within the target state that might affect U.S. efforts and hinder U.S. political and military goals.

Miller argues that success in "armed liberal state building" requires matching the state-building strategy to the type of state failure that the liberal power intervenes to correct. He identifies five types of state failure: anarchic, illegitimate, incapable, unproductive, and barbaric. To resolve these identified problems of anarchy, illegitimacy, incapability, and so on, the intervening state must select an appropriate matching goal to attain within the target state. The possibilities include enforcing order, building institutions, spreading liberty, and winning converts. The intervening state must also decide what degree of control to exert within the target state: it must monitor and encourage reform efforts; it must take an active role in training and equipping civilians and security forces; and it must assume authority to directly administer the government.[13]

If much of this advice is commonsensical, as Miller notes, his book does not provide a theory of counterinsurgency success and does not intend to. His focus on liberal goals does provide further reason to consider what actual level of achievement of reforms appears across successful counterinsurgency cases. Like Schadlow, Miller does not address the nationalism problem within the targeted state, or reasons why leaders within the target state might resist U.S. efforts, and neither author explains how to change elite interests to align with those of the United States.

Eli Berman, Joseph Felter, and Jacob Shapiro explicitly note that they are not presenting the way to defeat insurgencies in *Small Wars, Big Data: The Information Revolution in Modern Conflict*. They do argue that their prescription for reducing violence in areas within a country experiencing military intervention into an internal conflict can potentially lead to overall success. Their theory focuses on the provision of information useful for targeting insurgents and insurgent sites. Governments provide services to civilians. Civilians who feel sufficiently safe in government-held areas or who yearn for the goods and services the government will provide if it controls their area will provide immediately useful tactical information on the insurgents to the counterinsurgent. The counterinsurgent will use their information to target the insurgents, their leaders, their supplies, and their activities. The question of how reducing violence in one area can lead to overall success in asymmetric conflict is one to which the authors return several times. They argue that "quelling violence locally can open up opportunities for larger political bargains that did not exist when the insurgency was strong." The assumption seems to be that the tactical effects of reducing violence in one area or another weakens the insurgency overall and, in the example they provide of Colombia, can shape public opinion in useful ways. The cases they examine include Afghanistan, Algeria, Colombia, India, Nigeria, Pakistan, the Philippines, and Vietnam: "That breadth should provide some confidence in the generalizability of the theory," they write.[14]

Berman, Felter, and Shapiro do not spell out how reducing violence locally adds up to campaign success. The authors also do not question the assumptions of the governance model, including the assumption that civilians want the provision of goods and services and those desires trump civilians' political goals, which may include regional, ethnic, cultural, class, religious, nationalistic, economic, and other interests and identities. The book focuses on the provision of tactical intelligence for immediate action, setting aside the problem of understanding the political interests of the actors involved in the conflict.[15] The authors argue that their process for local success—providing services in exchange for information on the insurgency, acting on that information, protecting civilians, and minimizing harm to civilians in targeting insurgents—can "win the village." They say that this "approach was implemented successfully in many parts of South Vietnam in the late 1960's and early 1970's, in most of Iraq from mid-2006 through 2009, and in many parts of Afghanistan in 2010–2012."[16] Those familiar with the history of the Vietnam War, the Iraq War, and the war in Afghanistan are unlikely to find this statement cheering.

The authors say the value of their work lies in enabling Western states to continue extended military interventions in which "the local ally lacks the capacity or the political will to fully extend governance over hostile territory" and when public support for the intervention is low within the intervening state. Their information approach can, they argue, "win the village using methods that domestic public opinion and the international community can support—and has done so repeatedly—albeit in wars whose strategic outcomes have been less than satisfactory (as of this writing)."[17]

Berman and coauthors, Miller, and Schadlow are important and influential voices in U.S. policy discussions of what liberal military intervention can achieve. Their ellipses and assumptions, their attention to points other than the political interests of the other actors in the conflict, and their interest in how to extend interventions in continued hope of success constrain policy debate on when, whether, where, and how Western great powers choose to intervene in internal conflicts. Their prescriptions raise human and moral costs by providing hope of success without evidence of success in achieving liberal political objectives.

The internal logic of the good governance approach is clear, but supporting research suffers from two main problems. First, it lacks theoretical rigor. This hinders consideration of which types of counterinsurgent behavior are more likely to contribute to success in which types of cases. Second, it is based on unexamined empirical assumptions. These assumptions make analysis difficult by drawing attention away from potentially important elements of counterinsurgency campaigns such as divergent political interests among the counterinsurgents. Additionally, critics note the deterministic or even teleological beliefs that theorists of modernization bring to their work, which is foundational to belief in good governance and to its flaws. Robert Packenham points out, for example, the liberal assumption that "all good things go together" when it comes to state, political, economic, and social development, including liberalization in all these spheres and the building of liberal institutions of state.[18] Further, research shows that the goal of democratizing a counterinsurgent state may in fact not attain the great power patron's goals. Democracies are not more likely than authoritarian states to have better outcomes in health and education, they are unlikely to experience less crony capitalism and clientism, and democracies are not necessarily more redistributive.[19]

There has been little research proposing or testing a theory of the good governance approach, including specification of the conditions under which the approach succeeds. Research that supports the approach generally does not delineate the domains in which best practices operate to best effect.[20] Researchers rarely engage in a systematic comparison of cases, and they pay little attention to external validity—one author generalizes his findings on defeating insurgency based on his experience as a military officer in two unusual campaigns.[21] Recent data-driven quantitative research asks specific questions about the potential costs of the government's use of force and effects of goods provision but rarely asks what causes counterinsurgency success, whether successful campaigns included an increase in popular support for the government, or whether governments gain useful effects from the exercise of organized violence.[22]

Moreover, much of the research that supports the governance approach makes potentially unwarranted empirical assumptions about the politics of these campaigns. An example is the widespread assumption that counterinsurgent governments deliver what they promise, which is also assumed to produce the expected positive effects on the populace and negative effects on the insurgency.[23] A related assumption concerns actors' interests and reforms, including that the counterinsurgent government has the capability and will to institute democratizing reforms; that the populace desires democratizing reforms; and the contradictory belief that the majority of the populace has no political preferences and will support the stronger side.[24] Similarly problematic is the assumption that the intervener has the ability to decisively shape events.[25] In addition, good governance proponents rarely note that authoritarian states are likely to constrain military effectiveness as a coup-proofing effort. Interveners intent on helping the counterinsurgent gain the necessary capabilities to provide good governance, including a military willing and able to avoid unnecessary civilian casualties and respect human rights, may assume that military professionalization requires money, arms, and training, but this calculation fails to account for the political reasons why a counterinsurgent government might prefer a less professional military. These reasons include efforts to avoid a military strong enough and effective enough to mount a successful coup, and the use of the military for patronage and preferment.[26]

Exacerbating these problems is the fact that many supporters of the good governance approach have confined their examination to the secondary literature on successful counterinsurgency campaigns. Although work by counterinsurgency practitioners presents normatively appealing narratives, it often plays down less palatable counterinsurgent choices.[27] Military history as a literature is didactic, determined to deliver lessons rather than analytical or explanatory arguments, and much of the counterinsurgency literature falls within this bailiwick.[28] Another problem is considering the government, the insurgency, and the populace as unitary actors, sometimes even conflating the counterinsurgent government and the intervening power backing it.[29] Assuming away domestic politics within the state experiencing the insurgency confounds analysis because insurgency is a domestic political problem.

The argument that good governance causes counterinsurgency success also rests on the assumption that success requires popular support and thus that the populace is the center of gravity, "the hub of all power and movement, on which everything depends."[30] It is not empirically obvious, however, that popular support is necessary for government success. Similarly, insurgencies that rely on financing from the sale of natural resources such as gems or timber need little popular support and thus are unlikely to face difficulties if they lose civilian support. Distribution of public goods to the populace may not be relevant if the fundamental issue is the redistribution of power. Indeed, provision of public goods may increase the flow of resources to the insurgency.[31]

There are other difficulties with the governance approach as well. First, governments willing and able to make reforms do so, meaning that it is the most challenging insurgencies that continue to burn, campaigns in which reforms are least likely to be implemented by governments fighting to survive.[32] Second, a government willing to make reforms may not have the ability to execute them, even with patron support. Third, violence hardens actors' positions and changes their calculations. It can exacerbate actors' sense of playing a zero-sum game and make resolving the conflict harder.[33] Fourth, reforms require coalition building within the elite because they are likely to constrain the interests of multiple elites and this process may be quite difficult.[34] Fifth, establishing democracy is challenging. Violence heightens this difficulty, and democratization efforts may even increase violence.[35] Sixth, there is an inherent tension between the strategic goals of the governance approach and the tactical necessities of defeating an insurgency. The government's need to accommodate warlords or other leaders to gain information and fighting power undercuts the good governance goal of empowering the populace.[36] The good governance literature seeks a prescription for an ethically acceptable way to defeat insurgencies, but that is its weakness. It asks what should be, not what is.

What Succeeds in Counterinsurgency

I argue that counterinsurgency campaigns backed by great powers succeed when the counterinsurgent government forms a coalition with rival civilian and military elites who cooperate in exchange for personal or group gain, and when the government uses the resources provided by the new coalition to cut the flow of support to insurgents, most often by targeting civilians with brute force to control their behavior, as well as targeting the insurgency directly.

This first element of my theory, accommodation of elites, is nonmilitary, noncoercive, and nonviolent. It is also fundamental to success, which means "marginalization of the insurgents to the point at which they are destroyed, co-opted, or reduced to irrelevance in numbers and capability."[37] Accommodation is necessary because the government needs the cooperation, information, and military capabilities rival elites can supply.[38] Accommodation strengthens the government politically and militarily. Accommodations weaken the insurgency indirectly by gaining for the government the military force and political information that it will need to attack the insurgency. The second element of my theory is the use of brute force to control civilians, cutting the flow of resources to the insurgency to weaken it indirectly and using force directly against insurgents, their resources, their communications, and their bases. The compellence element of my theory lies in the government's use of these tools to break the will and the capability of the insurgency to fight on.[39] Accommodation plays a role in the creation of this compellent ability and in its use against insurgents and their resource flows. Compellence involves the prudent use of power.[40] In counterinsurgency, as in compellence, "the object is to make the enemy behave."[41]

This argument challenges widely held beliefs about the need to gain popular support for the threatened government by meeting popular interests and avoiding harm to civilians. When democratic great powers fight insurgencies, either directly or through a client government, they talk of winning hearts and minds and report that they helped institute good governance, but in fact they use violence like any nonliberal power seeking to protect its own security.[42]

COUNTERINSURGENCY AS STATE BUILDING

My theory of compellence counterinsurgency differs from the conventional wisdom in four important ways. First, I analyze the process of countering an insurgency as one of violent state building rather than political competition for popular allegiance.[43] Second, I identify the achievable outcome as political stability rather than liberal democracy.[44] Third, I focus on the domestic interests of the counterinsurgent government and other elites rather than on the efforts of the intervening great power. Finally, I identify useful as well as costly counterinsurgent uses of force.[45]

My compellence theory considers counterinsurgency as primarily a domestic political process of violent state building. The state-building process toward political stability has historically been convulsive.[46] Political order arises from elite efforts to come out on top in violent political rivalry. Elites rule to protect their own interests, not those of the populace.[47] Once elites have determined through violent competition which of them will dominate the rest, and at what cost to which actors, then political stability will follow as long as the elite bargain holds.[48] Elite control of institutions, meanwhile, whether in a captured democracy or an authoritarian state, means that making reforms will be difficult because implementation would be costly to elites who benefit from the status quo.[49]

The desired end state in the compellence theory is a stable political system in which the intraelite bargain to rule holds long term, at least five years based on the usual standard for coding when an internal conflict has ended. Governance capability may increase because it benefits elites, but democratization is neither planned nor intended and attempting it is likely to be destabilizing.[50] The state-building enterprise may focus on producing a particular regime type, but it need not do so and, in my theory of counterinsurgency success, does not do so. It is agnostic on the type of regime produced as long as it is capable of maintaining political stability longer term—that is, for at least five years.[51]

THE PLAYERS

The four actors in this process are the government and elites (those within the government, including the military; those outside the government but with power or influence, such as religious, social, political, and militia leaders; and elites within or aligned with the insurgency); the populace (itself comprising multiple individual and collective actors); the insurgency (also comprising multiple individual and collective actors); and the government's great power backer or backers, which identifies the client government's survival as very important or important to its own security.[52] I focus my analysis on the government and elites of the counterinsurgent state. By elites, I mean political entrepreneurs and entrepreneurs of violence.[53] These entrepreneurs have information and influence that can help the counterinsurgent target the insurgency directly and indirectly.[54]

Political entrepreneurs include religious, cultural, and community leaders, as well as those whose primary role is organizing and supporting violence. Entrepreneurs of violence are elites who have an armed force. Elites include defectors, other sources within the insurgency, and social, intellectual, and business leaders. As prominent members of their community, elites have local knowledge useful to the counterinsurgent as partners or potential partners. These actors have or create influence, and their abilities can serve the counterinsurgent's goals if it can tap into their power structures. These entrepreneurs may persuade others to cooperate with the counterinsurgent, or to not cooperate with the insurgency, for example. They may persuade fighters to defect to the government side. Political entrepreneurs play "critical parts in activating, connecting, coordinating, and representing participants in violent encounters."[55] Their networks can shape the choices of multiple individuals. In internal conflict, much contestation and violence occurs over local issues and conflicts rather than over the "master cleavage" of the war, and political entrepreneurs and entrepreneurs of violence know about these local cleavages and interests, which can help the counterinsurgent government target challengers.[56] Contestation over power and resources can provide an opportunity for the counterinsurgent to partner with one side or another to gain access to information and influence.[57] Political entrepreneurs and entrepreneurs of violence such as police, media, and criminals can shape popular behavior—for example, by inciting and quelling religious riots.[58] Warlords and other armed actors can help the counterinsurgent forcefully control the populace, while political entrepreneurs can encourage quiescence among their followers.

The key relationship in the compellence theory is that of elites, those formally and informally holding power and their rivals for power, including members of the insurgency. The goal for those in power is an arrangement that co-opts rivals and enables those in power to retain their wealth and power. The goal for rival elites, including insurgents, is to gain sufficient wealth or power to stop fighting and benefit from their newly acquired wealth and power. Elites, ruling and rival, mediate relationships between popular formal and informal groups and the government. Elites, as the counterinsurgent government, control the populace to weaken the insurgency and thus remain in power. Civilians who consider their interests channeled by elites assent to control, may or may not gain from accommodations provided to their leaders, and are likely to retain their preexisting political preferences even when receiving government benefits.[59] Popular interests are not critical to the outcome of the elite competition because elites shape insurgent and civilian choices about what positions and actions to take.

The government needs the cooperation of rival elites because they are likely to have knowledge and skills necessary to successfully target the insurgency politically and militarily. The average civilian may have tactical information on such subjects as where he or she last saw insurgents or who is related to whom. They are less likely to have politically significant information on subjects such as the interests of leading insurgents and rifts or factions within the insurgency, or the interests of civilian groups. Elites are not important for so-called actionable intelligence, information that the military can use immediately to send out military forces to attack the insurgency. What matters at the political level of analysis of counterinsurgency is elites' knowledge of political players, groups, interests, and dynamics, and their willingness and ability to use that knowledge to benefit the government.

The process leading to success begins with the government co-opting powerful individuals such as insurgent defectors and rival political and military leaders in order to build its information base and military capabilities. The government accommodates the interests of these actors by providing benefits targeted to the individual or small group, such as impunity, status, or a sinecure. Public goods serve all, while "private goods cover a wide range of government policies and actions that produce benefits for particular individuals, such as state-granted monopolies, access to hard currency, stores in economies with shortages, and kickbacks and bribes secured by government officials."[60] Economic and other assistance from the great power patron can be channeled to this end. Finally, the government uses its enhanced military and information capabilities to go on the offensive against the insurgency to deny it the ability to succeed: harrying its forces and support networks, using large and small operations to destroy its supply caches and lines of communication, denying it freedom of movement, putting insurgents on the run, and blocking the flow of resources to the insurgents. There are a variety of ways to use brute force to cut the flow of resources to insurgents. The most frequent choice in the cases here is to use brute force to control civilians, including by putting them in prison camps, destroying or moving communities, putting communities under military lockdown, and controlling the flow of crucial resources such as foodstuffs. The process ends with the insurgents' and supporters' will to fight broken. The government need not kill all the insurgents. It only needs to show them that they cannot win.[61]

Compellence Theory

In the compellence theory of counterinsurgency success, the independent or explanatory variable is compellence. There are two intervening variables. One is political and the other is military. I operationalize the first, the political variable, as accommodation—the use of threats and rewards to gain the cooperation of political and military leaders in exchange for information on the insurgency and populace and provision of military capabilities to the government.[62] I operationalize the second, the military variable, as a military campaign to destroy the insurgency's capability and will to continue fighting. The military campaign has two facets, direct and indirect. The direct military effort is an attrition campaign against the insurgency.[63] The indirect military effort uses brute force to block the flow of resources to insurgents, often by using force to control civilians.[64] The process involves the use of compellence to break the insurgency as a fighting force and organization based on the threat, display, or application of force to change other actors' behavior.[65]

The government gains the cooperation of elites by making accommodations to individuals' interests. *Accommodations* are benefits provided for some, but not all, political actors, specifically those who provide political and military power. They do not directly benefit the populace as a whole, though recipients may use their gains to reward their own supporters. These benefits are relatively low cost to government elites.[66] Therein lies their appeal. They may include direct payments; the granting of impunity for criminal activity or violence; access to material resources such as timber or revenue-producing checkpoints; and access to nonmaterial resources, such as the granting of an official position (which may also prove lucrative in material terms) to a rival member of the elite. The government uses accommodations to co-opt elites because accommodations are far less costly to government elites than are good governance reforms, which lie at the opposite end of the spectrum of possible political and economic change.[67]

Reforms serve all. They resolve popular grievances against the government. Accommodations serve a few. They do not resolve popular grievances. A government may implement reforms or merely promise them. The counterinsurgent's accomplishment of promised reforms counts as high-level reforms. Repeated attempts at implementation, without full success, count as moderate-level reforms and suggest a lack of capability rather than will. Low-level reforms are the promise alone, or repeated promises of reforms, with few or no implementation efforts. In contrast, accommodations benefit only a subset of elites who provide something in exchange.

Reforms are counterinsurgent efforts to gain popular support by making structural changes to political, economic, or social elements of governance. At their strongest and most widely felt by the populace, they represent major, permanent adjustments in structures or policies governing the distribution and exercise of power that affect all residents of the state. Reforms are intended to resolve or at least reduce the popular grievances driving the insurgency. Reforms include political liberalization (that is, creation of institutions ensuring free and fair elections, freedom of political expression, protection of civil and human rights, and redistribution of property or income).[68] At this high end, reforms are quite costly to government elites because long-term, systematic political or economic changes, such as imposition of the rule of law, establishment and implementation of a tax system, reduction in corruption, redistribution of land for a more just economic system, and similar steps, reduce elites' power and influence.[69]

Toward the middle of the spectrum of political change, limited or symbolic reforms cost government-associated elites less than would actually implementing reforms. Limited or symbolic reforms are delivered sporadically rather than systematically, and in specific geographic areas or to specific groups rather than to all members of the populace. They do not resolve the grievances believed to be fueling the insurgency and are not intended to.

At the lowest end of the spectrum of political change are accommodations. Accommodations are the most narrowly targeted offers that the government can make to gain another actor's assistance. They benefit the few rather than the many. Accommodations do not resolve popular grievances against the government and are not intended to. Accommodations are the normal stuff of politics, including the exchange of benefits that supports formation of a minimum winning coalition to retain power or otherwise reinforce and extend patronage networks.[70] For ruling elites, accommodating rivals is the process of absorbing opposition in order to swing the political and military balance of power with the insurgency to the government's favor. Weak accommodations are those that help prevent government collapse, while stronger accommodations widen and strengthen the elite coalition by co-opting rivals.

The interests of elites within the state determine what degree of reform or accommodation is possible, if any. Pressure from the great power patron is unlikely to achieve significant change in client elites' perceptions of their own interests.[71] Government elites are likely to want to retain as much of their power and wealth as they can while also preventing the insurgents from attaining their goals. Reforms mean regime suicide. Further, governing elites who see the competition to rule as a zero-sum game are less likely to be willing to trade accommodations for help against the insurgency because they fear losing, and that giving up something will lead to the loss of everything. Elites who see the potential for a positive-sum game, on the other hand, are more likely to extend accommodations to rival elites in an exchange of value. The adversary's attitude plays into the government's attitude as well. An insurgency demanding revolution is likely to focus the minds of elites on the unlikeliness of compromise, fostering a zero-sum attitude. Conversely, demands for a larger slice of the existing pie are less likely to appear as an existential threat to ruling elites.

A client may make relatively low-cost accommodations such as implementation of a civic action program providing one-time or irregular military delivery of goods such as food, clothing, entertainment, and medical care to one community or another. A counterinsurgent government is likely to announce major projects intended to serve the people of the state. It may also make symbolic gestures meant to show good faith to its great power patron and, perhaps, also to its people. Reforms restructuring the political or economic order, however, are rare.[72] Reforms to extend political power—for example, through democratization efforts such as free and fair elections—could cost the government by diluting its influence or even throwing it out of office. Reforms sharing wealth, such as implementing or strengthening a system of taxation, would cost the wealthy some of their wealth if they began paying taxes or paying more taxes. Modernizing reforms such as strengthening the administrative state would cost elites by removing sources of personal power—for example, the ability to appoint officials based on factional interests or patronage rather than experience or ability.

The likelihood of accommodation depends on the characteristics of the actors involved. I identify four characteristics enabling accommodation. First, accommodation is most likely when elites see room for gain through cooperation. Otherwise, logically, there is no deal to be made. Second, accommodation is more likely when both sides are making relatively limited demands. Counterinsurgent elites are already fighting to retain their wealth and power. They are unlikely to yield more of either than they consider necessary. They will rebuff elites who make unlimited or too-costly demands. Third, accommodation is more likely when it is relatively less costly than reforms intended to defeat the insurgency. The logic is the same: elites are unwilling to give up more than necessary to remain in power. Fourth, accommodations are more likely when counterinsurgent elites do not see the insurgency as an existential threat. The fear of losing everything makes elites less willing to give up anything. It is this condition that produces accommodation within the client elite but not between government elites and rival elites.

I identify three types of elites and three types of accommodation among them. There are elites in government, elites outside government, and elites in the insurgency. These types of actors combine into three types of interaction. First, elites within government accommodate other government elites. Second, government elites accommodate elites outside government. Third, elites in government accommodate insurgent elites.

Intragovernmental accommodation is likely when elites see the insurgency as an existential threat and want to band together to ensure continued great power support for the counterinsurgency campaign. It is less costly to accommodate one's fellow elites than it would be to implement the good governance reforms sharing power and wealth demanded by the great power sponsor. Governmental-nongovernmental accommodation is likely when government elites identify their need for specific counterinsurgent capabilities, whether political or military, that they cannot build themselves or are reluctant to. Government-insurgent accommodation is likely when the insurgency is more interested in gaining a bigger slice of the pie than in overturning the system, and when neither counterinsurgent nor insurgent is primarily driven by ideology.

For example, government elites might accommodate their fellows in power in order to present a united front to their great power sponsor. Those making the decisions, in such a case, might decide that serving the interests of their fellows by using military forces for security in home areas is more important than sending those forces out to fight insurgents. Such a decision suggests that government elites do not see the insurgency as an existential threat. Otherwise, they would fight with all they had. An example of governmental-nongovernmental accommodation is government elites raising tribal or other nonstate militias through entrepreneurs of violence rather than focusing on expanding their own military capabilities. Nonstate violent actors provide a certain amount of distance between their uses of force and the counterinsurgent government, which might be useful in dealing with the great power sponsor or international audiences.[73] Such actors may also have greater knowledge and skills than regular military forces.[74] A political alliance with outside elites might help government elites' position with their external sponsor or might prove influential domestically. Finally, an example of government accommodation of insurgent elites is winning over a rival to gain his or her political support or military power, or share in resources under the control of the defector.

Questions for Cases

I ask six questions of each of my six cases:

1) When was the counterinsurgent successful in marginalizing the insurgents "to the point at which they are destroyed, co-opted, or reduced to irrelevance in numbers and capability"?[75]
2) How did it succeed?
3) Were there reforms? If so, to what extent were they implemented, and when did they occur relative to the defeat of the insurgent threat?
4) Were there accommodations? If so, when did they occur relative to the defeat of the insurgent threat?
5) Was there an increase in popular support for the government? If so, when did it occur relative to the defeat of the insurgent threat and any reforms or accommodations implemented?
6) Does the strength of the insurgency vary with any of the key elements in my theory?

Timing is important to this test: if reforms take place *before* the government defeats the insurgent threat militarily, or if popular support for the government rises *before* the government defeats the insurgent threat militarily, or if elite accommodations occur only *after* the government defeats the insurgent threat militarily, then my theory has limited explanatory power.

Compellence theory cannot explain counterinsurgency success if any of the following three conditions apply: first, if the government does not control the populace targeted to cut the flow of resources to insurgents, which I identify as necessary for success and the conventional wisdom decries as destructive to the government effort; second, if the government implements reforms benefiting all, gaining support among the population while reducing support for the insurgency, then defeats the insurgent threat after making reforms, because I argue that reforms and popular support are not necessary for success; and third, if the government systematically avoids harm to civilians even at military cost, because I argue that using force against civilians is necessary for success, and uses of force may well involve harm.[76]

Structuring the Analysis

This book provides a rigorous, policy-relevant examination of the causes of counterinsurgency success when a great power intervenes militarily to back a threatened government. I define success as the "marginalization of the insurgents to the point at which they are destroyed, co-opted, or reduced to irrelevance in numbers and capability."[77] In short, the threatened government remains in power at the end of the campaign and the state is territorially intact.

The scope conditions under which my theory operates include Cold War and post–Cold War campaigns targeting insurgents who survive on civilian support willingly or unwillingly given,[78] and cases with and without an ethnic component. The universe of cases is the Correlates of War's intrastate wars data set involving intervention (129 cases between 1945 and 2007).[79] I focus on the post–World War II period for policy relevance because norms on government treatment of noncombatants have changed since 1945 and government treatment of civilians is generally believed to play an important role in counterinsurgency. I do not distinguish between irregular and conventional conflict because many insurgents and counterinsurgents engage in both. I do not include continuing campaigns such as those in Iraq and Afghanistan because there is no outcome to analyze.

The dynamics of Cold War cases are similar to and thus relevant to contemporary conflicts in four ways. First, the insurgencies that I examine are like many contemporary insurgencies in that they are not unitary actors. They are made up of a variety of groups and leaders with a variety of interests, goals, strategies, and tactics. Second, these groups used ideology to advance their goals just as insurgencies do today. Third, the client state today as in the Cold War period is less a unitary actor than a conglomeration of elites pursuing their own interests in tandem.[80] Fourth, the international environment is different in that today's world is no longer bipolar, but the U.S. focus on advancing good governance within other states remains despite the disappearance of its illiberal superpower rival, so the examination of good governance counterinsurgency efforts remains policy relevant. Similarly, I sought cases often presented as model Western democratic great power successes because they should be hard cases of success for my theory of compellence to explain.[81]

These cases are all examples of great power military intervention. The degree of great power support for its threatened partner varies across time and place. The cases of Iraq and Afghanistan, like Vietnam for the United States after sending in combat troops in 1965, are outliers in that Western states rarely invade and occupy smaller countries in the current era. Military intervention can range from provision of intelligence and diplomatic backing to larger projects such as providing military aid, arming and training forces, providing air power to support the counterinsurgent government's own ground troops, and sending military advisers to work with the client military, with interventions climbing upward in cost and quantity of support all the way to sending in combat forces and even occupation. In all of my cases, the great power believed that partner survival was an important security interest and was also unwilling to commit combat forces to preserve its partner's rule. I made this choice for policy relevance. Cases of limited intervention are far more common than those involving occupation and thus more useful for informing policy choices.

I examine only successful cases. Doing so leverages my ability to consider the variation on my independent variables of compellence (political and military) within each case. It also helps explain the processes at work and provides the ability to see whether my predictions are congruent with the empirical evidence in the cases.[82] Selecting on the dependent variable also helps me identify which possible factors are not necessary or sufficient conditions for success.[83] This is useful because the leading view of what causes counterinsurgent success (good governance) produces very different predictions from those produced by my theory.

I analyze the campaigns to determine what the counterinsurgent or client government did and when and where it did it, geographically and temporally, rather than focusing on what it said it would do but may not have attempted or achieved.[84] Asking what governments actually did in their successful campaigns identifies choices overlooked or downplayed in most existing work on counterinsurgency. If showing intent to reform is sufficient for success, or popular perception of the government's good intentions is sufficient for success, then even when reforms are limited, the process of public support shifting to the government and thus weakening the insurgency should still be evident. Public support is difficult to assess and becomes more so in wartime, so I assess participation in efforts the counterinsurgent government or intervener itself presented as indicators of support and present my findings in this area with caution.[85]

My research includes review of the counterinsurgency literature, scholarly work in other fields on the states and issues involved, contemporaneous military and civilian government documents in ten U.S. and British archives, and participants' personal collections, memoirs, and oral histories. I also interviewed participants when possible.

I make an empirical contribution to the historiography of all of these cases, as well as a theoretical one. Examination of primary sources and secondary literature outside the counterinsurgency domain in five of the six cases shows that the campaigns included elite accommodation rather than reforms gaining mass support, higher levels of force against civilians than previously shown in the counterinsurgency literature, and earlier military defeat of the insurgent threat than previously recognized. My findings on the sixth case, Turkey combating the Partiya Karkeren Kurdistan (Kurdistan Workers' Party; PKK), synthesize the secondary literature into a more cohesive analysis of the campaign than many extant.

In the cases I analyze, Greece, El Salvador, and Turkey display a particularly high value on the use of force against civilians. Malaya, Dhofar, and Turkey provide particularly strong examples of elite accommodation. Malaya—now Malaysia—and Oman are examples of notably long-term political stability. The Philippines, Greece, Turkey, and El Salvador have remained relatively stable, but there have been military coups in the first three and a high level of criminal (rather than political) violence in El Salvador.

The five earlier cases (Malaya, the Philippines, Greece, Dhofar, and El Salvador) are often claimed as good governance successes exemplary for their relatively high level of reforms and relatively low level of intentional uses of force against civilians.[86] These are also cases in which the democratic great power patron insisted that reforms were necessary to defeat the insurgency and pressed its client hard to attain them despite elite resistance.[87] These campaigns should constitute cases that my compellence theory cannot explain, if the conventional wisdom on the role of good governance in counterinsurgency success is correct. My theory does explain these cases, however. In addition, analysis of the Turkey case establishes that my theory holds beyond the five canonical examples of claimed good governance success by liberal interveners. Turkey was a notably brutal campaign. It was also conducted by a democratic state with less direct military patron support than in the earlier cases. And yet my theory explains success in Turkey as well as in Malaya, Greece, the Philippines, Dhofar, and El Salvador, demonstrating its relatively high predictive and explanatory value.

Cases

THE MALAYAN EMERGENCY

In the British campaign, 1948–1957, the colonial government defeated a small, isolated Communist insurgency that failed to gain political traction even within the population of impoverished ethnic Chinese rubber plantation workers that it targeted as its often-unwilling base of support. Elite accommodation took the form of the British and ethnic Chinese and Indian elites agreeing to continued ethnic Malay political dominance with entry of ethnic Chinese and ethnic Indian elites into the ruling coalition. The military campaign began with a widespread crackdown to deter further challenge to the government, then continued weakening the insurgents by forcing ethnic Chinese and other residents into prison camps, reducing the insurgents' ability to obtain resources from them. Finally, the government chased the remaining bands of insurgents into the jungle and hunted most of them down. British reform efforts to create a modern pluralistic democracy to defeat the insurgency foundered on ethnic Malay insistence on continued political domination of the economically dominant ethnic Chinese and ethnic Indian communities. Like the ethnic Chinese, the indigenous Malay community and the ethnic Indian population had little interest in Communism. Malay elites did, however, have an interest in independence from Britain, which they gained in 1957. The British had been planning for Malayan independence since 1942. It was not a reform introduced to gain popular support. The government defeated the insurgency without gaining the popular support it believed it needed to do so.

THE GREEK CIVIL WAR

In Greece in 1947–1949, the United States backed the repressive, fragile post–World War II Greek government and built its military capacity sufficiently to defeat the Communist and nationalist insurgents. The insurgents received broad popular support for their calls for a more representative, less repressive government but faced determined resistance from the right-wing oligarchy that remains powerful today. Accommodation took the form of efforts to retain elites' support for the government in power in order to keep U.S. support flowing. The military campaign imprisoned thousands of civilians in horrid conditions on island camps, cleared the mountains of communities that might provide support to the insurgents, and broke down insurgent formations through military force. The U.S. government believed that reforms were necessary for success but ultimately decided that stability in the form of insurgent defeat had to come first. The U.S. contribution to the effort included military and political advisers, as well as economic support, military training, and materiel.

THE PHILIPPINES' WAR ON THE HUK

In the Philippines in 1946–1954, the government faced a geographically isolated challenge from peasants in one area of the island of Luzon. The insurgency included a Communist urban element aligned with the nationalist rural membership fighting for a return to what they saw as the more just patron-client relationship that had existed before the advent of modern agricultural techniques intended to increase the profits of the great landowners. The insurgency had wide support in central Luzon but failed to spread into areas where socioeconomic conditions differed. The United States backed the Philippine government as a bulwark against Communist expansion in Asia, pressing for major governance reforms while building Philippine security forces. Elite accommodation took the form of agreement among members of the government, professionals and landowners, and the Catholic Church to strengthen the state's military sufficiently to defeat the insurgent threat while making gestures to soothe peasants' frustration. In the military campaign, the government used massive clearing operations against civilian communities, extrajudicial execution, and prison camps to cut the flow of resources from populace to insurgents, then used large offensive operations against the weakened insurgents, driving them into the mountains to die or surrender.

DHOFAR, OMAN

The British-led campaign in Dhofar, Oman, ran from 1965 to 1976. The sultan of Oman faced a popular nationalist and Communist insurgency in its remote southwestern corner. His British backers pressed reforms on him, which he resisted, but he welcomed the buildup of his military. In a palace coup in 1970, the sultan's son replaced him and gained additional British and regional support for the campaign. Accommodations took place in the form of empowering warlords and others, including insurgent defectors and tribal leaders. The British-formed militias led by these men were better able to fight the insurgents and gain information from the populace than was the regular army.

The British-led military defeated the insurgent threat by controlling civilians to cut the flow of resources to insurgents, physically blocking the flow of resources from the insurgents' safe haven across the border with Yemen, and controlling the populace in the guerrilla-ridden mountains. Limited reforms such as construction of clinics followed the military's success against the insurgency rather than causing insurgent defeat.

EL SALVADOR

In El Salvador from 1979 to 1992, the U.S.-backed government fought the Communist and nationalist insurgency to a draw, preserving the government from an insurgent takeover. Elite accommodation took place largely among civilian and military officers in the government as hard-liners and slightly more liberal political and military entrepreneurs jockeyed for influence. The Salvadoran government resisted U.S.-pressed reforms but accepted U.S. efforts to strengthen its security forces. It used its increased fighting ability to clear civilian areas, creating vast refugee flows that reduced provision of material support to the insurgency. It used U.S.-provided air power to break down the insurgency's conventional formations but was never able to successfully pursue and destroy the smaller bands of insurgents or gain more popular support than it began the war with. Continued insurgent political and military strength, along with the end of the Cold War, forced the United States and the hard-liners within the military to accept peace talks and a political settlement to the war rather than the military victory they had pressed for. UN-led talks ended the war.

TURKEY AND THE PKK

The case of Turkey against the PKK in 1984–1999 differs from the rest in that it is generally considered a notably brutal case rather than a model for democratic great powers to follow. It involves a democracy conducting a counterinsurgency campaign on its own territory against its own populace. This circumstance is similar to the situation in the Philippines, Greece, and El Salvador, but the focus in these latter three cases in the counterinsurgency literature is usually on the great power patron's role in the campaign rather than that of the client government. Including Turkey in my analysis helps reframe all these cases by focusing attention on the counterinsurgent government itself. Elite accommodation in Turkey took the form of government support for the great Kurdish landowners of the southeast, providing impunity for illegal smuggling and other accommodations in exchange for the provision of organized violence, controlling civilians to cut the flow of resources to the insurgency. The militia and military campaigns cleared vast areas of the region of their inhabitants. The campaign defeated the PKK threat militarily. It captured and imprisoned its leader, Abdullah Ocalan, with U.S. assistance, and the insurgency withered. It was the structural change of the U.S. invasion of Iraq in 2003 that created the opportunity for remnants of the PKK to regroup and reopen their campaign from northern Iraq, as well as within Turkey.[88] Turkey shows the external validity of my theory because it is considered a particularly brutal campaign and thus should bear little similarity to successful campaigns conducted by democratic great powers and lauded as models if the governance approach explains counterinsurgency success.

All of the cases analyzed in the following chapters show evidence of governmental accommodation of rival elites in a coalition-building process that provided the cooperation, information, or military power necessary for counterinsurgent success. The case with the least evidence of elite accommodation of rivals outside the government, El Salvador, is also the one case in which the government did not militarily defeat the insurgency, though Greece also shows little evidence of rival accommodation.

All cases also reveal governments' intentional and systematic use of brute force against civilians in ways that contributed to counterinsurgent success. The cases all show governments promising reforms, but little evidence of implementation. The El Salvador and Philippines cases are particularly rich in examples of promised reforms, though in El Salvador domestic politics returned only to the status quo ante bellum rather than to a new height of political openness or economic opportunity. Reforms in El Salvador followed the peace agreement. They did not contribute to it. All the cases show, as far as the evidence allows, a lack of increase in popular support for the government. Individually and collectively, these cases provide strong evidence of the explanatory power of the compellence theory, with its emphasis on coalition building among rival elites and a military campaign targeting civilians as well as insurgents.

Not the Wars You're Looking For

Malaya, Greece, the Philippines

The Malayan Emergency may be the best-known modern counterinsurgency campaign. It has gained iconic status. U.S. pundits and practitioners turned their attention to the campaign most recently in the early 2000s, when the Iraq War began going badly for the United States and its partners. It re-emerged, as it had during the Vietnam War, as the emblematic right way to defeat insurgency: relatively quickly, once the British figured out what they were doing wrong by using excessive force; cleanly, with carefully limited uses of force to avoid civilian harm; and through democratizing political reforms that resolved popular grievances believed to drive the insurgency. The U.S.-backed Philippine campaign against the Huk insurgency, from the same post–World War II era, may also be familiar to those interested in counterinsurgency as a case in which the United States enabled the threatened government to make democratizing reforms and thus emerge from the conflict as a stronger, more stable long-term partner in the Cold War and after. The Greek Civil War, which also followed World War II, is less well known in counterinsurgency circles but does sometimes make an appearance in the prescriptive literature.

All three campaigns share an era, a democratic great power concern about Communist insurgents, and domestic political interests and rivalries present well before the insurgencies began. There are important differences as well. In Malaya, the British ruled a relatively capable colonial state in an area where they had known the players, terrain, languages, and cultures for generations. They also faced an insurgency of limited popular appeal without significant external support. In the Philippines, the United States was familiar with the people and terrain from the counterinsurgency campaign it waged at the turn of the twentieth century and its role in the Philippines until the Japanese occupation during World War II. It also faced an insurgency with limited appeal, though in this case because of geography rather than ideology. The Huk also lacked an external sponsor. The United States, unlike the British in Malaya, did not have a relatively highly bureaucratized and capable state to work with. In Greece, the United States took over supporting the weak and divided Greek government when the British bowed out because of their struggle with the costs of waging World War II. The United States lacked familiarity with the country and its politics, and it faced a strong insurgency making relatively popular demands of a widely unpopular government. All three cases share a successful counterinsurgency outcome.

In this chapter I find support for the compellence theory in all three cases, Malaya, the Philippines, and Greece. I analyze the cases by providing background on the conflict and presenting my analysis using material often overlooked by previous counterinsurgency authors. I find that in all three cases, elite accommodation played a significant role in the counterinsurgent's ability to defeat the insurgency militarily, with the type of elite involved varying by case; uses of force included forcefully controlling civilians; and uses of force broke the insurgency before reforms were implemented, if they were implemented at all, as the compellence theory predicts.

Readers may find themselves shaking their heads at the differences between the familiar tales of these campaigns and my analysis. If I am "not telling the story right," as an interlocutor once objected, it is because I have recovered, from the archives and from scholarly literatures other than that on counterinsurgency, elements of the cases overlooked by previous commentators.

Malaya

Great Britain entered Malaya as the private British East India Company in 1786, following the Portuguese and Dutch into the lush islands of Southeast Asia in their search for natural resources and trading opportunities. Malaya, by World War II a British colony, was occupied by the Japanese during the war. The British retook control after the Allied victory. The Communist and nationalist Malayan National Liberation Army (MNLA) began a terrorism campaign against economic targets in 1946. In 1948, the MNLA included about twelve thousand lightly armed guerrillas (a high estimate compared with other sources) and a political organization based in the ethnic Chinese community.[1] Most of its support came from tin miners and rubber tappers living in squalid camps on the fringes of the jungle. The MNLA used violence, fear, extortion, and coercion to dominate the isolated camp dwellers.[2]

There was limited popular support for the insurgency's goals. The MNLA presented a narrowly appealing message of Communism to poor communities and a more broadly appealing message of independence from Britain, but British moves toward independence and toward forming a multiethnic Malayan nationality were already well under way.[3] Malaya's population of approximately 4.55 million was 49 percent ethnic Malay, 38 percent ethnic Chinese, and 12 percent ethnic Indian, with a sprinkling of other ethnicities.[4] The ethnic Chinese community was fragmented by origin (mainland versus Taiwan versus Singapore and so on), views on the Chinese Revolution (pro and con), and type of employment (businessmen, traders and shopkeepers, laborers, etc.).[5] This mixture of interests provided stony ground for an appeal to either Chinese or a new Malaysian nationalism. There was also relatively little anti-British feeling for the insurgency to draw on, particularly in the wake of the brutal Japanese occupation.[6] The insurgency gained resources primarily from the communities of ethnic Chinese squatters because of their isolated locations and lack of government protection. Most residents of Malaya showed little interest in politics. British authorities found that the masses cared little for independence. Independence appealed to Malaya's elites, though only under certain conditions, while Communism did not.

The British government feared communal conflict and attempted to lessen the possibility in its constitutional developments for the future of the colony, but did not consider the MNLA a communal or ethnic insurgency. The "'Emergency' is not a national movement [and] . . . steps must be taken to prevent the communist campaign becoming a national movement," the Ministry of Defence was informed from the region in 1950.[7] The director of operations noted in 1954 that the terrorists were mostly Chinese but the movement was not a national one.[8] Indeed, Malaya experienced little or no ethnic tension before the British effort to liberalize the state raised questions about the distribution of opportunities and resources.[9]

Support for the insurgency, coerced or willingly given, came from residents of all communities. In one attack on a police post in Negeri Sembilan in 1954, Malay police did not resist. Government officials bemoaned the apathy of the predominantly Malay community toward the insurgents.[10] The MNLA itself avoided sparking communal violence, according to captured documents.[11] It made little or no known effort to appeal to ethnic Chinese identity.

Characterization of the MNLA as a specifically ethnic Chinese movement grew from the elite story developed in the independence era. Successive Malaysian governments shaped a narrative of the insurgency that emphasized its ethnic Chinese membership to underline the outsider status of ethnic Chinese residents and the heroism of Malay fighters in defeating this domestic threat.[12] Later analysts of the counterinsurgency campaign rarely extended their knowledge to domestic politics and thus assumed the accuracy of this narrative. But historian Karl Hack notes that "far more Chinese joined the Home Guard (at its peak 250,000 with the vast majority being Chinese) and the MCA [Malayan Chinese Association], which offered information and practical help, than the MCP [Malayan Communist Party], its MNLA (peaking at fewer than 8000) and its auxiliary Min Yuen. . . . Many Chinese opted to become a part of the machinery of population control, protecting perimeters, checking people for smuggled goods at New Villager gates, or giving information."[13]

Ethnic Malay elites included the traditional rulers of the peninsula's states and their English-speaking administrators. Both feared losing traditional Malay dominance when Malaya gained independence from Britain.[14] Ethnic Chinese and ethnic Indian elites were anxious to protect their economic and financial interests within the new state.

The ethnic Malay population lived mostly in rural, self-supporting communities and was less prosperous than the more urban ethnic Chinese and ethnic Indian communities. Ethnic Malay and ethnic Indian elites grew increasingly concerned during the Emergency that independence as a liberal democracy (the British goal) would mean ethnic Chinese domination because ethnic Chinese constituted the second-largest ethnic population in Malaya and were its most prosperous residents.

The British wanted to gain popular support for the campaign and the coming independent state of Malaysia but never did so, according to their own accounts. It was important instead, they found, to accommodate the interests of local elites to gain their cooperation for the British independence project and a strong future political and economic relationship with Britain. Elites supported British efforts to control civilians in order to cut ties to the insurgency, for example. The prosperous ethnic Chinese MCA was important in acceding to the destruction of rural ethnic Chinese communities and the imprisonment of their residents in camps.

The counterinsurgency campaign varied tactically over the course of the conflict as security forces broke down the MNLA and its members fled into the jungles, but it remained the same strategically from beginning to end. The British focused on cutting insurgents off from resources, most notably by controlling the populace, and on targeting the insurgency directly with large military sweeps through insurgent areas and eventually jungle operations against the surviving bands.

Once the insurgency was broken down into small groups deep in the jungles, unable to mount coordinated attacks or even communicate in a timely manner, the government gradually began providing public goods to individual communities on a case-by-case basis. Systematic political reforms took place in the form of the British design of plans for Malayan independence, which began in 1942, well before the inception of the insurgency. British plans for Malayan independence were well known at the time.

The conventional wisdom on the Malayan Emergency is that after Britain's initial failure to defeat the insurgency through its indiscriminate use of force, including collective punishment, forced deportation, and imprisonment without trial, the military learned to seek popular support through reforms and the careful use of force to avoid damage to civilian interests.[15] Typically insurgent defeat is dated to 1954.[16]

Contrary to the conventional wisdom, in returning to contemporaneous political and military documents, I find that uses of force against civilians continued throughout the campaign. I also find that the reforms credited to the British were not a response to the insurgency but preceded it and thus could not have been a driver of success, when it comes to the granting of independence; or were not implemented at all, in the case of equal citizenship for all; or were not implemented until after the insurgent threat was defeated, in the case of basic services provided in scattered ways and at irregular times in the so-called New Villages that held civilians forced from their homes.

In addition, the record shows that the British never gained the support they believed they needed from any of the communities in Malaya beyond some members of ethnic elites, weakening the claim that popular support played an important role in counterinsurgent success. These findings support the predictions of the compellence theory in finding Britain's accommodation of elites to be crucial to success, along with its systematic uses of force against civilians. The lack of reforms while the insurgency was still a viable fighting force means that reforms cannot have driven insurgent defeat. The lack of increased popular support for the government means that it too was not important for counterinsurgency success.

In brief, the British began planning for Malayan independence in 1942, its formation of the liberal Malayan Union in 1946 drew immediate protests, and the same year a small group of Communist residents began violently targeting the Malayan economy. The British, with greater local input this time, replaced the Malayan Union with the Malayan Federation in 1948 and declared the Emergency the same year. The British began resettling civilians and controlling their movements and the resources available to them in 1948. Also in 1948, the government defeated the insurgency as a threat, reducing it to a violent nuisance by separating it from its civilian support system. It broke the MNLA as an organization able to plan and coordinate in 1951, the year insurgent violence peaked as the insurgents withdrew to the jungle. In 1952, aid deliveries to the New Villages began, led by private organizations rather than as government reforms. In 1952 the MCA and United Malays National Organization (UMNO) agreed to share out electoral seats and join forces with ethnic Indians in the Alliance Party, all steps intended to avoid ethnic political competition that also restricted British efforts at liberalizing reforms. In 1954 the insurgency consisted of small bands of individuals trying to elude military pursuit in the jungle. Malaysia declared independence in 1957.

MALAYA ANALYSIS

Insurgency Broken by 1948. The insurgency was broken as a threat to the state by 1948, based on my definition of success as the "marginalization of the insurgents to the point at which they are destroyed, co-opted, or reduced to irrelevance in numbers and capability."[17] The usual date for the end of the conflict is 1954. The date matters in this case because counterinsurgent success preceded any attempts at reform.

The MNLA was rendered unable to achieve its political and military objectives in 1948 and never regained its strength. One official wrote in 1949 that "militarily the bandits are already beaten in Malaya in the sense that they cannot now hope to succeed in their objects."[18] The UK government deemed a coordinated insurgent offensive unlikely based on the group's inability to communicate.[19] A third assessment was similar: "It is evident that the initiative has largely passed to the security forces and that the bandits are in considerable difficulties."[20] Insurgent attacks were becoming significantly less frequent; insurgents were broken down into smaller groups; they were short of money, ammunition, food, and medical supplies; and communications were difficult. "It is most improbable that they will be able to launch the coordinated offensive throughout the country which they had intended," British officials reported.[21] Captured documents showed the British that insurgent morale remained low in March 1949 and that the state's sweeping up of civilians into armed camps to separate them from the insurgency was denying insurgents funds and food, as intended.[22]

By June 1951, the insurgency had disintegrated.[23] With their withdrawal to the jungle, they could no longer effectively mass force, communicate, or plan.[24] The MNLA could no longer fight because of its battle losses and the imposed costs of government controls on civilians and the resources insurgents needed to survive. Insurgent losses were on the increase from surrender, starvation, and suicide.[25] In June 1951, surrenders were up about 180 percent over the three previous months and insurgent casualties had risen 42 percent.[26] The number of insurgent-inspired incidents fell from a monthly average of 507 in 1951 to 89 in 1954, with deaths and the economically costly slashing of rubber trees significantly down as well.[27] In 1951, two-thirds of attacks had been taking place in the states of Johore and Perak, at the southern and northern ends of the peninsula, indicating that the insurgency was geographically divided, which made communications all the more difficult.[28] Ambushes of security forces were rare by 1952, with insurgent bands isolated in the jungle. That same year, it took seven thousand man-hours of patrolling to see one insurgent. Insurgent attacks were rare.[29] Monthly major incidents fell from 169 in May 1952 to 10 in May 1953 and a still-negligible 30 in 1954. By 1953 in one area of Perak, "the bandits survive[d] only in small groups of dispirited men and women."[30] The number of insurgents killed or captured in ambushes rose dramatically each month from 1952 to 1953, from about 30 in May to about 50 in June, 100 in July, about 150 in August, about 175 in September, about 200 in October, about 250 in November, about 275 in December, about 300 in January, about 325 in February, about 350 in March, and about 400 in April. Overall, by April 1953 aggressive insurgent action was gauged at "a very small amount."[31] "The present level of the Emergency is such that the life of the country proceeds without significant interference," the director of operations wrote in 1955. "There is no great impact on any one district or any particular race. Most of the incidents are not of a serious kind and those of an aggressive nature are barely one a week."[32]

Authorities reported in 1957 that violence peaked in 1951 and had been declining since. "Every aspect of the Emergency is dwindling and has been dwindling steadily for four years." The insurgents' "primary aim for the past four years has been to evade contact," authorities in Kuala Lumpur reported. There were about 2,100 insurgents in 1957, down from an estimated high of 11,500 in a population of about 6 million.[33]

Elite Accommodation. The British accommodated local elites in playing their long game for political stability. Colonial authorities hoped to use elites' influence to gain popular support.[34] Authorities recognized, for example, that citizenship mattered little to most ethnic Chinese but mattered greatly to their leadership, "whose access to power depended on the votes of his potential supporters."[35] Britain hoped in 1950 to persuade Malayan rulers to let ethnic Chinese elites enter the higher ranks of government service as a way of ensuring ethnic Chinese support for British goals.[36] The British sponsored or supported communal organizations of local elites to channel their communities' interests, and ultimately lead political parties as well.[37]

The elites important in the Malaya case were communal leaders aligned with the British, including the Malay sultans and ethnic Chinese and ethnic Indian business leaders. The British focused less on ethnic Indian elites, primarily businessmen and members of the civil service, than on the ethnic Chinese and Malays.[38] Malay elites who played a significant role included Tunku Abdul Rahman, son of a sultan and known as the Father of Malaysia, and Dato Onn Jaafar. Onn, raised as a member of the royal family of Johar and educated in England, cofounded UMNO but broke away when it rejected his call for membership for all ethnicities. Leading ethnic Chinese included Tan Cheng Lock, a wealthy leader in the rubber and banking industries, and tin magnate Henry S. Lee, who cofounded the MCA and later the Alliance with UMNO.

The ethnic Indian community was smaller and received less government attention than the two larger communities. The Malayan Indian Congress (MIC) had access to patronage and legislative seats only through support from ethnic Indians and national Alliance leaders.[39] Ethnic Indian leaders in Malaya, primarily Tamils, threw their lot in with the Alliance starting with municipal elections in Kuala Lumpur in 1952. The MCA, UMNO, and MIC agreed to run candidates of their respective communities in wards dominated by that community. Their experiment in communalism succeeded and set the pattern for future party behavior. The MIC joined the Alliance in 1954.[40]

The British addressed each ethnic community's interests based on that group's relative power and role in supporting British goals. They shared elites' communal concerns and fear of communal violence (the government did not identify the insurgency as a communal conflict). British-backed elites supported British plans for independence and the counterinsurgency campaign. The British also hoped they would help gain them popular support for the campaign, but according to the British themselves, this never occurred. I discuss this point at greater length later in this analysis.

Elites participated in processes useful to the British. They shared information with each other and with lower-level leaders and interested members of the populace; they channeled popular concerns upward for potential British course adjustment; they gave the imprimatur of local support to the government; and eventually the ethnic Chinese MCA provided basic services in the New Villages, possibly forestalling outbreaks of violence.

In return, these elites gained local status and the status of British support at a time when there was little anti-British feeling; they gained a share in governmental and informal power without political violence and at relatively low risk; they gained authority with official positions in government; they gained support for their official organizations and unofficial roles; and they gained a voice for their communities. The outcome, as I discuss in more detail in a later section on the lack of reforms, included ethnic Malays retaining the greatest share of power in the government as well as other privileges, while ethnic Indians and Chinese eventually gained some rights in the form of things like limited land ownership and some possibility of citizenship.

As an example of accommodation, British authorities repeatedly stressed the need to include local elites on Malayan government boards. A 1950 memo emphasized the importance of adding a Malay and a Chinese to the government's war council to represent planting and other commercial interests. "I consider it of prime importance that some leading local personalities should be associated with the decisions of the War Council. There is a tendency among Asians here to regard the Emergency as 'a white man's war,'" the memo said.[41] A report from the high commissioner of Malaya to the British secretary of state for the colonies stressed the need to find Chinese spokesmen with courage and ability to challenge Communist propaganda.[42] A later memo, from 1954, revisited the subject. "In an attempt to associate the political leaders of the country more closely with the conduct of the Emergency, towards which they are prone, like the rest of the public, to adopt a casual and complacent attitude, the high commissioner has invited five members of the executive council to serve on the director of operations committee. The committee . . . has hitherto consisted only of senior government officials and representatives of the three services." The author noted that the effort also included governmental levels below the federal: "It is to be hoped that the Asian political leaders will now begin to identify themselves with Emergency measures in a practical and responsible way. Similar steps are being taken in the states and districts."[43] Early the next year, another report noted that it was cumbersome for the director of operations to work through committees, but important to put locals on his committee to associate the people more with the Emergency campaign.[44]

From early in the campaign, the British cultivated elite support within Malaya, including that of ethnic Chinese leaders. A 1949 security report said, "The Malayan Chinese Association which is now showing some signs of actively committing itself on the side of law and order can fairly be described as a government inspired and sponsored movement." Behind the scenes the high commissioner played a decisive part in forming the MCA.[45] The government also sought support from lower-level leaders, noting, for example, in 1951 that associated Chinese chambers of commerce were condemning the role of the Chinese People's Government in Korea and asking the British to withdraw recognition of that government.[46]

The MCA played a leading role in supporting government goals. Indeed, MCA leaders were either closely associated with the government or members.[47] A 1950 report to Whitehall credited the association with speaking out for the government, helping resettle squatters, and supporting British state-building efforts such as teaching Malaya and English in all government and government-supported schools and banning display of the Chinese flag.[48] The British government continued emphasizing the importance of the MCA to its goals as the Emergency continued.[49]

In turn, the MCA "saw the New Villages as an important political constituency."[50] It did relief work in the New Villages, including providing displaced residents with cash, building materials, clothing, and other necessities.[51] The organization served as the unofficial representative of the camps' inhabitants.[52] Tan Siew Sin, Tan Cheng Lock's son and also a prominent community leader, wrote in 1952, "We are just a sub-branch of the Organization of the Director of Operations, hoping to assist the Government to end the Emergency."[53]

The government struggled to balance the interests of the ethnic communities in Malaya with its own goals. At the beginning of the Emergency, the British identified the constitution as "a delicate balance of all the elements in Malaya, containing much compromise between the communities," and noted that "it is accepted by all sections as substantially equitable," recognizing the need to make sure that future arrangements were "acceptable to all the principle elements in the population."[54] Britain's long-term plan for its soon-to-be-former colony was democracy for all Malaysians.[55] But the British interest in bringing non-Malays into government clashed with the traditional rulers' interest in continued domination. In 1950, the high commissioner warned the secretary of state that the British must emphasize that they recognized the needs of Malaya loyalists.[56] The British tried to persuade the sultans to let ethnic Chinese into the higher ranks of government service.[57] An alarmed telegram from the commissioner-general, South East Asia, warned Whitehall that Gen. Harold Briggs's plan for "major political changes" should only be implemented if it would help with the counterinsurgency campaign. The commissioner-general expressed concern that plans to admit more ethnic Chinese and other non-Malays as citizens and to hold municipal elections in 1951, among other things, would alienate the colony's nationalists. At the same time, he pointed out, not widening citizenship would cost the British the support of the MCA and intensify the cooling of non-Malay support for the cause. Similarly, delaying the promised elections could be a propaganda coup for the Communists.[58]

Malays resented what they saw as British special help for ethnic Chinese residents. The high commissioner wrote in 1950 that Malays strongly felt they were neglected, thus "provision of schools and medical facilities in [ethnic Chinese] squatter areas will be politically impossible unless a program providing similar facilities for Malays is embarked upon simultaneously."[59] To assuage Malay envy of the welfare work that missionaries were doing in the New Villages, the British set up the Rural Industrial Development Authority in 1951, headed by Dato Onn Jaafar, to provide training and loans to Malay small businessmen.[60] The MCA also provided financial support for Malay economic development.[61]

Keeping Malay elites' support was an important British goal. Without it, an orderly transfer of power would be less likely, and the possibility of ethnic violence would rise. "It has become increasingly apparent that the questions of equality, language and citizenship . . . are most dangerous material from the point of view of inter-communal relations," one political official wrote.[62] A series of 1954–1956 intelligence reports from state officials reveals increasing ethnic Chinese concern and Malayan activism and violence against other ethnicities as independence neared.[63] "The MCA at last appreciate the paradox of pressing for elections in 1954 and thus hastening the process whereby the Malays will be enabled to swamp the polls while a large part of the Chinese population has no vote," a 1954 intelligence report noted.[64] Some ethnic Chinese feared Malay dominance sufficiently to ask the British whether they could change their minds and not support independence after all.[65]

Uses of Force against Civilians. The Malaya campaign has received more attention than perhaps any other counterinsurgency campaign, including recent work by scholars correcting the historical record as portrayed in the counterinsurgency literature. The conventional view is that the British quickly learned that their uses of force were only fueling the insurgency, corrected course, gained popular support for the government through reforms, and thus defeated the insurgency. During the first two years of the campaign, according to this narrative, the British relied on massive sweeps that only alienated the populace.[66] There are frequent references in the counterinsurgency literature to the costs of the use of military force in the early years of the conflict. "The initial C-I [counterinsurgency] effort of 1948–1950 proved inadequate, confused, and undermanaged," writes Robert Komer, who served as the U.S. pacification czar in Vietnam.[67] An often-cited RAND study takes a similar position, arguing that British forces first tried to break down insurgent concentrations by force and keep them constantly on the move but failed to weaken the insurgency, then began conducting large-scale multi-battalion jungle sweeps that also proved futile. Next, this account says, British "forces burned down whole villages and relocated their populations to eliminate civilian support for the insurgency. This tactic, too, was largely unsuccessful."[68]

Recent revisionist work, in contrast, restores attention to the ways in which the forceful character of the British campaign, including its systematic violence against civilians, supported government efforts to defeat the insurgency.[69] It nevertheless echoes earlier work in arguing that government uses of force against civilians declined in later years. In the revisionist literature, the first years of the campaign involved deliberate uses of force to intimidate ethnic Chinese and others into supporting the government. From 1948 to 1949, these authors argue, the government used mass arrests, property destruction, forced population movements, and lethal force against civilians, with British military assessments finding these measures effective.[70] British reassessment in 1950 led to more discriminate uses of force and also an increase in controls on the movements and access to resources of the civilian population, they argue. The British focus in this second period of the conflict included continued forced resettlement and collective punishment, although punishment was more likely to be applied to communities actually supporting insurgents, according to these authors. The third and final phase of the campaign included the conferral of material benefits on some members of the populace and more targeted offensive action against the insurgents.[71] This new element of phasing introduced by the revisionists is important because it shows that the delivery of benefits to civilians followed uses of force. This work rarely discusses political elements and effects of the campaign in detail but is of great importance in taking a first cut at dispelling the myths of the earlier accounts.

The British and Malayan governments were not shy about identifying the useful role of force even late in the campaign. A 1951 report said, "While the aim was always to kill bandits, the role of the RAF [Royal Air Force] was often in the nature of artillery, with the object of driving the enemy into areas where they would be more easily dealt with by ground forces."[72] In 1955, the director of operations noted the twin importance of the forceful control of civilians and attacks on insurgents. "Our food denial is still the most effective weapon which we employ against them," the director observed, although offensive operations in the jungle were also still necessary, as was a continued grip on the civilian populace. The use of air power and artillery, meanwhile, harassed the insurgents and had "a satisfactory effect on the waverers."[73] Two years later, rationing food for civilians in New Villages and other militarized communities remained the basis of operations and the director of operations expected it to remain so after independence in 1957 as well.[74] Food denial meant, for example, giving civilians only enough cooked rice to feed them for the day so they would not be able to pass any on to insurgents, and distributing only punctured tins of canned milk, which spoiled quickly in the heat.

It was large offensive operations and tight controls on the movements and provisioning of civilians that forced the insurgency to break down into bands on the run in the jungle. As early as 1948, area weapons such as aerial bombing[75] and other military tools were weakening insurgent capabilities and reducing the number of attacks.[76] Efforts to control the populace and resources increasingly hobbled the insurgency.[77] By 1954, insurgent action was so limited that the military radically changed its offensive focus from the "Briggs/Templar 'steady squeeze' plan" to control civilians in more populated areas to also pursue insurgents deep into the jungle.[78] Analysts attributed the dramatic fall in military contact with insurgents (from 939 contacts in 1951 to 350 in 1955) "to the elimination rates of terrorists (killed, captured, surrendered and died of natural causes) being higher than recruitment rates." The British reached the insurgency's tipping point and passed it.[79]

Increasing surrenders—an indication of breaking insurgent will—were the result of several factors, including the use of force to block the flow of resources from civilians to insurgents. Surrenders rose in proportion to killings and captures, with the most important factor identified as insurgent contact with security forces.[80] In Kedah state, food controls increased insurgent kills and surrenders.[81] At the end of 1954, reasons given for surrender included food shortages, security force pressure, and loss of faith in victory.[82] In 1957, the British counted 9,581 insurgents "eliminated" since June 1948 out of an estimated total of 11,500 individuals who had been insurgents at some time. Those eliminated included 6,398 killed, 1,245 captured, and 1,938 surrendered.

The British spoke of protecting the populace from insurgents because the insurgents often coerced material and nonmaterial support from squatter settlements at the edge of the jungle. Protection in practice meant controlling civilians through brute force.[83] By 1952, more than five hundred thousand people, including about 25 percent of the ethnic Chinese population, had been rounded up and forced into New Villages where individual behavior was closely monitored.[84] The resettlement process relied on force: "Squatter resettlement has been confined to physical removal of squatters to areas where they can be controlled."[85] New Villages included insurgents, though they were intended to separate civilians from rebels.[86] More than thirty thousand residents were deported.[87] Authorities would have liked to deport more residents: "General Briggs is of the firm opinion that, provided it is politically possible for all the detainees to be shipped to China and dumped somewhere on the coastline there . . . it would have a great effect on the situation in Malaya."[88] Other measures included detention without trial, seizure of food, and destruction of premises used by insurgents and supporters.[89]

MALAYA ALTERNATIVE EXPLANATION:
THE GOVERNANCE MODEL

Had the Malayan case reflected the predictions of the good governance approach, we should have seen the government making reforms that gained it popular support while weakening the insurgency, and we should have seen a reduction in uses of force to control civilians. The empirical evidence reveals neither reforms, nor increased popular support, nor reduced uses of force against civilians.

Reforms. The existing literature emphasizes a newly important role for political reforms instead of violence in the campaign with the arrival of Gen. Sir Harold Briggs in April 1950 as civilian director of operations under the British high commissioner. Briggs's strategy included the creation of New Villages, designed to protect civilians from insurgents and cut the flow of resources to the insurgency; the delivery of goods and services to civilians; and the co-optation of the insurgents' message about independence.[90] "The Malayan C-I approach was not primarily military," Komer says of this period, noting its civil, police, and psychological operations along with military efforts. All occurred "within the context of a firm rule of law and steady progress toward self-government and independence, which robbed the insurgency of much political appeal."[91] Focus on the independence promise is common, as with Julian Paget's claim that the decision to grant independence as of 1957 provided significant support for the counterinsurgency campaign by winning ethnic Chinese and Malay support against the Communists.[92]

Identification of other reforms is prominent in the literature as well. Several authors argue that the British goal was to make social and political reforms that would win ethnic Chinese support and keep that of the Malays.[93] Komer makes a broader claim about implementation. The government "undertook a variety of political, economic, and social measures, accompanied by an information campaign, to win 'hearts and minds,' along with the move towards independence," he writes.[94]

Authors typically discuss the reforms they claim took place without specifying them in any detail or providing clear ties to insurgent defeat. They also pay little attention to the timing of the events that they point to as driving defeat. For example, Komer lists goods to be provided to New Villagers, but without specifying when or even if they were delivered: "Each settler would get title to the land he tilled, and a sixth of an acre for his house and garden plot. But every effort would be made to see that the communities did not degenerate into mere detention camps. Schools, dispensaries, markets, electric light, and other facilities would be provided. Water would be piped in." Komer also lauds elections, but again without noting their timing or effects relative to the defeat of the insurgent threat, saying, "The first town elections were held in early 1952. . . . In May 1952, legislation was passed for electing village councils in the Malay kampongs [communities] and in the 'new villages' created by the resettlement policy. By 1955 more than 50 percent of the villages had elected local councils."[95] Similarly, the RAND study argues that an important contribution to success was "initiatives in the New Villages that would both accelerate their movement toward self-government, including local elections, and improve quality of life in general, including economic opportunities, community halls, traveling dispensaries, and other amenities," but does not consider the implementation or timing of these efforts or any effects relative to the defeat of the insurgency.[96]

The historical record provides little or no support for these claims about the role of reforms in government success in Malaya. There were no major reforms democratizing or liberalizing the state, and the limited expansion in political rights that did take place *followed* success of the counterinsurgency campaign, as did the provision of some limited benefits to civilians in New Villages. Even if we judge the insurgent threat defeated by the more traditional date of 1951, not to mention the usual date of 1954, instead of my dating of 1948, the claims that reforms defeated the MNLA are unsupported by evidence.

The British indubitably wanted to create a pluralistic society and a liberal democratic constitutional state. They planned and expected to establish a liberal democracy with a multiethnic military.[97] Not creating a liberal polity "would be to accept a major defeat in the war of ideas, and would encourage the growth of bitter communal strife, from which Malaya has hitherto been comparatively free," a Foreign Office official wrote in 1952.[98] Thus British authorities continued pressing for a liberal political order throughout the Emergency. "Even after the Emergency is over it will be essential, if internal strife is to be avoided, to continue to affirm that we shall not withdraw until a true partnership of communities has been established in Malaya," the director of operations said in 1955.[99] But local elite resistance repeatedly forced the British to scale back their plans for liberal reforms. The British ultimately focused on what a leading British police officer characterized as preserving the essentials of liberty rather than the trappings of freedom.[100]

The major political change the British instituted in Malaya during the Emergency was the grant of independence in 1957. It cannot accurately be characterized as a reform prompted by the insurgency or intended to quell insurgent violence. Planning for independence began in 1942.[101] These plans were no secret. By 1944, British officials were meeting with Malay leaders. The government announced its plan for the liberal Malay Union in the House of Commons in 1945.[102] In addition, within Malaya, there was no widespread call for independence. As the British made political changes, in fact, local concerns rose about what would follow. The British goal of creating a pluralistic liberal state was closely bound up with Malaya residents' fears about who would have what political rights and the possibility of communal violence.

The government gained ethnic elites' support for its counterinsurgency campaign by accommodating personal, communal, and nationalist interests at the cost of its reform goals. Two British choices stand out. First was the decision to bring ethnic elites into government as representatives of their communities and to create and support specifically communal interest groups, as discussed earlier in this chapter. In doing so, the government decided to try balancing communal interests rather than doing away with them. Second, the British abandoned plans for equal citizenship for all ethnicities and residents of Malaya in order to retain ethnic Malay support and reduce the possibility of communal violence.

The Malayan Union of 1946 was intended to give all residents equal rights. Britain wanted to create a Malaysian identity encompassing ethnic Malays, ethnic Chinese, ethnic Indians, and all other residents. Plans for the liberal union foundered on the dominant ethnic Malay elites' resistance to such reforms as sharing citizenship and voting rights with other ethnicities. The union was dissolved in favor of the Malayan Federation in 1948. In 1948, the government succeeded against the MNLA with citizenship for non-Malays still tightly restricted. Thus it is difficult to argue that citizenship reforms helped defeat the insurgent threat. Indeed, ethnic Malays still receive special treatment in Malaysia today.

The British continued trying to create a stable Malaysia based on a liberal political order, adjusting their case for greater reforms to try to gain local elite support.[103] Secretary of State for the Colonies Oliver Lyttelton made London's expectations clear to General Sir Gerald Templer when he was named to replace the assassinated high commissioner, Sir Henry Gurney. Templer was to "further our democratic aims in Malaya," including by providing a common citizenship for all.[104] Malay elites, however, as the dominant but not majority ethnicity, feared that democracy would swamp them demographically because ethnic Chinese and ethnic Indian residents outnumbered Malays. Malay parties opposed granting automatic citizenship to anyone born in Malaya (jus soli), which ethnic Chinese elites began demanding in 1956.[105] Some Malay elites argued that "it would be preferable to continue under a 'colonial' regime rather than to grant the Chinese the claim for 'jus soli.'"[106] Malay elites also resisted elite ethnic Chinese demands to make Chinese one of the official languages.[107] Even if we use the conventional date of 1955 to identify counterinsurgent success, the battle between elites for greater citizenship rights did not occur until after the MNLA was disposed of as a threat. Thus the eventual extension of citizenship rights to a part of the non-Malay population could not have contributed to counter-insurgent success. Indeed, ethnic Chinese in Malaya showed little interest in gaining citizenship. Even after qualifications were relaxed, in 1951, 433,000 ethnic Chinese who met the qualifications did not register and many others did not wish to apply for citizenship.[108] This lack of interest shows that increasing citizenship rights was not a reform that responded to ethnic Chinese demands and thus was not important for counterinsurgency success.

The British also acceded to local elites' decision to continue to use communal identities as the foundation of politics, dealing a severe blow to the British goal of a pluralistic democracy. In supporting a deal between the MCA and leading Malays to share electoral seats in Kuala Lumpur elections in 1952 as a way of sidelining a third, more pluralistic party, the British supported a new pattern of communal parties agreeing to electoral sharing by community in order to defeat less communally oriented parties.[109] The MCA-UMNO arrangement set the state for communally based politics in the form of the countrywide spread of the Alliance Party.[110] In 1954, the Alliance Party, comprising leading ethnic Malay, ethnic Chinese, and ethnic Indian parties, agreed on a quota system for candidates in federal elections, with three MCA candidates permitted for every four nominated by UMNO.[111] This agreement compromised liberal British goals but fostered elite cooperation with British authorities. It is difficult to see how British acquiescence to communal demands for an informally restricted democracy can be considered a reform, or how its timing contributed to the defeat of the insurgent threat in 1948 or even later.

The conventional wisdom argues that after the first, violent phase of the campaign, the government granted reforms in the form of benefits and goods that improved civilians' daily lives and thus gave the government popular support, drained it away from the MNLA, and contributed to insurgent defeat. The British themselves tell a different story. "At present it would be in general terms true to say that we are doing little to improve the lot of mass [sic] of the population beyond increasing taxation," British High Commissioner Sir Henry Gurney wrote in 1950.[112] There were "vast medical and health problems to be dealt with," the director of medical services in Malaya said in 1952.[113] In 1957, well after the insurgent threat was defeated, the director of operations reported in understated fashion that there was "still considerable discontent in the New Villages."[114]

The New Villages and other efforts to separate insurgents from civilians were supposed to be a way to bring the far-flung and often tragically poor residents of Malaya under the beneficent hand of the state so it could provide for their needs. These efforts are usually presented as such in the counterinsurgency literature. But there is increasing evidence from residents' own accounts that they did not consider themselves well or even fairly treated. A doctor described seeing four hundred civilians huddled behind the barbed wire of a resettlement community: "I shall never forget their pale and puffy faces: beriberi, or the ulcers on their legs. Their skin was the hue of the swamp. They stank. There was no clean water."[115] In one New Village, Templer berated the villagers in July 1952 about the need to provide information on the insurgency and punished them by imposing further controls on their movements and further rationing of food and other necessities. Villagers listened in silence, simmering at their "unjust punishment."[116] The resident commissioner in Penang state reported that in the capital, George Town, in 1955, ethnic Chinese considered the New Villages "small and remote concentration camps, devoid of any attraction whatsoever."[117] Unhappiness and frustration continued with resettlement, curfews, and food controls that led to shortages and a rising cost of living.[118] As late as 1956, in Penang popular frustration continued: "A meeting of several hundred hill folk took place in Balik Pulau during the month to protest against resettlement."[119] Again, these shocking health problems and resentments continued well after defeat of the insurgent threat, making it difficult to argue that reforms caused counterinsurgent success.

A few official reports of community satisfaction appear scattered amid accounts of unhappiness. Overall, however, in 1951, "the resettled population [were] not altogether satisfied," according to another understated British report. The populace did not appreciate "that they [were] immeasurably better off as the result of being resettled, and that they should positively help the government to maintain their security."[120]

The government began resettlement and control over civilians' movements and food supplies in 1948 and systematized its efforts over time. Goods and services intended to help camp residents survive, such as clothing, building materials, and cash advances, only began arriving in 1952, and they were provided primarily by charities and the MCA, not the government.[121] Missionaries and the MCA provided significant support to the "traumatized" New Villagers beginning in 1952–1954, after defeat of the MNLA threat. Villagers forced to relocate to smaller areas for easier control or into the armed camps resented the loss of their homes and vegetable or rubber plots. The presence of insurgents and criminal elements from secret societies within the militarized communities concerned the government. But it took several years to begin to remedy the deprivation. In 1952, Methodist missionaries were working in 42 New Villages. There were 438 villages in 1954, indicating just how little help was reaching villagers even after counterinsurgent success. In 1958, missionary work was under way in 333 of the 410 New Villages accessible to missionaries. Also in 1958, missionaries were proposing setting up cottage industries, cooperatives, and daycare centers for New Villagers, indicating that these services were not already being provided.[122] Only in 1955 in Penang, for example, were thirty-three-year leases for agricultural plots ceremonially presented to farmers in two New Villages. A fund-raising drive for a school took place in another.[123] But a light industrial effort in New Villages to make decorative high-heeled wooden shoes was not flourishing.[124] Though the conventional wisdom presents the eventual provision of land to some New Villagers as a major reform, in fact, many residents yearned to return to their old location rather than stay in the New Villages.[125]

Popular Support. Existing work argues that popular support was an important component of success in Malaya. The RAND study, for example, argues that the resettlement of civilians in the campaign "went beyond basic relocation, actually providing a community structure and amenities over and above what was necessary to meet the population's basic needs," and calls it a "defining feature of Gen. Sir Gerald Templer's successful efforts to win popular support for the COIN [counterinsurgency] effort." Julian Paget makes a similar argument, claiming that social measures, including the "major social reform" of the New Villages, helped win the populace to the government side. Komer too argues that success in Malaya involved "gaining popular support through effective, equitable government and by satisfying popular aspirations."[126]

The historical record shows that Britain did not gain the popular support it believed it needed to defeat the insurgency.[127] Statements ruing this lack appear throughout the Emergency, though officials had reason to claim that they were gaining support in their reports to superiors in order to gain praise. The director of operations reported in 1951 that "the efforts of government have been directed towards encouraging a spirit of Malayan nationalism among the Chinese in Malaya and encouraging them to play their part in the campaign, but so far with little success."[128] Even the traditional Malay rulers failed to see the Communist threat the British did, Templer complained.[129] One of many complaints about popular indifference was that "the public tends to regard the Emergency as a matter between the British government and its representatives in Malaya on the one hand and the MCP on the other."[130] The populace was largely apathetic, including ethnic Malays, authorities wrote in 1954, six years after breaking the insurgency.[131] Indeed, "the public has, as usual, done its best to disprove Aristotle's dictum that man is by nature a political animal."[132] The director of operations reported in 1955 that despite British efforts, "the majority of the people have so far been brought only to a state of 'reasonably friendly apathy.'"[133] Local leaders remained uninterested in the Emergency as late as 1956.[134]

In some areas, popular views of the government remained hostile into the independence era. The director of operations reported in 1951 that with 67,000 persons resettled or in the process of resettlement and 52,500 to go in priority areas, and 50,000 resettled or in the process of resettlement with 280,000 to go in nonpriority areas, those resettled were showing "increased appreciation of the security afforded them," but "active Chinese support [was] still generally lacking."[135] Several years later, in 1955 in Perak state,

"New Villagers around Ipoh still appear[ed] to be uncooperative, indifferent, or actively hostile."[136] Some state officials did report decreasing unhappiness with population and food controls over time.[137]

Fortunately for the British, there was also little support for the MNLA throughout the campaign. In 1948, a top-level report said that "they have failed to secure the support of the vast majority of the Chinese or any other community in Malaya."[138] After counterinsurgent success, in 1955, the director of operations reported that the insurgents were "feared and disliked by the mass of the people, but regrettably they [were] helped by a minority."[139]

MALAYA CONCLUSION

The evidence shows that the British defeated the MNLA threat through elite accommodation and uses of force, supporting the compellence theory. Rather than taking care to avoid damage to civilians and avoiding uses of force against them, and making reforms that gained it popular support, the government made the accommodation of rival elites a key part of its campaign, along with the use of force to control civilians.

In Malaya, government elites saw room for gain through cooperation with others, both sides made limited demands, government elites had found the reforms they wanted to make impossible because of their need to consider the interests of nongovernmental elites, and these actors did not see an existential threat in the insurgency. Government elites needed the cooperation of nongovernmental ethnic elites to create the long-term political stability they sought. Ethnic elites helped provide order and legitimacy, supporting the government's counterinsurgent efforts.

The British particularly accommodated the concerns of the ethnic Malay elites. As independence neared, the Malays increasingly feared the loss of status and privileges, though they were the poorest and least educated of the three largest ethnic communities in Malaya. The British attempted to demonstrate that politics in the independence era could mean gains for all. Yet they continued to privilege the Malays over other ethnicities for two reasons. First, this ethnicity was closest to a majority, which meant, in practical and philosophical terms, that its views mattered most. Second, the British needed the traditional leaders to continue their governance role in the political units within the peninsula.[140]

One point that stands out in records of the Emergency is that the goal of bringing all ethnicities into the polity as equals was specific to British goals for Malaya. There are no grounds for assuming it was or should be something all counterinsurgent governments do or should want. Indeed, it was not something that all residents of Malaya agreed on. It was certainly not a goal set by the British to respond to ethnic Chinese grievances driving the insurgency. The British themselves did not identify ethnic Chinese political grievances as a driver of the insurgency. To claim otherwise shows a fundamental misunderstanding of the case.

Greece

The Greek Civil War may be the least widely known of the counterinsurgency campaigns hailed as models of good governance. At the time, the United States considered defeating the insurgency a crucial U.S. security interest. Indeed, the war spurred President Harry S. Truman's doctrine declaring that the United States would support democratic states challenged by Soviet aggression. In this campaign, in 1947–1949, the United States took over supporting the repressive, fragile, post–World War II Greek government when London informed Washington that it could no longer afford to do the job. The U.S. government believed that good governance reforms were necessary but ultimately decided that stability in the form of defeat of the insurgency had to come first. As part of the Marshall Plan, U.S. advisers built Greece's military capacity sufficiently to achieve a decisive military victory over the Communist and nationalist insurgency, the National Popular Liberation Army, later known as the Democratic Army.

U.S. policymakers feared that Communist victory in Greece would disastrously provide the Soviet Union with access to the Middle East and its oil. "Greece and Turkey, without financial and other aid from either the United States or Great Britain, may become Soviet puppets in the near future," warned a report to the State Department. "Their loss to the Western world would undoubtedly be followed by further Soviet territorial and other gains in Europe and in the Near and Middle East. The resulting chaos would be accompanied by an immediate weakening of the strategic and economic position of the whole Western world, particularly of Great Britain, and the very security of the United States would be threatened."[141]

The civil war had been fought before World War II, during it, and after. Insurgents had popular support for their calls for more representative, distributive governance but faced determined resistance from Greece's right-wing, monarchist oligarchy. The insurgent political program included a broad coalition government; the end of the fighting; a general political amnesty; reform of armed forces policies and the civil service; disarmament of all armed bands, including rightist militias; dissolution of parliament; and fair elections.[142]

U.S. support strengthened the Greek military and improved its fighting capabilities and firepower, but the civilian state remained repressive and corrupt. Necessities were in short supply after years of war and German occupation. "There was an almost total lack of supplies and transport," one observer wrote. "Even the simplest items such as paper to write on or the pencil wherewith to write were unobtainable, or could only be obtained after days of effort."[143] The Greek government accommodated the interests of elites within it rather than challengers from outside Athens. It also supported and deployed militias to clear out civilian communities and hunt insurgents. The military campaign broke down insurgent formations through brute force, held thousands of civilians in fetid conditions on island prisons and in reeducation camps, and cleared the mountains of entire communities that might provide support to the insurgents.

The empirical evidence in the following sections is based on contemporaneous U.S. military and civilian documents and the work of scholars of Greek history. It presents a rather different picture of the campaign and the drivers of success from that provided in the existing counterinsurgency literature. I identify in my analysis when the government defeated the insurgency and how it did so (accommodations and hard fighting that included brute force against civilians), and I consider the relative strength of alternative explanations for success suggested by the existing literature: good governance reforms and popular support.

In brief, the insurgency in question began in 1946, following on political violence before and during World War II. The British handed over their military support mission to the United States a year later, in 1947, the same year that the Greek government banned the Communist Party and expanded its army. In February 1947 the United States expressed concern that the Greek government would soon crumble.

By July 1948 the military was pressing the insurgency from south to north up the peninsula. March 1949 saw the insurgents pushed out of the area near Athens. The government defeated the insurgent threat in August 1949 and the United States withdrew its advisers. Uses of force against civilians played an important role in separating insurgents from the resources they needed to survive. The military and militias destroyed civilian communities. Fetid military camps held thousands of civilians. Political accommodations took place among elites to retain U.S. support. The Greek government instituted no reforms, and U.S. concern for its survival severely limited its leverage. The government lost rather than gained popular support over the course of the war.

GREECE ANALYSIS

Insurgency Broken by 1949. The Greek military decisively defeated the insurgency in 1949, two years after U.S. backing replaced that of the British. In this case, there is little dispute over the date of the insurgency's destruction as a threat to the government. In February 1947, Dean Acheson had warned of "crisis and imminent possibility of collapse in Greece."[144] By that September, insurgents were massing in groups as large as a brigade and the U.S. military group commander saw "little promise of success."[145] The insurgency had strongholds along the northern border, in central Greece, and in the mountains of the Peloponnese to the south, near Athens.[146] Insurgent attacks were increasing in northern and central Greece and spreading in the Peloponnese. But casualties also rose, with the insurgency suffering 7,213 killed, 5,433 taken prisoner, and 5,222 deserted in 1947.[147]

By the end of July 1948, the military was making "striking progress in the face of immense difficulties." The insurgency took terrible casualties, including 6,686 from October 1948 through January 1949, 5,376 in March 1949, and 10,228 in April through June 1949.[148] In March 1949 the insurgency was driven from the Peloponnese, significantly reducing the threat to the capital. By April 1949 the Greek military forced it out of its northern bases in Vitsi and then from its previously secure base in the Grammos mountains, clearing Greek territory of rebels from south to north.[149]

The government's massive military operations from south to north harried and then drove the insurgency back into its mountainous northern strongholds,[150] inflicted terrible casualties, then broke the insurgency down into small bands on the run,[151] short of food and ammunition because of military uses of force against civilians.[152] Night air attacks hindered insurgent movement and restricted insurgent use of campfires with the goal of reducing insurgent efficiency rather than killing them outright, a hallmark of an attrition strategy.[153] A column of 1,500 insurgents fleeing to their Grammos mountains sanctuary in October 1947 included 800 armed and 700 unarmed fighters, indicating that the insurgents were already short of arms early in the conflict.[154] A batch of 108 insurgents surrendering in 1948 was in a "hungry and miserable condition."[155] The insurgency suffered 2,602 casualties in one operation alone that "virtually cleared" central Greece of insurgents.[156]

Monarchist and rightist General Alexandros Papagos was made commander in chief in January 1949. Papagos, who like the king and queen showed considerable interest in forming a dictatorship, was determined to achieve victory through violence.[157] "The war with banditry will be ended only by military force," he said. "Only this dynamic solution will permit of a diplomatic one."[158] A rightist in government, Gen. Napoleon Zervas, made a more picturesque vow: "We will answer terrorism with terrorism ten times as strong, disaster with disaster ten times as strong, and slaughter ten times greater. And this is not anti-Christian, because God has taught us how to behave to anti-Christian Communists, who have sold their souls to the devil."[159]

U.S. Gen. James Van Fleet, head of the Joint U.S. Military Advisory Group, described the military's target as insurgents, not territory, underlining the attritional character of the war. While clearing from south to north in 1949, forces were to keep the insurgents on the move "so that they could not sit down and organize supply centers and train forced recruits."[160] Indeed, in the second quarter of 1949, "aggressive GNA [Greek National Army] pursuit kept the enemy from establishing himself in any area." Insurgent casualties for the quarter were reported at 10,228, the lowest since October 1947, because so few insurgents remained. No large-scale insurgent attacks took place. The U.S. military mission had had to convince the Greek High Command to seize the initiative with "large scale coordinated operations designed to clear systematically the guerrillas from the infested areas of Greece." U.S. officers also prioritized areas to clear. U.S. advice was generally followed "with excellent results."[161]

Increasing army mobility was important to get troops into the mountains for clearing and other operations. "It [mechanical transport] could not help carry the battle beyond the roads into the rocky fastnesses of the mountains and hills where the guerrillas by virtue of their mode of warfare had been able very early to seize and maintain the initiative of a higher mobility." U.S. officials noted in the same report that conditions in Greece were so bad after World War II that they had to import horses for the cavalry and mules for artillery and pack bearing. "Prior to leaving the United States," the report noted, "these mules had been given special training for mountain operations."[162]

It was not only U.S. mules that helped the government succeed against the insurgency. U.S. military aid included hundreds of planes and ships, 4,130 mortar and artillery pieces, 89,438 bombs and rockets, 159,922 small arms, 7.7 million artillery and mortar rounds, and 455 million small arms rounds.[163] The might of the Greek military, even factoring in poor training and leadership, corruption, and bad morale, far exceeded the insurgents' capabilities.

Finally, the army overran the insurgent base at Vitsi in August 1949 after a three-day battle. Insurgents lost the majority of their equipment and supplies in their race north for the Albanian border. Next the military captured the huge insurgent base in the Grammos mountains. Four army divisions and five commando groups supported by air power took the two-hundred-square-mile base. The insurgency was down to 5,600 members by this time, the smallest number since U.S. records began in 1946. With the mopping up operations, the number fell to 3,580 by August 31, 1949.[164] Major hostilities ended in August and the United States withdrew its divisional advisers.[165]

Elite Accommodation. Three political accommodations supported government success in Greece. All three helped keep U.S. support flowing to the Greek government rather than bringing rival elites into a formal or informal coalition. The first was the centrist–right-wing cooperation that kept representatives of the Left out of the government. The second was the government's continued use of military forces to protect the home regions of parliamentarians, which retained elite support for the government at a time of political disarray. The third was the government's continued toleration of right-wing militias, including even bringing them under the government's aegis, which kept their politician-leaders from denouncing the government.

The center-right alliance was born after the Varkiza peace deal signed in 1945 between the government and the Greek Communist Party (Kommunistiko Komma Elladas; KKE). Both centrists and rightists in the Greek political system remained fearful of the Communist threat despite the agreement. The centrist Liberal Party and others feared the Left would take power through elections. They assessed that their alliance with the monarchist Right provided the protection of numbers despite policy disagreements with rightists, including over the need for military dictatorship versus support for the existing parliamentary system. "So long as the KKE seemed a serious threat—that is, until 1949—the distinction between many Centrists and the Right would consist of little more than personal antagonism."[166] Parliament outlawed the Communist Party in December 1947, but many insurgents were nationalists and leftists rather than Communists. Amnesty efforts to woo insurgents had little effect.[167]

Along with fear, the parliamentary alliance between rightists and centrists was based on professional affinities, personal and clientelist ties, regional loyalties, and patronage resources. The Greek political system was based on a traditional patronage order in which elites served their own interests through the centralized government down to the local level and back up again. "The monarchy, when restored in 1946, formed the apex of a hierarchy based on patronage and social deference."[168]

Traditional social, business, and political elites naturally feared the insurgent effort to rally the masses to political action. Along with parliamentarians, supporters of leading rightists such as Georgios Grivas (leader of the violent underground organization X) and Napoleon Zervas included businessmen who benefited from collaborating with the Germans during the occupation and from black-market profiteering. The security forces, formal and informal, were also dedicated rightists, forming a shadow state within the state. But the centrists needed these forces to defeat the insurgency. In Greek patronage politics, attention to the poor and social and economic issues was limited. Parliamentary deputies used their power at the national level to press the government on behalf of their better-off constituents back home.[169]

The Orthodox Church also allied with the rightist-nationalist-monarchist alliance against the insurgency. Though the insurgency did not "openly threaten" the church, religious fought on both sides, and both sides killed priests, the church feared the possibility of antireligious activity if the Communist insurgency succeeded in taking power.[170] The government permitted the church to remain an arm of the state that retained treasured privileges including "a major role for religious instruction in schools and exclusive control over marriage."[171]

The center-right alliance solidified right-wing power nationally and locally, and ended in near military dictatorship as well as counterinsurgent success. The Right stole the 1946 elections boycotted by center-leftists, leftists, and the National Liberation Front party associated with the insurgency. The government formed under rightist Constantin Tsaldaris responded to calls for repression of the Left, including filling posts from the local level up with rightists and purging teachers and the civil service. Under Tsaldaris, right-wing militias were brought under state control to officially continue the slaughter of the White Terror of the immediate post–World War II period. U.S. pressure helped bring Liberal Themistocles Sophoulis back to power in 1947, but right-wing domination of parliament and the security forces prevented him from reaching out to the Left beyond issuing an amnesty.[172]

An amnesty for insurgents might have provided an opening for accommodations, but U.S. officials opposed it, and Sophoulis agreed to limit its terms as part of a deal with the United States for the Liberal Party leader to take power as prime minister heading a Liberal-Populist center-right government in September 1947. The agreement specified that "individual ministers would be removed at U.S. suggestion if they [were] uncooperative," though the United States in fact had limited leverage. The amnesty, accepted by few insurgents for fear of death, lasted two months before the government returned to its policy of retribution.[173]

More broadly, U.S. pressure as well as Greek rightist convictions meant that the government rejected Communist efforts to seek a political solution rather than a military one. In 1947, the KKE sought formation of a centrist government under Sophoulis, who rejected the offer.[174] The United States made its position on talking with the Communists clear. "We consider [the] KKE's fair-sounding proposals to be insincere and dangerous, and that any serious discussion of them could only strengthen [the] Communists' hand," Secretary of State George C. Marshall wrote in July 1947.[175] U.S. support for the government meant that successive Greek leaders had no incentive to strike a bargain with the insurgency.[176] Accepting the political participation of the Socialist Party was beyond the pale for Greek elites and the United States. Even working with prominent Greek Liberal Party members who sought a political solution to the war and "were simply not as anti-Communist as the Americans" was out of bounds for the United States.[177]

After two years of U.S. frustration with political interference in the military and with military politicization and lack of ability, an agreement between the government and the United States made Papagos commander in chief in January 1949. He received extraordinary power. His suggestions were binding even on the minister of defense. His position also "facilitated the establishment of American influence, unhindered by political opposition." Papagos began professionalizing the military by lessening political interference in strategy and replacing brigade and battalion commanders based on ability rather than patronage.[178] Enlargement of the military enabled the offensive action that broke the insurgent threat, and Papagos was set on military victory.

The second significant accommodation supporting government success in Greece also involved elites already within the government. In this accommodation, the government continued providing military defenses to parliamentarians' home areas, and persuaded the U.S. government to fund an enlargement of the army that would permit these continued defensive operations as well as the offensive operations urged by the Americans. Military commanders were crippled by interference from parliamentary deputies pressing for protection of larger communities in their districts.[179] The army provided troops to protect specific towns and villages, limiting its offensive abilities. "All too often the GNA found itself obliged to submit to political pressure and maintain combat troops in the vicinity of certain vulnerable towns and villages," the U.S. military group commander reported in 1947.[180] In 1948, Van Fleet told Greek Minister of War George Stratos that it was difficult to explain to the U.S. government why an army of two hundred thousand men could not defeat a much smaller bandit force. It was even more difficult to explain, Van Fleet continued, why thirty thousand troops could not defeat 5,500 bandits in the Vista area. "Such a condition is unacceptable by American standards," Van Fleet said.[181]

U.S. officials pressured the government to free the military from these guard duties to go on the offensive against insurgents, but the government continued pressing for a larger army. The United States ended up enlarging the army to enable both defensive and offensive action. "There was apparently only one solution, that against which they had heretofore remained adamant, an increase in the strength of the Greek National Army." The United States finally authorized in September 1947 an army of 140,000, including a temporary increase of 20,000 men.[182] Enlarging the army enabled the government to both keep its elite allies happy by protecting their property—thus assuring continued U.S. support—and go on the offensive against the insurgency.

In the third accommodation among governmental elites, the government permitted right-wing militias led by elites to remain active. For example, the government ordered all Units for the Defense of the Countryside and mobile Units of Pursuit Detachments disbanded in January 1948 in favor of the official militia, the National Defense Corps, designed for static defense to free soldiers for offensive operations. The government, however, did not implement its order out of deference to the political leaders tied to these groups. The militias remained outside of government control.[183] The government saw little danger in the rightists' violence. Indeed, it worked in its favor. U.S. fears, like those of Greek elites, focused on leftists rather than the right wing that held power.[184]

Uses of Force against Civilians. The literature on the counterinsurgency campaign in Greece is limited, and much is produced by and for military practitioners. What exists focuses on reform plans rather than implementation, plays down or ignores systematic violence against civilians, and claims that the government learned from early uses of force against civilians to treat them better later in the war.[185]

The existing counterinsurgency narrative on the Greek Civil War emphasizes the government's change of approach after realizing that its early uses of force were counterproductive. A think tank study says the Greek military commander at war's end, Papagos, "discontinued unproductive sweeps and impulsive measures to counter insurgent activities and instead worked to clear, secure, and hold territory in well-defined areas, one at a time."[186] This account does not note that sweeps and other military action to "clear, secure and hold territory in well-defined areas" took place throughout the conflict in order to separate insurgents from civilians and their resources. Counterinsurgency authors also often ignore or downplay the government's systematic uses of violence against civilians. One influential report does not detail the government's population control programs but does note "the insurgents' poor treatment of the civilian population."[187] Existing work generally fails to recognize the intimate, inevitable relationship between military action and the use of brute force against civilians in this campaign. "Victory depended on maintaining the support of the countryside by securing villages through pacification programs while the army encircled and eliminated the guerrillas," writes one author who assumes popular support for the government and overlooks the uses of force integral to these "pacification programs."[188] Another mentions a program to resettle more than eight hundred thousand villagers as "largely considered successful in hindering insurgent intelligence acquisition and logistical and moral support" without identifying the effects of this program on civilians or explaining how it was conducted (by force).[189] One U.S. military officer's study of the conflict details the government's military operations without mentioning the civilian inhabitants: "Steep slopes, and poor, limited roads inhibited the Greek Army's movements. Slow moving government forces were unable to effectively pursue the Communist guerillas, and therefore resorted to clearing an area, then holding it, which caused the guerillas to go into defensive positions," he wrote. Later, the author continued, "the Communist fighters played right into the Greek government forces' advantages of being able to mass infantry, artillery and fighter bombers onto the Communist formations."[190] Another U.S. officer provides a similar view with an even more detailed account of military operations but no mention of any effects on civilians.[191] An analyst describes the reeducation camps set up on islands for suspected Communist sympathizers in the military in surprisingly inapposite terms. He compares them to "English public schools," dismissing "propaganda" about the camps' squalid conditions.[192]

Together, security forces and rightist militias targeted civilians to cut the insurgency's access to resources, including food, intelligence, and recruits.

Targeting civilians was a policy choice by the army and the government. Sources sympathetic to the insurgents identify the military's depopulation of villages as a main reason for defeat.[193] Tactics included controlling food supplies, driving civilians from their homes, barring those imprisoned in their villages from tending their fields and flocks, suppressing the media, mistreating surrendering insurgents, lynching, and conducting mass arrests.[194] The military used napalm in the mountains and destroyed civilians' farm machinery and livestock as well as food crops.[195] Civilian villages in insurgent areas and in areas considered insecure were denied aid in the form of food, clothing, and medical supplies, including UN relief food and supplies.[196] The military forcibly controlled villages and put civilians under curfew.[197] Clearing mountain villages cut food and recruits to the insurgency. "Large areas of the Pindus range and the Macedonian mountains were depopulated."[198] In 1947–1948 the government moved about fifteen thousand peasants a month into "security camps," while the number of refugees rose to seven hundred thousand at war's end in 1949. That figure represents about 9 percent of the population.[199]

The Greek military cleared hundreds of thousands of civilians from their homes to break the flow of resources to the insurgency at a time when the country was still largely rural.[200] About seven hundred thousand members of the rural population moved during the war, 18 percent of the rural population of Greece.[201] Some were forced from their homes. Others fled insurgents, militias, the military, or all three. In these two years of fighting, 1947 to 1949, the number of refugees and displaced persons in Greece increased from fifty thousand to seven hundred thousand.[202] In October 1947 the army had already cleared three hundred thousand civilians from their homes, primarily in the insurgent-dominated northern and central areas of Greece.[203] These evacuees would have preferred to go home even at the risk of insurgent attack at least in part because of their "tragic" living conditions as displaced persons.[204]

Operation Terminus in 1947 failed in its attempt to rout the insurgency from northwestern Greece, close to the Albanian and Yugoslav borders, but it succeeded in destroying the insurgents' support system, including through air raids and burning villages. In Operation Haravagi in 1948, in the same region of the northwest, two of the largest villages, Kastania and Amarando, lost half their population, a loss evident as late as the 1961 census.[205] Many civilians who could remain in their homes chose to do so, even with insurgents occupying their villages or holed up nearby. Insurgents committed terrorist acts against civilians, and the Right threatened them, but these peasants did not want to leave their homes or their land. They had been part of the insurgency, perhaps, or had sons and daughters fighting with them, and they sympathized with the insurgencies' goals. They also feared the army and the rightists, with their beatings and killings.[206]

One old shepherd said, "Why do the gendarmes, instead of taking after the guerrillas, beat us up—defenseless people—and then get out of the village to their garrison before nightfall? Of course, with no gendarmes here at night, the guerrillas come and we give them food. And of course they requisition food, too. But the army and gendarmes also requisition food from us. The guerrillas divide the burden fairly; the government men simply seize what they want. The guerrillas let us go and work where we please, in peace, and deal with us as friends; the gendarmes beat us."[207]

Throughout the war, the government imprisoned many people suspected of Communist leanings in filthy camps on islands in southern Greece. The government also held insurgents' families' hostage, controlled the supply of already scarce food products, and conducted mass arrests, including one sweep that imprisoned some nine thousand individuals, and mass deportations.[208] Many communities that the military did not evacuate were surrounded and controlled by force.[209] The military used air power against civilian communities day and night.[210] Along with mass arrests came mass executions. In 1947, 24 executions were reported in a single day.[211] The government noted in October 1949 that it had executed 1,223 people out of 3,150 condemned to die.[212] International protests rose at reports of mass executions. Winston Churchill himself protested. The United States expressed concern about world opinion.[213]

The state held suspected Communists from the army and elsewhere in squalid camps for "reeducation."[214] The U.S. ambassador reported receiving many complaints about the "deplorable conditions" of some eight thousand deportees on the "barren" island of Caria.[215] Some seven thousand former inducted soldiers alone were imprisoned in September 1947.[216] Others were leftists or liberals who opposed Communism, swept up and sent off en masse without trial to exile in the islands.[217] Food in the camps was scarce; prisoners had to buy their own if they could. The state provided no shelter. Cooperation with local residents gained prisoners some food and shelter "at a very low level." Prisoners organized self-help efforts such as schools. The situation would have been worse but for the prisoners' "initiative and the government's willingness to let them profit from local advantages," the U.S. ambassador wrote in November 1946.[218] After visiting a so-called reeducation camp on one island, a British officer reported "a broken rib is an occupational disease on Makronisos," referencing the guards' casual brutality.[219]

The government made little effort to count or care for refugees until late in the war and after counterinsurgent success. The army forced civilians to move and left them to their fate, while civil authorities had no procedures in place to support them. The government agreed in November 1947 to end all community evacuations but those absolutely necessary, but according to a top U.S. official in Athens, the degree of implementation was unknown.[220]

In May 1949, the government tried to begin regulating relief and repatriation programs for some civilians.[221]

GREECE ALTERNATIVE EXPLANATION:
THE GOVERNANCE MODEL

Had the Greek case supported the governance approach, we should have seen reforms gaining popular support and in turn weakening the insurgency, and a reduction over time in the use of force against civilians. None of these three elements is evident in the historical record.

Reforms. The assumption that reforms bruited or planned are reforms implemented appears in much of the counterinsurgency literature. One author, for example, explains the Greek government's plans for addressing the needs of civilians driven from their homes "to deprive the insurgents of the popular support necessary to continue their armed struggle." These plans included clearing communities only when militarily necessary and after warning inhabitants. The military would transport the civilians to camps. Civilians would only be allowed to return home when it was safe to do so, and "the state would provide to the refugees daily family benefits, daily bread rations, farming equipment and animals, clothing and housing materials." The author notes that by May 1949, 705,000 civilians had been removed from their homes—roughly one-tenth of the population of Greece—and the government decided to provide additional relief services to refugees. Several pages later the author mentions that postwar support for refugees was not implemented well or fully, but does not provide details on implementation of the war or postwar plans he identifies.[222] Scholars writing about macro-level reforms, meanwhile, identify the goals of the Marshall Plan and the Europeans working with the United States to rebuild Europe, while underlining how difficult it was to implement reforms such as restoring basic infrastructure and rebuilding the economy during a civil war.[223]

The perilous situation of the Greek government facing a popular insurgency prompted the United States to create and implement the Marshall Plan to save Europe and indeed the world from Communism. The Truman administration's explanations to Congress about the need for the plan "added up to intervention on a massive scale, upon the request of the Greek government, to make Greece a strong, independent, self-supporting, democratic state."[224] In drafting Truman's speech to Congress asking for funding for the Marshall Plan, adviser Clark Clifford wrote, "The seeds of totalitarian regimes are nurtured by misery and want. They spread and grow in the evil soil of poverty and strife. They reach their full growth when the hope of a people for a better life has died."[225]

In practice, however, U.S. officials became more pragmatic. The United States sought greater elite unity, military effectiveness, and economic efficiency, but there was little discussion among U.S. officials about plans for systematic government liberalization or good governance.[226] Long-term U.S. goals for the repressive, corrupt[227] Greek government discussed in private focused on political stability rather than democratization or liberalization. A committee named to study aid to Greece and Turkey identified the desired end state for Greece as "maintain its independence and restore domestic tranquility."[228]

U.S. Secretary of State George Marshall's itemized goals for Greece in May 1947 did not include democratization,[229] though he did inform the Greek prime minister that the continued presence in the cabinet of "such [right-wing] irreconcilables as Zerves is not reassuring."[230] Marshall summed up U.S. policy objectives as "a) maintenance of the independence and integrity of Greece, specifically to keep Greece from falling into the Soviet orbit and b) development of the economy of Greece on a self sustaining basis as soon as possible." Marshall prioritized destruction of insurgent forces and establishment of internal security above other goals.[231] Marshall also noted that "judgment should not be passed against the existing regime because it fails to meet American economic or financial requirements."[232] Successive Greek governments remained fragile during the war but attained greater stability in the 1950s ahead of the right-wing military coup of 1967 that led to the rule of the Colonels until 1974.[233]

U.S. pressure for political reform had little effect on the Greek government. Marshall urged the government to observe the rule of law in arrests and executions to keep world opinion supportive of the government.[234] The government did not do so. Dean Acheson, as undersecretary of state, urged U.S. diplomats to seek a moderate unity government in Athens that would push the rightists out.[235] The Greeks did not form a moderate unity government or force the rightists out. U.S. Ambassador Lincoln MacVeigh urged Greek officials in 1947 to avoid such tactics as summary arrests and deportations, "which can possibly be characterized as dictatorial, especially at this time when U.S. govt seriously considering aid to Greece." The Greek government did not avoid such tactics. The U.S. ambassador urged the removal of the rightist Zervas, at the time minister of public order, in favor of a liberal "who could protect state [sic] just as efficiently, but less spectacularly, and with greater observance of due process of law."[236] The Greek government did not remove Zervas. The State Department's Division of Near Eastern Affairs noted the pernicious role of rightists as well as leftists in the government and urged moderation on Athens, but Greek leaders made other choices.[237] The Americans suggested to Prime Minister Sophoulis and Deputy Prime Minister Tsaldaris in April 1948 that they hold municipal elections, but the Greeks thought it a bad idea.[238]

Similarly, the government might pass laws, but enforcement was another matter. "They pass tax laws but cannot collect the taxes. They declare amnesties but cannot enforce them. Real power lies in the bureaucracy, the army and the police, and nothing has been done to purge these instruments of the most vengeful pro-Nazis not to mention the reactionary monarchists," CBS newsman Howard K. Smith said in 1949. While tax revenues rose substantially under U.S. tutelage, it was the result of indirect taxation that hit the purchasing power of the poor most painfully, hardly a reform intended to help the populace.[239] BBC correspondent Kenneth Matthews concluded in 1948 that "'democracy' in Greece is a paper façade, and beyond a quarter-mile radius of the hotel district of Athens and Salonika, where the foreigners live, not even the façade exists."[240] Further, the British ambassador reported in late 1948, there was "an all too prevalent attitude, not only that Greece has a right to practically unlimited foreign aid, but that" Greece was absolved "from the obligation of making determined efforts or real sacrifices."[241] Indeed, the United States joined Greek efforts to curtail freedom of the press in Greece and on the part of U.S. media. CBS correspondent George Polk was assassinated in 1948 after criticizing the government's reactionary policies. U.S. officials quashed an Overseas Writers Association investigation that tied rightists to Polk's death.[242]

U.S. commitment to Greek government survival limited U.S. leverage. U.S. officials considered reducing support because of the "incompetence and irresponsibility of the Greek government" in the winter of 1948–1949. They faltered because of the American fear that its withdrawal would mean imminent Greek collapse to the Communists.[243]

There are Greece scholars who take a harsh view of the U.S. failure to press reforms. One argues that "Greece for all practical purposes ceased being a sovereign nation. . . . Political parties came to or fell from power only with the prior agreement of the United States; . . . and finally, the army, which was already under the direction of foreigners, became even more dependent on non-Greeks for its day-to-day decisions," writes one scholar, Yiannis P. Roubatis. "Acheson envisioned the creation of a government that would exclude from active participation at least one large part of the political spectrum, the left. The United States government had demonstrated that, apart from occasional statements of displeasure, it was prepared to work with the most reactionary elements in Greece."[244]

Both Greek and Western policymakers presumed that circumstances would soon return to their normal prewar state and that the economy would recover. They focused on the immediate problem of feeding the populace after the famine of 1941–1944 under German occupation, as well as on such tasks as the delivery of raw materials to resume local production, but had no development plans.[245] There were good reasons why the government might hesitate to try to stabilize the economy. Efforts to tax the government's elite political allies, merchants and industrialists, and impose price controls would have been likely to fail because of elites' opposition.[246] Such a breach in the government would have endangered further Western support. U.S. discussions of administrative reforms to make the state function more effectively and efficiently took it for granted that they would occur without linking them to the success of the counterinsurgency campaign.[247]

An independent U.S. survey of conditions in Greece in 1947 criticized the government's approach to recovery and the insurgency because it did not attempt to provide benefits to civilians. The survey team also criticized the Greek government for serving its members' interests rather than those of the populace. "Evidence is lacking that the present government has even begun to grapple purposefully with its economic problems," the team wrote. "It strives to restore order by suppressing the Left by force, but it makes little serious attempt to use for economic and social reconstruction the foreign financial assistance which Greece has received. . . . The government itself, with the exception of some cabinet ministers, looks to the rich industrialists and profiteers, and to the hierarchy of the army as now constituted, as its prime domestic support." The Greek government even sold UN relief supplies to industrialists to resell for substantial profit, the report said.[248]

Popular Support. Popular support for the government declined, rather than grew, over the course of the war. Even "important elements of [the] population which would normally support constituted authority" did not do so, an embassy official reported to the State Department in Washington in 1947.[249] Popular morale and confidence in the government continued to sink as the fighting continued atop the occupation-era famine and the rightist White Terror that preceded the civil war.[250]

There are relatively few references to any need for popular support within Greece in U.S. documents, particularly in contrast to contemporaneous documents on Malaya, the Philippines, Dhofar, and El Salvador. More frequent are references to the importance of U.S. and world opinion, as with the message U.S. Ambassador Lincoln MacVeagh delivered to acting Foreign Minister Panagiotis Pipinellis in person. MacVeagh urged the government to "refrain from further indiscriminate arrests or other unnecessarily drastic measures and endeavor mitigate [*sic*] inevitably bad impression created abroad by measures already taken." The ambassador underlined that "public opinion abroad" on Greece's policies concerned its friends, meaning the United States.[251]

GREECE CONCLUSION

The successful Greek counterinsurgency campaign looks very much like that of the British in Malaya on the military side, with large operations clearing civilians from the countryside and imprisoning many of them in camps. There is less evidence of the government drawing in rival elites through accommodation in Greece. Successive governments did take care to guard the interests of members of parliament and other elites already within the fold, including by bringing them into government and keeping them there despite U.S. objections, and by protecting areas of the countryside important to leaders. The limited degree of political accommodation of rival elites in this case may help explain Greece's subsequent lack of political stability.

Government elites saw the possibility of gains through cooperation with other government elites, gains in the form of continued U.S. support. Their demands of each other were not only limited but congenial to their political preferences. Accommodations were also less costly than reforms, which the government refused to make. Accommodation was limited to intragovernmental elites because the elites saw the insurgency as an existential threat to their power and wealth. As predicted, government elites banded together to ensure continued great power support.

The government saw two possible outcomes of the war: it either retained power or lost everything. The insurgency had considerable popular support for goals such as an end to government repression and for free elections, which would severely constrain elite power. The greatest accommodation that government elites were able to manage was to stay united against the insurgency in order to keep U.S. support flowing. The Greek Right's fundamental goal of retaining power provided no room for talking with the enemy, or even admitting political elements into the government who did not share the Right's goals. The Right's cataclysmic view of its adversary was more than rhetorical. A U.S. team surveying conditions in Greece in 1947 attributed at least some of the Right's ferocity to fear. Rightists feared the Left taking power and stripping them of all they had. Prosperous rightists also feared punishment for collaborating with the occupying Germans during the war. "Such fears combined to create a peculiarly indiscriminate and blind fury on the part of the more extreme partisans of the government, and on the part of the government itself, as reflected in its acts against its opponents," the survey team wrote.[252] The military still roundly defeated the insurgency on the battlefield, suggesting that accommodations limited to government elites do not necessarily reduce the likelihood of military counterinsurgency success.

There is little evidence of reforms taking place or of the great power intervener pressing for reforms. The latter point reveals a distinct difference in the Greek campaign from those in Malaya and the Philippines, as we see in the next section of this chapter. The Greek uses of force against insurgency and civilians, as well as the lack of reforms, provide support for the predictions of the compellence theory, as does the government's success despite its lack of reforms and popular support.

The Philippines

The Huk insurgency in the Philippines grew from peasant resistance to landlord efforts to modernize and improve their yields after World War II.[253]

Traditionally, when landlord and peasant agreed on the terms of their relationship and both sides lived up to them, relations were relatively pacific.[254] But from the disruptions of the interwar global economic crisis through the Japanese occupation and into the postwar period, landlord-tenant relations worsened in the rich fields of the central area of the island of Luzon, near the national capital of Manila.[255] The peasants of Central Luzon wanted their government to protect them against what they saw as the increasing depredations of landowners, but landlords' and security forces' abuse and extortion forced them to seek safety with the Huk.[256]

Unfortunately for these sharecroppers, the landlords ruled the state. The oligarchs filled official positions and used the law as they wished. Political loyalty determined promotion within the government and military. Personal gain trumped professionalism. Nepotism, patronage, and other forms of corruption were not a problem to be solved, one that lessened efficiency and reduced productivity. Corruption was, as in many places, normal politics in the Philippines.[257]

Patron-client tensions worsened in April 1946, when President Manuel Roxas preserved his two-thirds majority in Congress by refusing to seat six candidates elected from an alliance of peasants, progressives, and nationalists in Central Luzon. Political violence increased in the area. Security forces, including the army, the military police (renamed the Philippine Constabulary in 1948), and civilian guards, used mortars, machine guns, heavy artillery, and aerial bombing to try to repress the peasants. Peasants' top priority became protection from attack by security forces rather than agricultural reforms. Many joined the Huk, guerrillas who had fought the occupying Japanese during World War II.[258]

The insurgency was a shifting mass of networks and organizations with changing and overlapping names and memberships, including an alliance and shared leadership with the Philippine Communist Party.[259] It was the peasants who had the numbers and the organization, however, so the party had to tailor its plans to their interests.[260] As a political movement, the Huk were winning mayoral and town councilor races in Central Luzon by 1950.[261] As a social movement, the Huk did what the United States, supporting the government, and the peasantry, appealing to the government, wanted the government to do: as best it could, the Huk protected peasants against official violence and landlords' bullying, enforced the law, and provided services. They stood guard and helped with planting and harvesting. They caught and punished thieves, rapists, and murders. Huk insurgents did commit atrocities and there was unsanctioned violence, most of which occurred later in the conflict, but generally the insurgency had a supportive rather than a coercive relationship with the populace it relied on for support. The Huk slogans included "Land for the Landless" and "Prosperity for the Masses." The Huk and their supporters wanted the rule of law; free and fair elections; a return to the more cooperative, mutually supportive traditional landlord-tenant relationship, including a larger share of the harvest for tenants and free or lower-cost loans from their patrons to get through a bad year; recognition of the anti-Japanese role played by the Huk during World War II, which stood in contrast to the collaboration of many elites; and economic and social security. Mostly the peasants wanted the government to be on their side. They did not seek to abolish the tenancy system or overthrow the government.[262]

The Philippines was a U.S. possession from 1898 until 1934, when President Franklin D. Roosevelt signed a bill making it a U.S. commonwealth until 1946, at which point it became independent. With the start of the Cold War after World War II, the United States was intent on keeping as much of Asia as possible within its sphere of influence. It also wanted to keep access to Clark Air Force Base and the Subic Bay naval base, which gave the U.S. military a crucial toehold in Asia.

U.S. policymakers and the military agreed that stability in the Philippines required "eliminat[ing] the basic causes of discontent among the Philippine people."[263] As they did elsewhere in the region, U.S. officials argued that the problem "could only be resolved by instituting political, social, and economic reforms that eliminated the underlying causes of unrest." Specific U.S. reforms pressed on the government included social and economic modernization and military civic action. Other demanded reforms included fair elections, financial and tax reform, minimum wage legislation, and agrarian reforms for tenant farmers. To this end, U.S. aid to the Philippines totaled $1.3 billion between 1946 and 1956, including $117 million in military assistance from 1951 to 1956, nearly 40 percent of Philippine military spending.[264]

In brief, in 1946 the government refused to seat opponents elected to Congress from Central Luzon and increased repression in the region. By 1950, the Huk were winning local political office and the counterinsurgency campaign was in full swing against civilians and insurgents. Attacks on civilians and the control of civilian communities continued throughout the war. Also in 1950, the United States judged the Huk likely to soon collapse, the military began more aggressively seeking out insurgents specifically, and Ramon Magsaysay was made secretary of defense. Magsaysay led accommodation efforts to cooperate with other elites and made low-cost gestures toward meeting peasant interests. In 1951 the government defeated the Huk as a threat, held relatively free and fair national elections based on a U.S. military presence, and began construction of the first site in a program intended to house surrendered guerrillas and former soldiers. Magsaysay was elected president in 1953. Huk leader Luis Taruc surrendered in 1954.

PHILIPPINES ANALYSIS

Insurgency Broken by 1951. Existing work on the campaign typically dates defeat of the insurgency to 1954, when Taruc surrendered. Existing accounts credit Magsaysay, installed at U.S. insistence as secretary of defense in 1950 and then elected president in 1953, with making political and economic reforms that brought many Huk back into the fold and ended the insurgency. These authors agree that the military's role was important to success but generally give greater credit to Magsaysay's professionalization of security forces while failing to mention continued systematic uses of force against the populace.

The government struck out against the people of Central Luzon as a whole, using brute force while promising its patron, the United States, that it would make the reforms it demanded. It herded civilians into prison camps, practiced collective punishment, and killed some peasants as a deterrent to others, all to break the flow of resources to the insurgency and weaken the Huk. After disrupting the insurgency's urban lines of communication and operations with sweeps and other large operations, the military used its increased manpower and firepower to chase insurgents in the mountains, penetrate to their bases, and track and attack them in transit.

It defeated the Huk as a military threat by 1951, three years earlier than generally claimed and well before any government reform efforts. The movement grew from a few thousand fighters in 1946 to about fifteen thousand guerrillas, one hundred thousand militia members, and one million sympathizers that controlled four provinces in 1950.[265] By 1954, there were fewer than two thousand fighters and few supporters. Operations consisted only of small raids, mostly for food and supplies, and banditry.[266]

The summer of 1950 was the turning point. Huk leader Taruc himself identified the end of 1950 as key. He hoped that expanded Huk political activity, even into the outskirts of the capital, would lead to a major uprising. In fact, he wrote, "we lacked sufficient numbers, and coordination between those in the city and those outside was poor. And we had no definite, well-thought-out plan."[267] Similarly, the U.S. ambassador reported in August that the Huk were likely to disintegrate soon militarily if the state kept the pressure on.[268] Both were correct. That year was the Huk peak and the beginning of the end. The insurgency essentially controlled four provinces in Central Luzon.[269] But by November of that year, the insurgents were fleeing the newly aggressive and strengthening security forces through the Sierra Madre mountains. Insurgent ambushes were no longer stopping the troops. Under Magsaysay, the military began patrolling more aggressively and irregularly, going farther from roads into the jungle to search for Huk camps and even staying out for several days at a time.[270] "They know our plans now; they know roughly our dispositions," wrote a former U.S. GI on the run with insurgent leaders.[271]

After more than four years of the government's "mailed fist" following the depredations of four years of Japanese occupation, in 1950 Huk and supporters alike were longing for peace. Their will to fight was broken. Surrenders rose. Many guerrillas simply returned to their old lives. Some saw nothing to be gained by fighting on. Others saw no hope of beating the army.[272] In the end, "most Huk surrendered because they were tired of living on the run from the government's increasingly effective security forces."[273] With observation planes always overhead, army patrols a constant, and ambushes frequent and costly, insurgent bands were disintegrating. In 1951 the government began limiting how much food civilians could buy to prevent any reaching the remaining bands of insurgents on the run. Insurgents received a share of supporters' rations but were still going hungry.[274]

American insurgent supporter William Pomeroy saw surrenders skyrocket by July 1951. Defectors passed on information to the government to try to avoid punishment. Individuals surrendered for a mixture of reasons including fear, hunger, concern for relatives, and loss of faith that their cause could triumph.[275] Many decided that the masses wanted peace above all, even without democracy, and gave up.[276] "We live and move in the same space that the enemy occupies," Pomeroy wrote. "There is no place to retreat, no place that is not accessible by road, by plane, or by a couple of days on a trail."[277]

By February 1951, the insurgency no longer existed as an organization or a fighting force. Taruc identifies 1951 as when the insurgency's final fight for survival took place. Communication among Huk units was difficult to impossible. Spies were joining them. Discipline was breaking down.[278] The insurgents had been driven out of the south and pursued into the forests of northern Luzon, where they barely survived, or did not survive, their lack of resources and government pursuit. By July, raids were overcoming the remaining bands. Surrenders were snowballing as insurgents starved in the forests. By August 1951 the guerrillas considered themselves defeated. Pomeroy added, "The sea is always at our backs. . . . It is no longer victory that preoccupies us. It is survival."[279]

After 1951, insurgents had difficulty getting weapons and ammunition and communication was increasingly difficult, as their courier system was vulnerable to patrols and security forces were targeting supply lines running between insurgent hideouts and villages.[280] By 1952, only an estimated 2,300 fighters remained and they were running for their lives. The insurgency lost 1,300 members to combat or surrender between 1950 and 1952. Insurgent casualties rose 12 percent in the first few months of 1952 while security force casualties fell 23 percent. In the spring of 1953, the army raided the heart of Huk territory, demonstrating that it was free to come and go as it pleased throughout Luzon. From this time, the remaining guerrillas were forced to remain constantly on the move.[281] "The more aggressive spirit of the Philippine armed forces and improved discipline and training have prevented the Huks from carrying on their activities on a scale comparable to that of 1949 and 1950," a U.S. diplomat wrote in 1953.[282]

Along with the military evidence, contemporaneous political discussions involving Philippine and U.S. authorities confirm this dating for the defeat of the Huk threat. In August 1949, President Elpidio Quirino told U.S. President Harry S. Truman that "the Huk movement had been cut down to a point where they are no longer a source of worry."[283] Quirino was desperate for continued U.S. aid to keep his government afloat and thus unlikely to play down the insurgent threat when speaking directly with the U.S. president. A U.S. Defense Department official made a similar point about the Huk threat to Assistant Secretary of State Dean Rusk in June 1950, saying, "It is not believed that the Communist-led dissident elements will be able to unseat the government in the immediate future."[284]

The number of Huk operations was dwindling as the scattered bands sought refuge farther from their homes. "The magnitude of Huk operations has decreased considerably since the army was assigned to suppress them in April," according to a September 1950 memo to Rusk. "For several months it has appeared that Huk outbreaks have decreased in size but that the organization has been expanding. . . . [Yet] the military advisors are confident that the army can handle any outbreaks *apparently now* [emphasis in original] in the making. Army forces could and probably would overcome any force that can be foreseen now."[285]

A U.S. National Security Council study in November 1950 confirmed the lack of threat posed by the Huk, identifying the insurgency as merely an indication of the weak Philippine state rather than a problem in itself or a cause of the weakness. "Although on the basis of military factors *alone* [emphasis in original] the Huks lack the capability to acquire control of the Philippines, their continued existence, growth, and activities reflect the ineffectiveness of the Philippine armed forces and the generally unsatisfactory social, economic and political situation in the Philippines," the authors wrote.[286] Given the increasing U.S. fear of Communism in this period, it seems unlikely that officials would downplay the threat in the Philippines.

U.S. State Department researchers assessed yet again in 1952 that the insurgency did not pose a serious threat to the government.[287] The U.S. ambassador reported to Washington in March 1953 that Magsaysay was going to run for president that year on his "record as defeator of Huks," a characterization that suggests the Huk were widely considered defeated by this time.[288] The U.S. ambassador reported in November 1953 on what Magsaysay was going to do as president. He made no mention of any need to defeat or mop up the Huk.[289] If the Huk were still a threat, such an omission would be inconceivable given the U.S. belief in the importance of the Philippines to Western defenses in Asia. Similarly, a 1954 memorandum references the successful campaign against the Huk rather than identifying the insurgency as a threat to address.[290]

Elite Accommodation. The hero of the conventional narrative, Magsaysay, did not conjure up changes in elite interests or impose them by force of will. He recognized political opportunities presented by chance and seized them. These opportunities included U.S. pressure for political, economic, and social reforms, and U.S. willingness to fund and support his efforts overtly and covertly. The key domestic opportunity was growing fissures among government elites. Crucially, Magsaysay was creative in devising programs that acknowledged peasant concerns without threatening elite interests.[291] His accommodations took the form of symbolic gestures intended to reassure elites concerned about unrest, including members of the insurgency.

Magsaysay and his U.S. partners tapped into shared interests among the landed class, professionals, Huk backers, and common people to form his coalition and take power as secretary of defense and then president. His accommodations were enabled by intraelite competition, discomfort over the high level of corruption and brutality displayed by the Roxas and Quirino administrations, and a desire for an end to the conflict in Central Luzon. Intraparty competition had paralyzed the central government by the spring of 1950, with corruption scandals within the ruling Liberal Party and disagreement over the conduct of the counterinsurgency campaign.[292] Magsaysay and the United States used the balance of power within the political system and relatively independent elite institutions, such as the press and the Roman Catholic Church, to ensure his election and accommodations that responded to popular frustrations without making structural changes to redistribute elite power and wealth.[293] Even so, the landed interests in Congress blocked many of the reforms he proposed.[294]

Magsaysay made short-term, ad hoc political gestures. They were not reforms, because of their lack of structural change and their symbolic character.[295] They cost elites little. Military lawyers represented peasants against landlords in court; peasants could send a free or reduced-rate telegram to Magsaysay to complain of army misbehavior (and get a response within twenty-four hours); a peasants' union was set up to rival the one allied with the Huk; and vulnerable ethnic Chinese moneylenders were forced to reduce the interest rates they charged peasants.[296] Taruc notes that Magsaysay's public relations efforts and improved treatment of surrendered insurgents damaged Huk morale.[297]

The government and military reportedly built more than four thousand schools, did road and bridge repairs, dug wells, and distributed food and medicine in scattered operations.[298] What goes unstated in reports of these civic action efforts is when and where they were accomplished. The effects such efforts may have had on the insurgency or populace are unknown. Once again, reforms require structural change to ensure that their effects on the populace as a whole continue into the future.

Magsaysay came closer to reforming the military than the political system. His accommodations strengthened the military's fighting ability, serving elite interests in combating the insurgency without exacting high costs from the patronage state.[299] Magsaysay's efforts did improve tactical military effectiveness. They did not professionalize the military by reducing its fundamental role as a patronage system. Magsaysay conducted unannounced inspections and spot promotions, fired more than four hundred officers, and sent hundreds more officers for training in the United States.[300] He famously court-martialed nine officers for extortion, illegal confiscation of rice from peasants, the selling of arms, and falsification of government documents as another of a number of low-cost gestures.[301]

In a negative form of accommodation, the military blackmailed local officials sympathetic to the insurgency into providing information in exchange for personal gain. For example, a mayor was called into his village square and "amidst great pomp and fanfare" was thanked by Col. Napolean Valeriano for helping his troops kill an insurgent courier. "Although unaware of the circumstances surrounding the courier's death, the mayor and his family appeared on the colonel's doorstep 0300hrs the following morning. In exchange for information, the government resettled the mayor and his family to another island." The military tapped into minority resentment of the insurgents by using the Negritos, an indigenous mountain people, as guides and informants against the peasantry.[302]

Other low-cost gestures also displayed the government's interest in helping the people without enacting structural change. For example, a doctor and nurse were sent to help the wife of an insurgent commander who was giving birth. A plane overhead announced congratulations to cheers from the community. Later the wife asked whether her husband could surrender, he did, fifteen fighters followed him, and the family became a legend.[303]

Uses of Force against Civilians. The conventional wisdom is that the radical change in the military's role from oppressor, rapist, torturer, murderer, arsonist, and thief to helper plays a dominant role in the campaign's success. Before Magsaysay took over as defense chief, local governments required people to buy passes to leave their own barrios and towns; set curfews; armed forces drove civilians from their own communities into larger towns for easier control; and held arrestees for years despite habeas corpus laws.[304] The security services were known for their brutality. They were the landlords' enforcers.[305] "Civilian guards and the constabulary arrested anyone they wanted, burned houses, took food, and raped. These men were absolutely the worst," one peasant recalled. "Travel wasn't safe in those days," another peasant said. "You never knew when the PC [Philippine Constabulary] or police would stop you, ask for money, even arrest you."[306] Many members of the security forces were collaborators who had scores to settle from the Japanese occupation.[307] They treated the populace as the enemy. Officers were little better, "more interested in graft, corruption, and a comfortable life than with fighting. Without logistical support, state forces lived off the villagers.[308]

They manned checkpoints and guarded estates; patrolled only roads close to base, never learning the terrain although they were posted in the same area for years; and only occasionally conducted major sweeps of up to three days.[309] Troops lacked intelligence and there was no campaign strategy. Command and control consisted of orders issued in Manila going directly to units in the field. A major offensive in March 1947, the most organized yet, included three battalions of regular forces and military police units, two thousand men accompanied by "reporters, food vendors, and sight-seers." They captured about one hundred suspects.[310] Taruc described how security forces controlled civilians under Roxas and Quirino: mass arrests and torture amid a "terror campaign, aimed not merely at annihilating us but at smashing our mass base." Other methods used by security forces included evacuating communities into larger towns with no provision of living space or other support, burning houses and stealing livestock, raping women, shelling civilian communities, and destroying crops in the fields.[311]

Under Magsaysay, forces were barred from using reconnaissance by fire—that is, "firing into areas where guerrillas might be, without concern for the civilians who might equally well be there." Troops were no longer to make a threatening display of their weapons unless they faced a clear and present danger. Instead, their conduct with peasants was to be as though they were among friends.[312] Existing accounts say that Magsaysay's military turned to small unit and constabulary tactics instead of big, ineffective sweeps through communities, and soldiers were expected to do social work.[313] The government reorganized, retrained, and equipped its forces; taught guerrilla warfare; disbanded abusive civilian militias; and began paying and feeding troops regularly. Government forces are said to have reduced or ended their use of heavy artillery, armored cars, tanks, and planes against peasants in their fields and communities.[314]

In fact, the state pursued its military campaign against civilians as well as insurgents throughout the conflict, and it is unclear to what degree individual members of the security forces improved their treatment of civilians. Security forces kept a tight hold on civilian communities they had taken under control earlier in the conflict, meaning fewer new reports of atrocities and human rights violations arose over time. The government also shifted to using unofficial proxies to control civilians. Insurgents complained of losing access to resources, meaning that control of civilians was weakening the insurgency, and the United States continued complaining about government abuse of civilians.[315] A report from the U.S. ambassador in Manila to Washington reported in 1950 that the military was driving civilians into larger towns and cities and a very large number has been displaced.[316]

Control of civilians was central throughout the campaign. Taruc said that the military's ability to control communities and thus prevent food from reaching the Huk brought insurgents "near starvation, subsisting solely on what we could find in the swamps."[317] Troops looted and burned villages, creating refugees and strategic hamlets.[318] They destroyed food; slaughtered farm animals; imposed curfews; required the purchase of passes for travel; arrested and held peasants, sometimes for years; and rounded up noncombatants to parade before masked informants.[319] Army checkpoints were extortion sites.[320] On Good Friday 1950, the army killed one hundred men, women, and children and burned 130 homes to avenge the killing of an officer. In another community, security forces lined up fifty farmers at a dance in front of a wall and executed them as "suspected Huk." The military shelled suspected Huk areas, damaging only civilians.[321] The air force used U.S.-provided P-51 Mustangs to strafe and bomb suspected Huk areas, but these attacks mostly damaged the civilians who lived there.[322] The Nenita death squad and its successors spread fear among insurgents and supporters, according to leader Col. Napolean Valeriano and his American coauthor, Lt. Col. Charles T. R. Bohannan.[323] Peasants reported that Nenita members wore the skull and crossbones on flag and sleeve. Its members broke bones, killed, and decapitated civilians.[324]

Troops continued to make arrests without trial, destroy food and shelter in Huk areas, take hostages, make reprisals, and forcibly relocate communities.[325] The government also formed village militias, led by soldiers, with the stated intention of having them protect their own communities, but the Huk usually did not target peasants.[326] These militias arrested and held peasants, sometimes for years.[327] With civilian communities largely under the control of security forces by 1952, the military formed civilian units led by army noncommissioned officers to control neighborhoods. These units grew to include ten thousand individuals by 1955.[328]

Throughout the conflict, the government used sweeps and other large operations against both insurgents and civilians. The military was sloppy but effective in breaking down the insurgency as an organization, and then it used its increased intelligence abilities, manpower, and firepower to pursue the remaining bands into the mountains and jungles. It was not a campaign involving surgical uses of force. Operations against civilian communities were common throughout the campaign as part of the effort to degrade insurgent capabilities. What improved over time was not the military's targeting of insurgents rather than civilians but rather its ability to pursue insurgents and control civilians.

Increased military power enabled the government to strike at more targets and to strike more effectively. In 1946, government forces stood at 37,000 poorly trained, armed, and led men, including 25,000 members of the Armed Forces of the Philippines and a variety of police forces. Armed Forces strength rose to 30,952 men in July 1950. In 1950 the army added a canine corps for tracking, scout rangers for long-range reconnaissance, and horse cavalry.[329]

With Magsaysay taking over as defense chief, the United States agreed to fund expansion of the armed forces by 6,000 men to about 60,000 total, providing a four-to-one margin of manpower over the insurgency, not including the constabulary and other police forces.[330] Army strength was increased nearly 60 percent over the previous year in 1951. The air force received fifty P-51 Mustang fighter planes in 1951 to support ground operations. One of the army's innovations was a homemade napalm bomb made from coconut shells and gasoline and dropped from a plane along with incendiary grenades.[331]

Magsaysay organized his forces into brigade combat teams, starting with two and eventually building up to twenty-six.[332] These mobile units of approximately one thousand men each were designed to spend their time in the field rather than on guard duty, and were supplied so they did not need to forage or steal from the populace.[333] The goal was small unit operations, mobility, and firepower. The brigade combat teams had rifle and reconnaissance companies, for instance, instead of artillery and heavy mortar batteries.[334] Troops were trained in guerrilla warfare, paid regularly, and promoted and paid for good work.[335] Prisoners taken by the military no longer automatically disappeared.[336] The United States fretted in 1952 that the military was still not sufficiently aggressive, but the army was getting better at targeting Huk units "with a minimal disruption of normal life in the countryside," in large part because civilians in Huk areas were by this time already under the control of security forces.[337]

With these increased military capabilities, the government targeted Huk civilian networks and base areas, and used information from infiltrators, informants, and aerial reconnaissance to disrupt supply lines and destroy crops just before harvest to deny food to the insurgency.[338] A defector's tip in October 1950 led government forces to the capture of 105 top officials, major weapons caches, and five tons of documents.[339] This major intelligence coup enabled the government to roll up important civilian elements of the organization and render it nonfunctional as a national force.[340]

Military intelligence collection and analysis improved with U.S. funding, advising, and training. Information came in from captured insurgents and friends and relatives who hoped to help the prisoners by helping the government. The government planted spies in jails and prisons, where criminals who had worked with insurgents would trade information for personal gain.[341]

Every battalion was ordered to develop information on all known and suspected members of the movement and on its local intelligence and logistics systems, and to build on other information developed by the new scout ranger units that conducted reconnaissance missions. The battalions kept the information on index cards and passed it along to their replacements. It was also periodically collected and consolidated for headquarters in Manila. The state eventually also acquired aircraft for observation and receipt of coded messages from agents in Huk territory.[342]

Smaller efforts struck at Huk morale as well. Starting in 1950, the state targeted the insurgency with a dirty-tricks campaign that the military claimed sowed dissention among Huk leaders and supporters. Rewards were put on the heads of guerrilla leaders, but higher amounts were promised for lower-level fighters, and local officials known to support the Huk were embarrassed and driven out of town.[343] Supplies were poisoned and ground glass was put into rice. Ammunition was scarcer and prices were skyrocketing, limiting insurgent firepower.[344] Scout rangers planted propaganda leaflets in areas the Huk thought were secure and seeded Huk supply stockpiles with exploding radios and flashlights and booby-trapped ammunition that exploded when it was fired, wounding the shooter, destroying the weapon, and spreading distrust. In Operation Coverup, teams moved into a village as farmers and laborers, collected information, ambushed Huk patrols, and kidnapped Huk officials, destroying the area as an operational base for the insurgents.[345]

The pseudo-gang called Force X was formed by Valeriano, also a leader of the Nenita death squad. Force X infiltrated the Huk at a time when the guerrillas "operated freely in Central Luzon but when their command organization was loose and inexperienced." The goal was to gather intelligence and kill or capture Huk and disrupt their activities. The unit was trained by captured guerrillas. In its first foray into the field, it infiltrated a Huk base camp, killed eighty-two suspects and a local mayor and captured three squadron commanders, then went on a two-week search-and-destroy mission with two infantry companies.[346]

In 1951, insurgents hiding in the mountains and forests were reduced to eating river snails, soft-shell crabs the size of a U.S. quarter coin, and tree grubs. By early 1952, the insurgency had been cut off from the populace by government control of civilians. Barrios had been emptied into military-held towns. Guards accompanied workers in the fields, cities were under lockdown, highways were patrolled and dotted with checkpoints, and grassy areas were bulldozed and the soil smoothed to show the footprints of any passers-by. There were watchtowers on the plains of Central Luzon. Security forces covered known insurgent trails with searchlights and machine guns. Insurgents lacked food, paper for propaganda, weapons, and ammunition. Discipline was disintegrating.[347] Arrest without trial, destruction of food and shelter, hostage taking, reprisals, and forcible relocation and military control of civilian communities all were integral to the campaign.

THE PHILIPPINES ALTERNATIVE EXPLANATION: THE GOVERNANCE MODEL

Had the case supported the governance approach, we should have seen reforms gaining popular support and weakening the insurgency and a reduction in the use of violence against civilians. This is not the case.

Reforms. The defeat of the Huk is usually presented as a narrative in which the government learns to treat its citizens properly by respecting their rights and meeting their needs, thus weakening and ultimately destroying the insurgency by reducing the grievances that fueled it.[348] The key player in this drama is Magsaysay, who did not grow up as a member of the elite and was a guerrilla himself during the Japanese occupation, unlike many elites who chose to collaborate. Some credit Magsaysay's U.S. adviser, Edward Lansdale, though this view may reflect an inability or reluctance to recognize the agency of local actors.[349]

Magsaysay, one author argues, saw the Huk as the symptom of a disease, of poverty, rising expectations, and an uncaring and corrupt government. His solution, along with military action, was reforms to "improve Philippine living conditions and remove the base of guerrilla strength—popular support. He demanded that each soldier, regardless of rank, be dedicated first to the people, then, to killing the guerrillas."[350] Treatment of the disease included the resettlement program Economic Development Corps (EDCOR). Magsaysay's civic action programs even helped peasants get their harvest to market.[351] Troops were instructed to provide medical aid to peasants while out on patrol and help solve other local problems.[352]

These reforms, according to the existing narrative, undercut the Huk and co-opted their message, reducing their popular support and thus weakening them militarily. "With hope and progress," one author writes, "the people would follow. . . . Ramon Magsaysay understood the people he grew up with, and knew what their aspirations were. . . . He was able to provide what his countrymen wanted and stop the Huk at the very peak of their influence and power."[353] One expert, unlike many counterinsurgency authors, points out that Magsaysay's reforms meant little or no political or economic change but "appealed to peasants' hope that they could stop fighting."[354]

Magsaysay's gestures toward reform took the place of actual reforms. Reforms were impossible given the political context of the time. Many political entrepreneurs, including government and economic elites, saw any structural change toward a more equitable sharing out of resources as an existential threat. Taruc believed that reforms would defeat the insurgency. "Peace depended entirely on Quirino's implementation of his promises, which failed to develop," he wrote.[355]

The United States wanted reforms, initially. It set up the Joint U.S. Military Advisory Group in 1947 to train Philippine forces, "foster a public spirit orientation, help in depoliticization, root out corruption and professionalize the promotion system to weed out incompetents and encourage 'officers showing readiness for combat.'" But the military was "enforcing politicians' interests, often under orders," and those benefiting by politicization, abuse of public authority, and corruption saw no need to end it. The government welcomed military assistance insofar as it made repression more effective and less costly.[356] Early in August 1951, then-Senator Ramon Magsaysay presented his plan for a more refined military approach to President Quirino, who named him secretary of defense at the end of August, after the Huk were already broken as a fighting force, which means that the changes he instituted could not have caused success.[357]

The United States wanted to see good governance reforms if its support was to continue. "The vital interests of the United States require that the Philippines must become and remain stable, anti-Communist, pro-American, and an example for the rest of Asia of progressive and responsible government," the Department of State wrote in 1950.[358] For Quirino, this meant "internal reform, a broadening of his government, and the initiation of a sound and constructive development program."[359] Specifics included "tax legislation of an equitable nature" and "a minimum wage law for all agricultural workers . . . to improve the living conditions of agricultural and industrial workers."[360] A report to the U.S. National Security Council in 1953 credits the Philippine government with saving the state from near bankruptcy in 1950, passing a minimum-wage law in 1951, adopting a law strengthening unions in 1953, and passing laws providing better rural credit facilities and agricultural extension services, but says nothing about implementation. It also reports that "it [the government] has shown no inclination to come to grips with the fundamental problems of land tenancy."[361]

American policymakers were damning Quirino for his lack of reforms at a time when the Huk were already breaking down as an organization and as a fighting force. If any of the laws mentioned in the previous paragraph were implemented, the timing indicates that they did not precede counterinsurgent success and thus could not have contributed to it. Unrest was increasing in the Philippines, Secretary of State Dean Acheson concluded in April 1950, but it was not due to Huk activity. He blamed the Philippine president. "All indications are that he [Quirino] would prefer to see his country ruined rather than compromise with his insatiable ego or accept outside assistance on any terms except his own."[362]

U.S. reports from Manila were similarly grim. The chargé wrote in April 1950, at the time the Huk was disintegrating, "The Philippine Constabulary, instead of winning popular support, has in general so behaved that it has alienated the rural populace."[363] The military, he continued, must become disciplined "with respect to the treatment of the populace. If they are, they may win and retain popular support, which now is passing by default to HMN [Huk] forces; dissident [Huk] forces may thereby be deprived of the intelligence, the supplies, the shelter from pursuit and the new recruits which a disaffected populace too willingly gives anti-government guerrillas. So long as the Constabulary seize foodstuffs without paying for them, become drunk and disorderly, extract information by inhumane methods, abuse women, shoot up country towns and generally mistreat the populace, just so long will they continue to lose the Philippines to the HMB [Hukbalahap]," he wrote, concluding on a bleak note: "The Embassy perceives few causes for optimism" regarding the continuing reorganization of the military. "Political conditions and economic trends suggest that the future will be favorable to the recruiters of dissident forces."[364] By November the Huk were broken and on the run despite the lack of reforms.

EDCOR, the land resettlement program, is claimed in the counterinsurgency literature as a major systemic reform. However, it did little for the peasants or Huk of Central Luzon and reflected no systemic redistribution of land ownership. It was billed as the provision of land to insurgent defectors when it was announced in 1951, after the Huk threat was defeated, but in 1954 only 246 former Huk lived in EDCOR communities out of a total of 1,046 settlers. By September 1959 that figure was down to 221 out of 5,709 people in EDCOR settlements. Many beneficiaries were soldiers, an accommodation of a small group of armed fighters rather than a reform benefiting many or all and certainly not one reducing the popular grievances in Central Luzon over the shortage of land for peasants. Furthermore, this accommodation did not address the fundamental problem of too many people and too little land. Indeed, the problem was getting worse. Between 1948 and 1952, after Huk defeat, the percentage of farmers who did not own their land rose from 37 percent to 46 percent. By 1963, 70 percent of farmers in the Philippines were landless tenants.[365]

The relatively free and fair midterm elections of 1951 were symbolic rather than indicative of structural change for two reasons.[366] First, U.S. forces played a major role in reducing violence, indicating not systemic government reforms but an unsustainable ad hoc U.S. effort.[367] Second, elite interests happened to coincide on the need for a cleaner vote after the particularly dirty, violent elections of 1946 and 1949. Quirino feared losing in 1953 if violence in 1951 approached previous levels, while disarray within his party left him without a bloc to back in 1951, reducing his interference. Finally, Vice President Fernando Lopez, hoping to retain power himself, allied with the opposition Nacionalistas, Secretary of Defense and U.S. ally Magsaysay, the United States, and civil society groups to attempt to ensure a fair vote.[368] U.S. and Filipino troops were sent out as observers for the balloting.[369] Troops also protected opposition members, polling stations, and ballot boxes, as did citizens' groups, which broadcast vote counts as soon as they were announced.[370] The Nacionalistas won big, and the chairman of the independent national elections commission deemed the vote 75 percent fair, compared with 30 percent fair in 1949.[371]

Similarly, the 1953 presidential election that Magsaysay won by more than two to one was relatively clean, and ensured by covert U.S. support. The United States mobilized civil society and the church and again sent troops to polling sites. More quietly, Magsaysay benefited from covert CIA backing.[372] There were no systemic changes to ensure fair future votes. The slightly cleaner elections were a function of individual choices by those in power at the time, including the United States, rather than structural changes that would continue no matter who was in power.

There was a bow to reform in April 1950 when Quirino put the constabulary under armed forces control, a move the United States intended to provide greater political oversight, but operational control was given to the interior secretary, an ultraconservative landowner who focused on military destruction of the insurgency rather than reforms.[373] The United States also provided "public administration experts to professionalize, depoliticize, and clean up the government bureaucracy." It put watchdogs inside the state to eliminate corruption, manage aid, and improve administration. It larded technical advisers throughout all strategic departments and placed field observers with the army.[374]

Magsaysay himself indicted the government's lack of systemic change in his letter of resignation as defense secretary, telling Quirino in his letter of resignation, "Under your concept of my duties as secretary of national defense, my job is to just go on killing Huk. But you must realize that we cannot solve the problem of dissidence simply by military measures."[375] Similarly, in his first State of the Nation address as president, in January 1954, after counterinsurgent success, Magsaysay said it was time to keep faith with all those who voted for promises of an end to insecurity, fear, poverty, and want. He promised to use the military for public works and economic development projects, provide land for small farmers, encourage charities to continue providing clean water to communities, and root out government corruption.[376]

The United States had few illusions about the likelihood of significant political or economic change. Officials demonstrated a typical degree of frustration with their client. Of Quirino, who replaced President Roxas in 1948, U.S. Ambassador Myron Cowan said the Huk "evidently seem[ed] to him the less immediate danger to his position."[377] As long as "the United States gives the appearance of a call girl, we shall . . . continue to serve as a refuge for weaklings and incompetents," a State Department analyst wailed in 1951. "Can we not be a little harder to get . . . ? Darn it, they are the ones who are threatened with a fate worse than death—not we."[378] The lead author of a U.S. white paper on development in the Philippines shared with Truman "the depressing details of the inefficiency, corruption, and antipathy toward the common people that characterized the Quirino government." He did not think major changes likely.[379]

Discussing reforms under Quirino, Secretary of State Acheson told Secretary of Defense George Marshall in January 1951, after counterinsurgency success, "I regret, therefore, to have to inform you that the changes which have been made so far are in effect little more than a reshuffling of the present incompetent and corrupt leadership. The executive order [on reorganizing the armed forces] so far appears to be only another one of those paper declarations which receive little practical implementation."[380]

Ambassador Admiral Raymond Spruance told Acheson in January 1953, after counterinsurgent success, in no uncertain terms that he held out little hope for reform, conveying his views in abrupt telegraphic shorthand:

> We are dealing with an administration intent first of all on political survival led with a few notable exceptions by men of mediocre stature. Incompetence and corruption have led to widespread lack of confidence in government. Unhappily minority party offers little prospect improvement. Leaders both parties generally old school politicians that cannot realize that basic social reform is required if communism is to be defeated and a stable economy and democratic government to survive. They and virtually all government officials in upper levels come from wealthy landowning families never seriously concerned about welfare of less fortunate and basically hopeful maintenance status quo.[381]

Similarly, a 1953 U.S. memo said, "Although Magsaysay believes that social reform, particularly with respect to land tenure, is essential for the maintenance of peace and order, it is doubtful that if elected president he could institute any very drastic measures since these would by their very nature run counter to what most members of Congress consider their personal interests."[382]

Popular Support. The government failed to gain popular support over the course of the successful campaign. Early reports underline this lack of support. "The communist-led Hukbalahap movement has taken advantage of the deteriorating economic situation and exploited the antagonistic attitudes of the people toward the government in order to incite lawlessness and disorder," a National Security Council study reported in 1950, the year the government defeated the Huk threat.[383] The problem for the Philippines, wrote a top State Department official in May 1950, was not the Huk but rising popular discontent with the government.[384]

In December 1952, after counterinsurgent success, a U.S. State Department memo mentioned, in telegraphic style, that cleaner elections in 1951 had hurt the Huk cause "by increasing confidence [of the] people in orderly democratic processes of Phil Govt. [the Philippine government]," but the insurgents were already on the run in 1951, so increased popular confidence in the state the following year cannot have contributed to the Huk defeat. Currently, the memo stated, "politically country in disturbed state, with people largely convinced government venal and corrupt and determined remain in power even by stealing election."[385] These documents indicate that the populace supported, even revered, Magsaysay personally, but they do not indicate that this enthusiasm extended to their government as a whole.

As late as October 1953, when Huk remnants were on the run in the mountains and forests and posed little threat to few but themselves, the U.S. embassy feared an armed revolt if Quirino was reelected in November, so disliked was he. "Such a revolt could muster an armed force at least equal to that loyal to the government, but would be backed morally by an overwhelming majority of the people," according to one memo.[386]

There is evidence that civilians brought under government control provided information to the government; there is evidence of a popular turn away from the insurgency after it was broken, when smaller groups turned to forced recruitment and banditry; there is evidence of civilian war weariness reducing support for the insurgency; and there is evidence that Magsaysay's personal popularity and symbolic accommodations won him popular support. It is difficult to argue on the evidence, however, that reforms or accommodations caused an increase in popular support that in turn weakened the insurgency. The order of events does not follow that logic. Fighters alienated the populace after the insurgency was fractured, not before. Magsaysay's accommodations persuaded peasants that the state was on their side after the government's success rather than before it.

Peasants themselves reported that some were won over by the government once they saw and felt the effects of Magsaysay's accommodations, efforts to demonstrate his concern for their well-being, as with the telegrams anyone could send him. Promises of reductions in rent gave peasants hope that the fighting could end.[387] Peasants increasingly cooperated with the government by providing information on the Huk in exchange for payments and ad hoc delivery of goods and services such as a medic team's visit to a community.[388] Provision of information under duress, at a time of urgent need, is not evidence of popular support in and of itself.

THE PHILIPPINES CONCLUSION

In the Philippines, the successful military campaign targeted civilians throughout and insurgents whenever possible, with the military's ability to do both increased by U.S. support. The government's focus on the Huk, particularly its leadership, increased after much of the civilian population of Central Luzon had been brought under the control of security forces. Reforms involved promises rather than implementation. Elites, including some Huk leaders, were accommodated with low-cost benefits such as the provision of a doctor for a woman in childbirth, rather than costly reforms such as development of a system to provide access to medical care throughout Central Luzon.

The anti-Huk campaign supports the predictions of the compellence theory. The government's accommodation of rival elites was more systematic in Malaya and less so in Greece compared with the Philippines, where the process of coalition building among elites took place within the government. The government's uses of force against civilians were less systematic than those conducted in Malaya, and less drastic than those conducted in Greece, but the military nonetheless persistently and effectively targeted civilians with force.

In the Philippines, we see primarily intragovernmental accommodation, as in Greece. Elites saw room for gain, they made limited demands on each other, the choice to accommodate was far less costly than the U.S.-demanded reforms would be, and not all elites saw an existential threat in the insurgency. The perception of threat was sufficient for governmental elites to band together to ensure continued U.S. backing, but not overwhelming enough to prevent accommodation of some individual insurgents to present as models for others.

The insurgency did not see itself as an existential threat to the government. It and many supporters were fighting for a greater share of the pie in the form of more just treatment from the government and the landlords. Magsaysay's political acumen was crucial in identifying gestures to the populace that could reassure civilians and insurgents without costing elites wealth and power. These gestures bore fruit because the residents of Central Luzon wanted to know that their government cared. It is not evident that such gestures would suffice in a campaign in which insurgents and the populace wished to overthrow the government. As the war ground on, indeed, insurgents' and supporters' hope for change declined, making Magsaysay's gestures of accommodation all the more powerful. "Many were even willing to accept the peace of slaves, just as long as it was peace," after the years of occupation and civil war, Taruc writes.[389]

A New Laboratory

Dhofar, Oman

Oman is a Gulf country stretching from the Strait of Hormuz in the east to Yemen in the west, its northern border meeting Saudi Arabia's Empty Quarter and its southern coast the Arabian Sea. It has been a great seafaring and trading state.[1] Dhofar is Oman's southernmost province, five hundred miles southwest across the desert from the capital, Muscat. When Dhofar's insurgency began with the formation of the nationalist Dhofar Liberation Front (DLF) and scattered attacks on oil exploration sites, Oman's sultan was determined to use his anticipated petroleum wealth to modernize more wisely than had his Gulf neighbors.[2]

Oman was never colonized by a Western power, and Sultan Sa'id bin Taimur, like his forebears, tried to avoid British domination. He used his relationship with Britain to advance his own interests, including strengthening his control over the state's territory and building his military. The Omani state consisted of Sultan Sa'id and his advisers. Each province had a *wali* (governor) appointed by the sultan and a *qadi* (judge). The sultan's British advisers ran the civil activities of the state from Muscat and controlled the military at the time of the conflict in Dhofar, but Sa'id had his own circle of Omani advisers in Salalah, Dhofar's capital.[3] Sa'id's acerbic analysis shocked his British advisers. "We do not need hospitals here," Sa'id told the British officer commanding the Sultan's Armed Forces (SAF) at the time of an uprising in northern Oman in 1958–1959. "This is a very poor country which can only support a small population. At present many children die in infancy. . . . If we build clinics many more will survive—but for what? To starve?"[4]

Dhofaris numbered at the time of the conflict about fifty thousand out of an Omani population of about four hundred thousand.[5] The pastoral jebali (mountain-dwelling) population comprised about thirty thousand people; the rest lived settled lives on the plain or belonged to nomadic tribes living in the rocky highlands behind the mountains.[6] Dhofar's populace included the descendants of African slaves; migrants from Zanzibar, formerly ruled from Oman; and South Asian businessmen, but the most numerous groups were the Arab tribesmen of the plain and the *negd* (the high plain beyond the mountains), and the mountain-dwelling, non-Arabic-speaking tribes known as jebalis, though the term came to denote all of Dhofar's mountain dwellers.[7]

The crescent-shaped coastal plain in Dhofar stretches about forty-four miles along the Arabian Sea, extending about ten miles inland at its widest point.[8] The cliffs beyond the plain rise up to five thousand feet, and the mountains extend into a high plateau that becomes a rocky, dry highland merging into Saudi Arabia.[9] The mountains are cut with a multitude of rugged *wadis* (valleys).

Dhofar was poor, as was all of Oman and as much of the Gulf region had been until its recent exploitation of oil resources. In 1970, Oman's infant mortality rate was 75 percent. It had three primary schools, no media, and a literacy rate of 5 percent.[10] "In the villages of Oman there is often not a single healthy inhabitant in sight," journalist David Holdren wrote in the mid-1960s. "Trachoma, tuberculosis, malaria, rheumatism and decaying teeth, on top of years of self-imposed inbreeding and involuntary underfeeding, have made the Omanis as poor an advertisement for the life of the noble savage as any I have seen."[11]

British strategic interests in Oman shifted over time. They first centered on the passage to India and later on Gulf oil carried through the Strait, as well as on British credibility.[12] Britain also concerned itself with the Dhofar insurgency because it wanted to prevent further Cold War dominos falling after its withdrawal from Aden in 1967, and because it was committed to retaining its Royal Air Force base outside Salalah and continued air force use of Masirah Island, off Dhofar, as a stepping-stone to East Asia. With technological changes, the air force eventually no longer needed Masirah as a refueling point. In addition, the rising need for British officers in Northern Ireland in the 1970s and the realization that British domination of SAF did not endear it to its other Middle Eastern partners meant the British were increasingly willing to leave Oman to the Omanis. At the same time, a fortuitous factor played into the British-Omani relationship: the rising oil prices of the 1970s allowed the sultan to spend more on his military at a time when the British needed to spend less.

Many Dhofaris saw Sa'id's relationship with the British through the prism of Egyptian President Gamal Abdel Nasser's powerful call for pan-Arab nationalism. Communist bloc support for the insurgency, starting in 1968, fostered an already strong, broad-based movement for autonomy or independence from the perceived oppression of the sultan and his British backers. The insurgency received safe haven across the Omani border in the People's Democratic Republic of Yemen after the British left Aden in 1967, and some fighting support from the PDRY at the very end of the war. Some aid came from the Chinese and Soviet consulates in Aden as well.[13] China provided military and ideological training to a small number of insurgents and later a relatively limited amount of small arms, along with printed propaganda and money for shipping them. After 1971 the Soviet Union provided some aid, and support from both Communist states increased later in the conflict.[14] None of this support, political or otherwise, was crucial to insurgent development or survival. "The people were ripe for rebellion and the Communists provided the resources for them to rebel. The two came together," argued the commander of SAF from 1975–1977, Maj. Gen. Ken Perkins.[15]

The insurgency slowly gained strength through Sa'id's reign but had been forced into a stalemate by the time his son, Qaboos bin Sa'id, seized the throne with British backing in 1970. Two years into Qaboos's rule, SAF gained sufficient strength to begin pushing the DLF (renamed the People's Front for Liberation of Oman and the Arabian Gulf, PFLOAG) west across Dhofar's mountains toward its safe haven in Yemen. In battling the insurgency, SAF divided the mountains into three zones, the Eastern, Central, and Western Areas. It eventually secured the coastal communities, then swept the mountains mostly clear of insurgents from east to west. The sultan declared the conflict won in December 1975. The mopping up continued in 1976, but the conflict has not reignited. Oman remains a stable and sultanistic state today, with a powerful patronage system and limited political rights for its subjects.[16]

Despite the tenor of the existing counterinsurgency literature on the campaign, there are more similarities than differences between the two phases of the conflict, under Sa'id from 1965 to 1970 and under Qaboos from 1970 to 1976. Both Sa'id and Qaboos attempted to accommodate rival elites, though less is known outside Oman of Sa'id's efforts. Accommodations under Qaboos's rule played a significant role in campaign success. Both built their military with British support and used it against civilians as well as insurgents to deny resources to the insurgency and thus weaken it, though under Qaboos the military grew significantly stronger than the insurgency, including gaining air power, and was able to execute a military strategy that had proved too ambitious for Sa'id's smaller, weaker forces.

In brief, the government began responding militarily to scattered incidents of political violence in Dhofar in 1965. Sultan Sa'id continued developing and implementing plans for the slow, careful modernization of Oman but resisted British pressure for liberalization. He also built his British-armed and British-led military. In 1970, Sa'id's son, Qaboos, ousted him in a British-backed palace coup. The British hoped he would quickly dispose of the insurgency through reforms to satisfy popular grievances, but by 1971 the insurgents held most of Dhofar. Qaboos too resisted British pressure for liberalization while continuing with his father's slow development of state infrastructure but not political structure. He invested more in his military than Sa'id had and brought in regional military partners. In 1973 SAF was finally able to hold on to its few outposts on the jebel (mountains) year-round. Accommodation in the form of raising militias and empowering their warlord leaders helped SAF take land in the mountains and drive the insurgents into the west. SAF controlled the communities on the coast and used the militias to control civilians in the mountains. It reduced the insurgency to the level of an annoyance rather than a threat by 1974. In 1976 the sultan declared Dhofar free of insurgency.

The campaign provides support for the compellence theory. Accommodations played an important role in strengthening governmental military and political capabilities. Forming a coalition with insurgent defectors enabled SAF to cut the flow of resources to the insurgency directly, through military force targeting the insurgency, and indirectly, through military force controlling civilian behavior. In addition, like Malaya, Greece, and the Philippines, it demonstrates that little if any political reform is necessary to succeed against an insurgency. Reforms in Dhofar were limited to nonexistent. Furthermore, SAF forcefully targeted civilians as a group throughout the campaign, though some commanders did take care to avoid civilian casualties. Popular support for the sultan did not increase.

Dhofar Analysis

INSURGENCY BROKEN BY 1974

The insurgency in Dhofar was defeated as a threat to the government by 1974, two years earlier than the usual date applied. The date of counterinsurgent success is significant in this case because it precedes counterinsurgent implementation of development efforts. As with the other cases, it is a story of increasing military strength and the application of force against civilians and insurgents rather than increasing political openness or economic opportunity. SAF's direct and indirect advances against the insurgency reflected an increase in military capabilities begun under Sai'id.[17] Efforts for which SAF lacked resources in the 1960s paid off in the 1970s once SAF had increased its numbers and firepower and added air capabilities that enabled it to hold defensive and offensive sites it seized in the mountains.

In 1966, about one thousand troops were posted in Dhofar, including a SAF regiment, the British Royal Air Force contingent at the small air station (responsible only for its own defense), and the motley tribal levies known as *askars* who guarded the palace, the perimeter of Salalah, and other static positions.[18] From 1967 to 1970, Sa'id kept one 600-to-700-man battalion in Dhofar.[19] By February 1970, SAF strength overall stood at about 2,500, led by 70 British officers, including the British Army's seconded commander of the Sultan's Armed Forces (CSAF), 30 British loan officers, and 40 British and Commonwealth contract officers, plus 40 Arab and Pakistani contract officers.[20] Four months later, still under Sa'id, SAF had grown to 3,800 troops, with one regiment at a time serving in Dhofar.[21] Sa'id ordered six helicopters in October 1969, along with six hundred .303 Lee-Enfield bolt-action rifles (the insurgency was using AK-47s, but Sa'id was nothing if not cost conscious).[22] By 1970, SAF's armory included two .50-caliber Brownings and 81 mm mortars, putting it roughly at par with the insurgency.[23]

Under Sa'id, SAF officers increased training in basic infantry tactics, from picketing the heights and camouflaging vehicles to conducting night ambushes and locating sources of enemy fire.[24] "There were no roads on the jebel and few areas where it was possible to take a vehicle of any sort," one British officer reported. "Movement in any direction was inhibited by precipitous *wadis*, strewn with giant boulders and dense thorn, many of which took 24 hours to cross, many impossible even for donkeys carrying weapons, ammunition, and water to negotiate."[25] SAF intelligence gathering was limited under Sa'id, but he had his own sources, as well as counselors other than his British advisers.[26] SAF was better trained, better equipped, and better led by 1970.[27]

Corran Purdon, the seconded British brigadier who commanded SAF from 1967 to 1970, faulted the British for SAF's lack of progress, reporting that its refusal to better support SAF "prolonged the war by years and resulted in needless deaths and woundings." Purdon and Sa'id had requested helicopters, and Purdon also wanted a field surgical team and a Special Air Service (SAS) deployment. Help only arrived after Sa'id's fall. SAF did get two Dakota transport planes to lift troops and equipment, which speeded evacuation of the wounded, and Sa'id ordered Skyvans, small planes that could handle the short takeoff and landing strips SAF eventually built on the jebel. Purdon would have liked a full artillery regiment for fire support, and did eventually get approval for purchase of a new air-transportable light gun to support troops in the field. The UK Ministry of Defense agreed to send SAS teams to train SAF in ambushing and other skills and to help gain Sa'id popular support, and sent SAS commander John Watts to visit and make a plan. It also eventually sent a field surgical team for Salalah to improve survival chances for wounded soldiers and thus boost morale.[28]

State military capability continued increasing with spending by the new sultan, Qaboos, and with additional help from abroad.[29] From approximately 3,800 troops at the time of Qaboos's coup in July 1970, SAF grew to about 7,500 in March 1972, 10,300 in June 1974, and 18,300 in December 1975.[30] SAF set up a headquarters in Dhofar in July 1971 to enable local direction of the campaign, rather than running things from the SAF headquarters more than five hundred miles away in northern Oman.[31] Additions included armored cars, jets, heavy and light helicopters, and nearly three hundred surrendered insurgents and returned exiles formed into five firqats (militias), which I discuss in greater detail later in the context of accommodation. The firqats were built around political entrepreneurs and entrepreneurs of violence within the Dhofari community. With two battalions in Dhofar at a time, one on the plain and one on the jebel, SAF's strength almost equaled that of the insurgency's fighting force, but for much of the campaign it was outnumbered if the insurgency's supporters were included in the count.[32] The 641 British officers involved included an SAS squadron, a signals detachment, and the field surgical team that arrived under Sa'id.[33] At war's end, SAF was absorbing about two-thirds of Oman's gross domestic product.[34]

Additional British help quickly followed the coup. It took longer to persuade Arab neighbors and Iran to assist. SAF was training in Jordan in 1972, and in 1975 King Hussein provided engineers, a Special Operations Forces battalion for defense of the lone road into Dhofar from northern Oman, and sixteen aircraft.[35] The Arab League sent a peace mission in 1974 and 1975, and Saudi diplomacy and cash payments to both sides led to a cease-fire with Yemen, which had been providing safe haven to the insurgency, in March 1976.[36] The single largest regional contributor to the campaign was the Shah of Iran. Late in 1972 the Shah provided a Special Operations Forces unit, a 1,500-man battle group, three frigates, and helicopters.[37] These gains in military power contributed to the quick dispatch of the insurgency after SAF's fighting capabilities increased.

At the height of its military power in 1970–1971, the DLF had an estimated two thousand full-time fighters, up to four thousand part-time militia members, and countless supporters.[38] In 1971, the DLF controlled nine-tenths of Dhofar.[39] DLF fighters were increasingly better trained and led than SAF, with better field tactics, and operated against SAF in larger groups and with more firepower, including automatic rifles for all the hardcore fighters, 75 mm rocket launchers, 82 mm and 60 mm mortars, and 122 mm Katyusha rockets.[40] By 1972, the insurgency was strong enough that SAF operations in the mountains at less than company strength and without artillery support risked failure.[41]

SAF was bolstered by years of materiel purchases and training under Sa'id and further materiel acquired under Qaboos. The military began moving into the insurgent-held mountains from the coastal area—which was all of Dhofar that the sultan held at this time. Starting in November 1971, SAF took territory and cleared insurgents out from among civilians and from their bases in the relatively heavily populated Eastern Area, then did it all over again in the Central Area. It used indiscriminate area weapons such as airstrikes and artillery, weapons that recognize no distinction between civilian and fighter, against suspected enemy headquarters, supply dumps, and convoys while also sweeping communities for insurgents.[42] By November, SAF was seeing a rising kill rate from aggressive patrols and airstrikes.[43] In August 1972, CSAF Brig. John Graham's concept of operations was twofold: conduct offensive operations and interdiction.[44] That focus remained from November 1, 1973, to April 30, 1974: interdiction of insurgents and resources and aggressive mobile operations in the east to enable the SAS and firqats to set up a handful of outposts on the jebel.[45] Finally in 1975, the insurgency had been weakened sufficiently in the Eastern and Central Areas to shift to attrition and interdiction of resources flowing to the insurgency in the relatively lightly populated Western Area.[46]

It was not an easy fight. In February 1971, seven months after the coup was supposed to have removed all of Sa'id's stumbling blocks, from his indecisiveness to his parsimony, Graham assessed that the insurgency was outgunning SAF, was on the offensive, and had the freedom of the jebel.[47] In June 1971, top British officers agreed that SAF had to get up to the jebel to win, but it lacked the skills and the morale to do so.[48] In July of the same year, Oman's defense secretary, Briton Hugh Oldman, concluded that Oman could not win as things stood and could not afford to raise more troops.[49] In August 1971, the British ambassador warned Whitehall that SAF had to at least secure the coastal plain, and Oman's defense secretary warned that the British needed a plan in case Salalah fell.[50] More than a year later, fourteen months after the coup, in September 1972, CSAF Maj. Gen. Timothy Creasey reported after his first ten days in office that his troops were insufficient to hold the territory; two battalions did not provide decisive superiority over the insurgency's estimated six hundred hardcore fighters.[51] Three years into the campaign under Qaboos, there were still only three outposts on the jebel, and these were all in the Eastern Area, where insurgent support was weakest.[52] Only in 1973 did SAF become strong enough to spend the entire year on the jebel.[53]

SAF used small and large operations and varied its tactics according to mission. One 1971 situation report notes patrols of one company plus firqat plus their SAS team; one platoon plus firqat plus SAS; and two companies plus platoon plus *askar* platoon.[54] Operation Jaguar in the east in the fall of 1971 took territory tactically useful for offensive operations, as well as land good for airstrips, wells, and grazing.[55] Operation Panther, in January 1972 and also in the Eastern Area, used firqats to clear out a pocket of insurgents.[56] The SAF outpost at Akoot, in the Western Area, was established late in 1971 and served to draw insurgent fire as well as providing a base for ambushes, artillery, a firqat, and intelligence collection.[57]

Smaller operations continued along with larger ones, such as regular clearing of communities on the plain and a major operation in October 1974 in the Eastern Area to harass the insurgency and open a section of the coast road.[58] SAF spent much of late 1974 and early 1975 searching *wadis* for insurgent arms and supply stores, operating at up to battalion strength.[59] In December 1974, the Iranian battle group on loan from the Shah tried and failed to capture the insurgents' massive supply cache in the far Western Area. A second attempt by a battalion supported by SAS and firqats in January 1975 also failed, but SAF was able to set up guns covering the caves and prevent access.[60] In February and March 1975, major operations in the Central Area cleared out large enemy groups. These included Operation

Himaar, in which two battalions routed the headquarters and elements of an enemy battalion in the vast Wadi Ashoq.[61] SAF used air power and artillery in small and large operations, patrols and ambushes, sweeps for arms caches, and helicopter-borne assaults to seize territory. The outcome was fewer and smaller insurgent operations.

Keeping insurgents on the move and cutting them off from civilian resources began paying off by 1973. Shortages of supplies and constraints on movement reduced guerrilla morale and efficiency in the Eastern Area between 1973 and 1975 and led to additional casualties.[62] The reduction in supplies and its cascade of effects also led to increasing numbers of surrenders in the Eastern Area.[63] In the 1974–1975 period, a dramatic increase in surrenders and information followed whenever SAF set up a firqat in its own tribal area, where it would provide the highly desirable goods of water and medical care to cooperative jebalis.[64] Surrenders indicate that the campaign was breaking the insurgents' will to fight.

In 1974, estimates of insurgent strength were down to about 600.[65] By November 1974 the insurgency had taken all its heavy weapons west of the Hornbeam Line (more on this shortly) in the Central Area to try to protect them from SAF operations.[66] As SAF's hold on territory expanded, as surrenders continued, and as fighters faded back into their old lives, insurgent numbers dwindled. An estimated 30 fighters remained in the Central Area in August 1975, and in January 1976 about 70 remained in the Central and Eastern Areas.[67]

ELITE ACCOMMODATION

The government's accommodation of rival elites was the most significant political change over the course of the Dhofar campaign. SAF's use of insurgent defectors as fighting forces, firqats, was central to the military defeat of the insurgency, while the installation of their leaders as warlords on the jebel and Qaboos's later outreach to other political entrepreneurs in Oman supported long-term political stability.[68] Sa'id kept a close eye on events in Dhofar, where he made his home. He received photographs of insurgents slain in battle so he could identify them.[69] In addition, he was married to a woman from the powerful Dhofari tribe of the Qarra, providing a wealth of contacts.[70] In Dhofar and indeed all of Oman, Sa'id and after him Qaboos used patronage, "individualized favors, which benefit only some citizens to whom the regime considers itself particularly indebted." Sa'id's *rentiers* de facto" included former DLF member Sheik Abd al-Aziz of the powerful Bait Kathir tribe, and the family of Dhofar's wartime governor, Wali Buraik.[71]

Qaboos's political allies among elites included the Baluchis who made up the core of his British-led army without making political demands on the government, and Omanis returning from Africa who had little involvement in internal political and tribal matters.[72] Qaboos cemented his position in

Dhofar through alliances with tribes on the eastern and western edges of the jebel, the desert-dwelling elements of the powerful al-Kathir and Mahra tribes.

Although only a few major tribes inhabited Dhofar, they were splintered into groups as small as twenty-five and under little control by sheiks, meaning that turning Dhofaris to the government side could not be achieved by persuading a few of the traditional tribal leaders to change their allegiance.[73] The tribal structure also meant that individual Dhofaris would not necessarily have information about many other individuals.[74]

Political entrepreneurs and entrepreneurs of violence were nevertheless influential. Under Qaboos in 1970, al-Kathiri sheik and insurgent defector Mussalam bin Tufl was released from prison and sent to visit the community of Habarut with a SAF platoon. He told other al-Kathiri leaders that they could return to their lands and to Salalah and enjoy new benefits, including jobs for their followers in development projects and with Petroleum Development Oman, and brought the Bedouin sections of these tribes into the sultan's patronage network. Urban al-Kathiri members were given important positions by Qaboos, including one who he made petroleum minister after years of serving as a "go-between and fixer" in Dhofar.[75]

SAF accommodation efforts on Qaboos's behalf, along with those of the British SAS, also yielded information and manpower. SAS forces, here called civic action teams, moved into the coastal villages that were all that the government still controlled after Qaboos's accession in 1970. In the fall of 1971 there were four-man teams living in houses in the oceanside villages of Taqa and Mirbat.[76] The SAS medical officer and veterinarian visited regularly. SAS men pieced together information from their give-and-take with patients and other visitors.[77] The SAS also put a team in the coastal village of Sudh after recapturing it from the insurgency in February 1971.[78] The SAS teams living in the coastal villages identified men from the jebel who could be persuaded to join the government side and bring others with them and gained information from ex-insurgents living in Salalah and from influential men who had fled the jebel for safety.[79]

The single most useful continuing source of information and manpower was the firqats. The SAS raised the first one in 1971. The timing of their establishment in their own tribal areas on the jebel in the fall of 1974, after the insurgency was defeated as a threat, indicates that it was their earlier provision of information and fighting ability that contributed more to government success than their later provision of some goods to some civilians.[80] These tribally organized militias were led by and included insurgent defectors. Their formation was made possible by their SAS handlers' recognition of growing divisions within the insurgency and identification of what behaviors would gain the cooperation of disaffected elites within it.[81] A driving force in developing the firqats were insurgency leaders Salim Mubarak and Mohammed Suhail, who switched to the government side in 1970.[82] In many cases, insurgent leaders who surrendered brought their followers with them. About two hundred insurgents accepted an amnesty in the first month of Qaboos's rule and became firqats.[83] At the end of the conflict, in September 1976, 2,500 firqats were handed over to the civil government under the *wali* of Dhofar.[84]

The firqats provided information and irregular fighting skills.[85] They knew the territory and the people, and were good at what SAF was bad at, including reconnaissance, speedy maneuver, tactical awareness, and recognition of trails and individuals on the jebel.[86] Lacking military discipline, the firqats came into their own patrolling and ambushing in small groups from mountain outposts. The firqats were properly armed, trained, and supported by SAF. SAS teams worked with them at all times to ensure that they stayed on the government side and to handle artillery and air support.[87] The SAS men working with the firqats suffered a casualty rate as high as 30 percent, an indication of the aggressive military role played by the firqats.[88] The British had hoped to form inter-tribal militias as a foundation for more liberal governance, but the tribes squabbled and the first-formed firqat, which was inter-tribal, had to be broken up.[89]

The firqats were also better than SAF at information collection and, unsurprisingly, at communicating with other Dhofaris.[90] Firqats could identify insurgent leaders and supporters, round them up, and encourage them to publicly repudiate the insurgency.[91] The *firqats* could influence cousins and brothers with the insurgency, if they thought it was in their interest to do so, and they could get information from them.[92] On the jebel, firqats warned their families that enemy activity near SAF outposts would mean no more water, an important commodity in Dhofar. The firqats also made SAF look less like an army of occupation. In providing employment for fighting-age men and in feeding these men's families, the firqats were "a very expensive insurance policy" for Qaboos.[93] Payments to the firqats and bounties for insurgent weapons and ammunition continued after the conflict. Between August 1974 and August 1976, Qaboos paid out nearly a million British pounds.[94]

In political terms, the firqat leaders had become warlords by 1974. They controlled everything in their tribal areas surrounding SAF outposts, including grazing, watering, and the sale of government-provided food, and were kept busy with politics in Salalah.[95] Their continued alliance with the sultan supported the British goal of long-term stability. They became the liaison between SAF and the jebalis, and the government payments they received provided a way to distribute wealth to the jebel.[96]

Other accommodation efforts were either fruitless or symbolic. Qaboos was in touch with an element of the DLF's leadership in 1972, for example, but the contact appears to have come to nothing.[97] Symbolic accommodations sometimes resemble those of the anti-Huk campaign, though on an individual rather than governmental level. An eighteen-month-old baby was brought to the company of a British loan officer with SAF, Ian Gardiner. The child was very ill; a medical orderly said it would die in a few days without proper treatment. Gardiner ordered the baby evacuated by helicopter to a hospital. He was criticized for making poor use of resources, but he said, "I saw the gratitude and respect that this small, naïve, cost-inefficient act generated for the Sultan's Army, and felt sure that Qaboos sat just a fraction more firmly on his throne as a result of it."[98]

Both Sa'id and Qaboos recognized the value of extending accommodations to rivals and potential allies. They were both believers in politics as a positive-sum game as leaders of a patronage-based political regime. At the same time, neither was interested in structural reforms that would limit their power or cut into their authority. Thus the British goal of getting the sultans to implement reforms that would share power more broadly, even with the populace as a whole, was impossible to attain. The insurgency began as an effort to gain a greater share of the pie that was the sultan's wealth. The revolutionary Communist element of the insurgency saw a zero-sum game, but despite its contribution of Communist bloc training and support, it turned out to be weaker than the insurgents and supporters interested in getting a bigger share of the government's pie.

USES OF FORCE AGAINST CIVILIANS

The conventional wisdom is that SAF floundered about violently until the installation of Qaboos as sultan, when his acceptance of British direction of the campaign focused on avoiding damage to civilians while defeating insurgents. One scholarly work claims that "Sultan Sai'id did not have a viable strategy for defeating PFLOAG: applying repression and military force to what was essentially a political problem. On the other hand, the British provided the Sultanate [under Qaboos] with a real strategy, in the form of the Watts plan, which was based on their years of experience in several 'small wars.'"[99] Existing work also fails to consider similarities between the uses of force against civilians and insurgents under Sa'id and Qaboos. For example, when Qaboos took power, one scholar writes, "he . . . emphasized that the past practices of indiscriminate reprisals against civilians on the jebel had to end."[100] Another notes that, under Qaboos, SAF drew civilians away from the Western Area, "giving the SAF and SOAF [Sultan of Oman's Air Force] freer rein to target suspected *adoo* [enemy] positions without fear of causing heavy civilian casualties." The same author references the need to separate insurgents from civilians without detailing what uses of force such separation may require.[101]

Existing work presents a misleading sequence of events leading to counterinsurgent success and ignores the role of force in establishing and holding SAF mountain outposts amid the civilian population. This narrative creates unreasonable expectations about the ease of routing insurgents and gaining popular support, as with this description: "Civil affairs from 1971 onwards . . . usually began with the SAF establishing a garrison on the jebel. . . . Engineers would drill wells, and build a shop, school, clinic and mosque. Dhofaris would cluster around these ad hoc settlements for food, water, medical and veterinary care. . . . Civilians would in turn provide both intelligence and volunteers for the government's tribal militias."[102]

Accounts by officers involved in the campaign briskly dispose of events necessary for the scattered distribution of aid that eventually followed, suggesting where later authors may get the impression of a speedy process when the intent is to improve narrative flow. For example, Ken Perkins, SAF commander at the end of the war, summarized the civic aid process thus: "Military successes were immediately followed by the construction of access tracks and by provision of well-drilling equipment. The wells became points of focus for the population and were consolidated as government centers by the building of clinics, schools, and government shops."[103] But success did not come so quickly, and it did not come through provision of public goods to the mountain populace.

The evidence shows that the campaigns under Sa'id and then Qaboos were more alike than different. Both focused on an attrition strategy to starve insurgents of resources. SAF under Sa'id gradually grew strong enough to begin offensive operations to control civilians and attack the insurgency. The process continued under Qaboos. The effort began with controlling civilians on the plain and continued with offensive operations into the mountains and then control of civilians there, as well as massive blocking operations to separate insurgents from resources coming from civilians and from the DLF safe haven in Yemen across the border.

SAF commonly responded to attacks by targeting communities in the tribal area where the attack took place (usually by capping or otherwise destroying the wells necessary for the community's survival).[104] In 1968, a company of the Northern Frontier Regiment attempted to take a position at the village of Dalqut, on the coast near the Yemeni border, to cut insurgent supply lines. SAF withdrew after three days of taking fire from the jebel above, blowing up the village wells on the way out.[105] Operation First Night involved shelling an area for forty-five minutes to flush out any insurgents present before searching it. The contact report noted that civilian movement was seen but no casualties occurred.[106] Operation Final Fling included the burning of one in every five houses in a village after troops found incriminating items and the villagers provided no information.[107]

The military used small and large operations against civilians, including major clearing efforts to separate them from insurgents.[108] It largely succeeded in cutting off insurgents from civilian resources. SAF commander Brig. Corran Purdon, in Oman from 1967 to 1970, wrote that in the campaign, "above all we had to have the killer wish, find the enemy, seize the tactical advantage, dominate the theater of operations, crush his will to continue and so end the war. At the same time we had to win the battle for the hearts and minds of the Dhofar people."[109] Purdon cared more about the former than the latter, as will be seen.

SAF did not limit its uses of force in conducting broad sweeps and village searches. Some of SAF's British officers believed in taking a forceful approach to civilians, while some attempted to avoid unnecessary civilian casualties.[110] Regular British officers were almost uniformly suspicious of the Dhofaris, as evidenced by a comment from Purdon as he pondered the role of the Dhofaris going in and out of Salalah, selling their firewood and doing their shopping: "No doubt most of them were active rebels and presumably all bore with them intelligence as to what they had seen and heard of SAF and of the government." SAF raids on communities alarmed residents, though Purdon's concern was the signals civilians sent to insurgents. During one operation to seal off a village and search it, he wrote, "the women, once over their surprise, made their usual noise to alert their menfolk."[111]

In targeting civilians with brute force, SAF turned Dhofar's coastal capital, Salalah, into a prison camp surrounded by barbed wire, with all humans and pack animals searched coming and going to prevent transmission of money and supplies to insurgents.[112] Fields of sugar cane, vegetables, fruit trees, and coconut palms all lay inside the barbed wire encircling Salalah.[113] Surrounding the town in 1969, "the buffer zone was mined and fenced, the fruit groves uprooted, and all contact between the resident population and the nomads of Dhofar was prohibited."[114]

Eventually, as SAF built up its strength, the coastal villages were also turned into armed camps, with civilian behavior tightly controlled.[115] Everyone heading inward was searched for mines and weapons and everyone heading outward was searched for food and medical supplies.[116] The military moved uncooperative civilians to Salalah, confiscating cattle, over-chlorinating wells to make the water undrinkable, and establishing free-fire zones.[117]

SAF used these resource controls against civilians to weaken the insurgency. A food shortage on the jebel in the summer of 1971 increased the importance of resources from the plain reaching the insurgency, and a captured insurgent document confirmed that food controls and constraints on jebali movements on the plain were cutting into popular support for the insurgency.[118] The insurgency was trying to grow its own food in 1971 to replace that lost to military restrictions on the movement of foodstuffs, according to a captured report.[119] SAF had imposed a total ban on transporting food on the plain by February 1972.[120] Once SAF was able to establish footholds in the mountains where the insurgents sheltered, starting in November 1971, it controlled the distribution of food to keep it from insurgents and to use it to induce civilians to provide help.[121] Salalah was the biggest regroupment center for civilians driven from their homes, with jebalis housed in cheap, newly built units, given a salary, and kept under surveillance.[122]

On the jebel, food control was to be imposed as necessary as part of SAF's civic action campaign.[123] SAF burned crops from the air to punish the populace and deny food to the insurgency. In the 1971–1972 period, SAF made so-called burmail bombs from discarded Burma Oil drums filled with aviation fuel and dissolved polyurethane (creating homemade napalm) that it dropped from airplanes and fired by flares.[124] The CSAF from 1975 to 1977, Maj. Gen. Ken Perkins, denies personal knowledge of crop burning but suggests that the immediate provision of other goods, or payment, might have consoled Dhofaris for the loss of their crops in the field.[125]

SAF used force to punish Dhofaris and deny insurgents access to resources throughout the conflict. It targeted the tribes of Dhofar,[126] and with the increasing number and frequency of attacks in 1967, Purdon decided to widen the practice of collective punishment and establish free-fire zones to inhibit movement. SAF imprisoned any able-bodied males it came across, fired on anyone with a gun, and blew up wells and paths to the Yemeni border.[127] After insurgents shot and wounded a British officer, Purdon ordered another officer and unit to return to the site and "give them a bloody nose." The bodies of slain insurgents were put on show. After Operation Granite, Purdon wrote, "we took the corpses back to Salalah with us *'pour decourager'* any of *'les autres'* [to encourage the others], or sympathizers who might be inside the town perimeter."[128] Similarly, in July 1972, the bodies of the insurgents killed in their attack on the coastal village of Mirbat were put on display in Salalah along with captured weapons and ammunition.[129] CSAF Brig. John Graham made reference in 1971 to using fire and metal to punish one group and deter many more from fighting.[130] In 1972, Graham ordered the Dhofar Brigade to continue punishing Dhofaris who helped the enemy, using the firqats whenever possible.[131] SAF also booby-trapped corpses for insurgents (or civilians) to find.[132]

Qaboos too expressed a preference for the use of force. In February 1971 the sultan told SAF not to worry about wounding civilians in insurgent-held areas.[133] In 1972, Qaboos urged SAF to drop a bomb on a tribe that was slow to join his side.[134] In September 1973, he asked the British prime minister to do some bombing in Dhofar to dispel the regional belief that the UK was extending the war for its own purposes.[135] Sa'id had made a similar request of SAF, accepting Purdon's recommendation that SAF deal with an armed incursion in the north of Oman by shooting all of the intruders as a deterrent, rather than dealing with them the so-called British way, with minimal force.[136]

The greatest number of references to reprisals against civilians appears in accounts of the 1970–1972 period under Qaboos.[137] "*Bait* [village] bashing," or turning a community upside down in a search for insurgents, was common, and troops would detain any jebalis they came across. In July 1971, the British Ministry of Defense noted Dhofaris' scorn for SAF and its uses of force against the populace, and urged a shift from attempting to subjugate Dhofar to trying to ally with Dhofaris against the insurgency.[138]

With the increase in SAF's air capabilities from 1970 to 1975 under Qaboos, civilian suffering rose. SAF bombed insurgent areas to disrupt the lives of fighters and civilians.[139] Anyone outside areas of government control was subject to bombardment and starvation, and by 1973 malnutrition was increasing in DLF-held areas.[140] Civilians in the Western Area, generally referred to as thinly populated, had a terrible time once SAF began focusing on this border zone. They could not get to government-held areas without getting shot at. If they remained where they were, the air force was likely to fire on them, particularly if they owned camels. Civilians were living in caves to try to escape the fighting.[141]

Eventually SAF begin to show a greater sensitivity to civilian casualties.[142] When SAF troops saw insurgents moving with groups of women and children as cover, they ordered aerial bombardment wide of the group and fired machine guns over the civilians' heads to scatter them, rather than targeting the group to kill the insurgents.[143] Operational instructions for the Jebel Regiment's January 1975 move into the Central Area required clearance to fire in civilian areas unless troops were returning fire.[144] A training guide dated 1972 noted that SAF must not kill camels indiscriminately, but consider in each case whether a camel train or convoy constituted a legitimate military target.[145] John Akehurst, Dhofar Brigade commander at the end of the conflict, noted that SAF killed many camels to cut the flow of resources to the insurgency. The cruelty of it and concerns about alienating the camels' owners distressed the pilots who targeted the beasts, but the camel trains were a key element of the insurgents' supply chain. Iranian forces opened the single road into Dhofar in December 1973 and held it, freeing SAF troops for other operations.[146] But in November 1974 the Iranians had to be moved west, where there were fewer civilians to kill, wound, detain, or otherwise alienate. The U.S.-trained Iranians were known to shoot at anything that moved, including SAF.

SAF efforts to cut insurgents off from resources equally affected civilians, particularly the nomadic jebalis. First under Sa'id and then Qaboos, SAF struggled for years to build blocking lines slicing through the mountains to prevent resources reaching insurgents marooned in each sector. In July 1967, SAF had only three rifle companies in theater. One and a half companies, about 150 men, was all that could be spared from defensive duty at Salalah and on the Midway Road, the sole land link to northern Oman. That was too few forces to control the western border area, or even to gather sufficient information to guide operations. Hundreds of camel tracks were visible, but intercepting insurgent convoys was beyond SAF's abilities.[147] Patrols and ambushes did apparently keep insurgent fighters short of food and weapons late in 1967, however, since no large attacks were mounted in that period.[148] In 1969, SAF attempted to cut insurgents' lines to their rear base in Yemen, but found it lacked the troops and equipment necessary to do so.[149]

Physically blocking insurgent supply lines and destroying storage caches became a major part of the attrition effort that broke the insurgency, along with controlling the populace to help cut the flow of resources to insurgents. Lengthy barriers controlled insurgent and civilian movement to reduce insurgent resources and mobility. Once SAF was strong enough to begin executing its plans and remain year-round on the jebel, blocking efforts took shape in 1971 with Operations Leopard, Puma, and Cougar to construct physical barriers on the jebel.[150] The biggest, the fortified, mined Hornbeam Line, stretched thirty-five miles from the Arabian Sea north across the mountains. Hornbeam and similar fortifications, plus military operations clearing insurgents from inhabited areas, cut insurgents in the west off from 85–90 percent of civilians and their resources by war's end.[151] Preventing the resupply of munitions from Yemen while forcing the insurgency to burn up ammunition in battle and by firing on static SAF positions degraded the insurgents' fighting ability.

Construction began on Hornbeam's miles of mines and barbed wire in December 1973 and ended in August 1974. British Royal Engineers began building the line, and Jordanian forces later joined the effort, which took place under enemy fire and up and down steep slopes in temperatures rising above eighty-six degrees.[152] The Hornbeam Line was the last of the barriers forcing insurgents into their cross-border and Western Area bases and away from the population while SAF continued its military destruction of the insurgency's ability to fight and move within Dhofar.

As the blocking lines multiplied and SAF kept strengthening them, the lines choked the flow of insurgent supplies from Yemen.[153] In February 1972, SAF believed that Leopard, Puma, and Cougar were responsible for the decline in the number of 3-inch, 81 mm, and 82 mm mortars and rocket launchers in the Central and Eastern Areas.[154] A month later, British authorities attributed declining insurgent activity on the Salalah plain to a reduction in supplies.[155] The insurgency was short of arms and all other supplies east of the Hornbeam Line in December 1973, and fewer mortars and shells fired at SAF positions early in 1974 suggested a lack of big ammunition due to the effects of the Hornbeam Line.[156] Shortages of supplies and constraints on movement further reduced insurgent morale and efficiency in the Eastern Area between 1973 and 1975 and led to additional casualties.[157] The reduction in supplies and its cascading effects also led to increasing numbers of surrenders in the Eastern Area as insurgents' will to fight was broken.[158] Though Hornbeam was effective, it was not perfectly effective. An estimated two camel trains per quarter were getting through, and insurgents were manpacking in supplies, but that was a significant reduction from the pre-Hornbeam rate of two camel trains a week.[159] Reports on the blocking lines do not discuss their effects on civilians.

By December 1974, SAF had consolidated its hold in the Central and Eastern Areas. The insurgency was boxed in in the Western Area from three directions: by the Simba Line on the west, by the Damavand Line on the east, and by the sultan's navy to the south, on the sea. On December 2, 1975, SAF forces linked up on the Darra Ridge, and Qaboos declared the war over on December 11.[160]

DHOFAR ALTERNATIVE EXPLANATION:
THE GOVERNANCE MODEL

The counterinsurgency literature on Dhofar focuses on the 1970–1975 period under Qaboos as a time of dramatic reform and development as drivers of counterinsurgency success.[161] The first phase of the conflict, when Sa'id strengthened SAF as it attempted to execute the attrition strategy that succeeded with additional resources under Qaboos, is typically dismissed as a disastrous period in which Sa'id brought his troubles upon himself with his mean-spirited penury and penchant for brutality. Most authors pay little attention to the specifics of what changes were accomplished, where, and when. Authors also fail to identify both sultans' accommodation of elites in building a winning coalition.

These views appear in work by scholars and military professionals, distorting understanding of the events of the campaign, raising unreasonable hopes about how much change an intervening power can foist on a client, and significantly understating the amount of brute force used against civilians in a successful counterinsurgency campaign. Some mischaracterization of the campaign appears to be a function of authors' relying on secondary sources without considering specific campaign elements, timing, and geography. Authors also fail to recognize literary license in secondary works on Dhofar, including practitioners' need to focus on what is most likely to interest their intended audience. Authors also generalize about the case to support preexisting beliefs about what causes success in counterinsurgency. There is little work to date on the insurgency itself, which means that authors rely on victors' accounts without, perhaps, considering the biases inherent in those accounts or wishful thinking about what should, normatively, succeed for democratic great powers backing a counterinsurgent state.[162]

In existing work on Dhofar, Sai'id typically appears as a mean old man who rejected reforms out of miserliness and ill will, while Qaboos is portrayed as a young Britishized hero who immediately implemented reforms that served all his people based on the support of his British advisers.[163] "The sultan [Sa'id] made life horrible for his people," wrote a U.S. military officer in an elite graduate-level military program. "Sultan Sa'id was not willing to even consider a political solution or create programs for the support of the Oman [sic] people. Winning a counterinsurgency war with Sultan Sa'id was not going to happen." In listing the important features of Qaboos's successful campaign, the same author starts with "the sultan's accession and immediate liberal reforms."[164]

Another work states, "More enlightened than his father, Qaboos embarked on an ambitious program of political and economic modernization aimed at bringing about general reform," without providing details.[165] Another generalizes, "Sultan Qaboos opened his country to civil reform."[166] A scholar addressing a military audience echoes this claim about reforms: "The first thing he [Qaboos] does is to address the social, political, and economic concerns. . . . He started a vigorous nation-wide program of developments [sic]."[167]

As with most such statements on Dhofar, details on the implementation of any specific reforms are thin to nonexistent, references to the passage of time necessary for implementation are rare, and analysis of a possible connection between implementation and the weakening of the insurgency is limited. Authors typically lump together as "reforms" a sequence of events involving the irregular, limited provision of civic aid to individuals and small groups that occurred after years of building SAF under both Sa'id and Qaboos with a great deal of hard fighting and increasing control of civilians, first on the plain and several years later in the mountains.

Further, the events these authors give primary emphasis followed the defeat of the military threat rather than leading to it. This example from a lecture to a military audience is typical in its compression of events: "He [Qaboos] invites the 22d SAS (Special Air Service) to come into Oman. They start to do civil action programs, and they began to raise local civilian regular defense groups called firqats, which is Arabic for company. Those groups start to work in the jebel. They start working with the jebalis. They start building wells and doing things like cattle inoculation. They do a cattle drive to bring cattle to market there."[168] Similarly, in a scholarly article referencing the SAS leader John Watts's plan for Dhofar (in fact requested by Sa'id, not Qaboos) in 1970, the author says, "Civil assistance tasks were purposefully given precedence over military tasks in Watts' formulation," without addressing what tasks were given precedence—or what order they were performed in—in their execution, if at all. The same author notes that "between the costs of civil aid and military operations, the war in Dhofar was soon consuming 50 percent of Oman's GDP," without considering the relative allocation of resources between civil aid and military operations.[169] Another author provides a similar account of spending without explaining where, when, or how it might have driven counterinsurgency success: "Government expenditure on economic and social development increased from $60 million in 1971 to $1,000 million by 1975." The author goes on to conclude that "Dhofar shows the importance of identifying the grievances that fuel an insurgency, and of alleviating them as part of an integrated COIN [counterinsurgency] strategy."[170]

A volume on counterinsurgent success similarly generalizes: "The Qaboos government embarked on a major campaign to reduce the active popular support for the insurgents by, inter alia, bringing modern economic planning and techniques (especially with regard to animal husbandry) to the jebel, building schools, increasing health care, strengthening local administration, and promising the jebalis greater participation in running their own affairs. . . . The emphasis on social and economic development was facilitated greatly by the gradual shift of the military initiative from the insurgents to the government during the 1972–1974 period."[171] Unfortunately for this author's thesis, the civil development described followed defeat of the insurgent threat, and the largest insurgent defection preceded any political, economic, or social changes instituted by Qaboos rather than following them. Qaboos offered insurgents an amnesty upon ascending the throne.[172]

Both sultans promised economic development and both implemented less than promised, though a number of Sa'id's projects came to fruition under his son's rule, and Qaboos's projects were largely completed after campaign success. Neither leader provided political reforms. Under both sultans, leading British SAF officers varied in their concern for civilian casualties. Finally, neither sultan was particularly popular within Oman or Dhofar, even after the conflict.

Political reforms were anathema to both sultans. The provision of a few goods and services was acceptable to Sa'id and Qaboos under certain conditions because it did not threaten the political status quo. In a situation where the sultan had no interest in instituting major political reforms, the focus on accommodations kept the intervening state and the counterinsurgent client unified.

Had the case supported the governance theory, we should have seen reforms gaining popular support and weakening the insurgency and a reduction in the use of violence against civilians. We should not have seen the strengthening of the insurgency into the 1970s given Sa'id's and then Qaboos's development efforts. The trajectories of the insurgency and of Qaboos's claimed reforms, similarly, do not move in tandem as they should if the beliefs of the governance approach hold. The insurgency continued gaining strength until SAF's increasing numbers, firepower, and mobility cut its access to resources by controlling civilians and targeted it directly and consistently. Furthermore, if one argues that promises, gestures, or symbolic reforms suffice in counterinsurgency success, then it is worth noting that if it were so, Oman should have seen greater success under Sa'id, or at least less insurgent growth. In addition, the government succeeded against the insurgency without gaining popular support.

Reforms. Sa'id and Qaboos both promised reforms and began implementing development plans, including some begun by the father and completed under the son. A number of these plans were largely executed outside the jebel and outside Dhofar, making their contribution to counterinsurgent success logically tenuous. A significant number of efforts to aid the populace of

Dhofar only took place after the insurgency was broken as a fighting force in 1974 and defeated as a threat in 1975. The provision of minor accommodations took place during the conflict, along with the accommodation of elites discussed earlier in this chapter, in the form of limited goods such as distribution of water after well drilling, provided directly to specific communities rather than to all inhabitants of Dhofar or Oman. But these scattered efforts primarily occurred on the more secure plain and the highland behind the jebel rather than in the rebellious mountains, making it less likely that such irregular accommodations drove insurgent failure.[173]

The British government consistently pushed Sa'id and Qaboos to make democratizing reforms while also developing Oman's economy and infrastructure. During the conflict, however, while accommodations benefited useful individuals and groups, neither sultan implemented systemic political reforms.[174] Qaboos refused, for example, to let Dhofaris participate in the provincial government he had appointed.[175] Under Qaboos's rule, at the end of 1972, Whitehall wondered whether there was any point in continuing military aid to Oman if no reforms were taking place.[176] The British were near despair about the lack of reforms in 1974, when the insurgency had already lost two-thirds of its strength thanks to military action.[177] A month after Qaboos declared the insurgency defeated, the British still found no grasp within the Omani government of even the need for civil development to meet immediate popular needs, much less systemic reforms.[178] Political reforms to the sultanistic state that was Oman would have constrained the sultan's freedom of action, a price neither Sa'id nor Qaboos was willing to pay.

Sa'id, who wanted to protect the people of Oman from negative Western influences, had detailed development plans. He was cautious, however, in spending on civilian and military projects. After inheriting a bankrupt state from his father, he was determined to never be insolvent again and to retain his independence from Britain.[179]

When Sa'id ascended the throne in 1933, he modernized the state to a degree, including by centralizing power within himself and away from traditional tribal leaders. He "laid the foundation for a government apparatus that ultimately deepened and broadened the range of the government's role." Sa'id's modernizing reforms included refining the collection of customs and taxes, stabilizing the economy, and channeling most of his money to the army. Further, by taking up residence in Dhofar, he was living near his people.[180]

In 1958, Sa'id issued a statement describing the development efforts he was beginning and promising further changes with an ensured income from Oman's oil resources. He detailed expected revenues and development plans, including water and electricity systems for Muscat and Muttrah (in the north) and development in tribal areas, including Salalah. In 1965–1966 Sa'id commissioned a firm of London consultants to make a development plan for the capital area. By 1969, there was progress in building the port at Muttrah and the water system for Muscat, and in April equipment arrived in Salalah for construction of a power station and electrical grid.[181] By 1970, Sa'id's completed projects included a system of water pipes for Muscat and Muttrah, and two unstaffed and unfurnished hospitals (in Ruwi, outside Muscat, and in Tan'am, in the interior of northern Oman).[182] The ever-practical Sa'id told Purdon that he saw the need to train artisans and technicians, but not too many officials, because having more officials than there are jobs "will breed many discontented young men."[183]

Oman's first oil royalties arrived in October 1967.[184] Sa'id made a speech in January 1968 about his plans and began several big urban projects, including the Sohar road (in the north) and a girls' school in Muscat, both of which came to fruition under Qaboos.[185] An increase in health facilities followed, along with a plan to electrify the northern city of Sur.[186] By 1970, Oman had three "Western" elementary schools (in Muscat, Muttrah, and Salalah), with 1,200 students, and nearly fifty Quranic schools, with 4,800 students. There were four "rudimentary" health centers in Oman in 1970.[187] Other social programs developed in Sa'id's last decade of rule included a mobile medical service for the nomadic Bedouin of the interior of Oman; an irrigation plan for Jebel Akhdar, site of an earlier uprising in the north; and two experimental farms intended to help develop Oman's economy.[188] If such development efforts defeat or prevent insurgency, then the insurgency should not have grown in strength under Sa'id.

As one Oman expert writes, the portrayal of Sa'id in the secondary literature has developed from cartoon despot to a more accurate assessment of the sultan as a state builder who paid off Oman's debts, balanced its books, unified the coastal sultanate and the imamate of the northern interior, enforced the mechanisms of rule, modernized the armed forces, and introduced modernity and development to Oman.[189] This closer examination of Sa'id's reign makes suspect any claim that Qaboos's reforms played a significant causal role in defeating the insurgency in Dhofar. Development and state building in the form of the centralization and regularization of power had been going on throughout Sa'id's rule. Contra the conventional wisdom on the conflict in Dhofar, Qaboos did not change course from his father's path.

Under both Sa'id and Qaboos, SAF distributed scattered small benefits here and there, now and then, in efforts to immediately improve the lives of a few Dhofaris. Sa'id agreed in 1969, for instance, to allow SAF patrols to provide medical care, food, and cash to individual Dhofaris in exchange for information (some SAF troops had been supplying ill jebalis whom they came across with eye ointment and aspirin for months).[190] SAF troops attempted to push the boundaries by providing cooked rations from regimental allotments and medication as well.[191] These efforts did not win over large numbers of people. Indeed, small-unit operations became more dangerous. In 1968, operating at less than half-company strength, about fifty men, was forbidden as too dangerous.[192] The belief that the provision of goods to civilians would gain their support did not hold true in Dhofar. SAF's relationship with the populace worsened over time. In the summer of 1969, a reconnaissance platoon on a mission to provide food and medical aid to jebalis was fired on.[193] Villagers continued to warn insurgents when troops approached, and SAF guides tipped off insurgents to SAF's operational plans despite SAF's sporadic provision of food and medical care.[194]

Both sultans were able to resist British pressure for reform. A British official noted that a coordinating secretary for development was hired because of British pressure, but after he arrived in Oman on August 9, 1969, he was given no work to do.[195] Omani Defense Minister Hugh Oldman was eager to distribute food to the jebalis in cleared areas in 1971. Qaboos refused.[196] Clinic staffers brought in under Qaboos to replace SAS medics in communities on the plain quit because they were not getting paid.[197] In 1974, the year the insurgency was broken as a fighting force and as a threat to the government, the British were near despair: the only driving force for development in Dhofar was the civil liaison officer, and he had been transferred to a position in the Royal Stables.[198]

Implementation of reforms does not even necessarily mean delivery of benefits to the populace. Construction of a hospital is not the same as provision of medical care, for example. An oil executive long familiar with Oman visited in 1990 one of the first new hospitals opened in Dhofar during the conflict. There was no electricity the day of his visit, fifteen years after the end of the conflict, because the ministry in Salalah had not gotten diesel fuel delivered, leaving the eighteen-bed, two-doctor hospital limited in what it could provide the populace.[199]

SAF's effort to immediately ameliorate want among Dhofaris and begin longer-term development efforts largely took place on the plain and on the *negd* behind the jebel, rather than among the insurgency's mountain-dwelling supporters. Much of the civic action and initial stages of development that did occur on the jebel was accomplished after the insurgency was broken as a fighting force in 1974 and defeated as a threat in 1975. John Akehurst, Dhofar Brigade commander from 1974 through the end of the war, took a realistic view of SAF's limited ability to serve the people of Dhofar. He wrote that military civic action teams sent to military outposts on the jebel after operations to take territory in 1974 were only expected to set up "the rudiments of what were later to become government centers." He specified that only in October 1974—more than four years after Qaboos's accession and the period when the insurgency's capabilities were already badly degraded—did the policy of taking territory from the insurgency on the jebel, installing firqats in their tribal territory, and then plowing a track, digging a well, and so on actually begin.[200] The first building erected at one of the four jebel outposts went up in 1974.[201] SAF was also providing minimal goods from the Dianas, artillery observation posts established on the crest of the jebel to call in fire against insurgent attacks on coastal sites.[202]

It was in January 1975, after insurgent failure, that Qaboos decided to establish six regional development centers at military outposts on the jebel. Each site was to get a mosque with an imam or teacher, a small Quranic school, a water well, a clinic, and a representative of the *wali*. Later that year, Qaboos announced that centers were to be established at twenty-five locations, with thirty-five wells drilled and a flying doctor service introduced.[203] Again, civil development took place but reached the jebel primarily after the insurgent threat was defeated, an argument supported by the constant British complaints about the slow delivery of civic aid in the form of small provisions of goods and services to communities.[204]

In December 1975, the month that the sultan declared the conflict won, civic action in the Eastern Area had been consolidated, civic action in the Central Area had begun, and civic action in the Western Area, where the hard fighting had been taking place, had only an initial presence.[205] CSAF Maj. Gen. Ken Perkins reported in December 1975 that the little civic action and civil development achieved so far in Dhofar was due to the Royal Engineers, and complained of the lack of government direction and prioritization.[206] A month after Qaboos declared the insurgency defeated, the visiting chief of the British General Staff found no grasp within the government of the need for civil development.[207] In 1976, after counterinsurgency success, the chief of the defense staff paid a visit to Oman from London and reported that Qaboos knew that civil development was important for stability but preferred to spend his money on his military.[208] Again, the timing indicates that even minor accommodations like intermittent provision of food were not a key driver of government success because they followed rather than preceded the defeat of the insurgency.

Popular Support. The conventional wisdom overstates the degree of popular support gained by Qaboos compared with support for his father. Authors usually claim an increase in popular support and attribute it to reforms such as "the construction of new schools, hospitals, housing and wells by the government side" without citing specific evidence or causally linking the latter to the former, or even specifying the timing of the events.[209] One scholar writes without further explanation or evidence that "British engineers completed invaluable military and civil aid projects [*sic*] the latter being particularly appreciated by the people."[210] In another work, a scholar says that popular support for the insurgency weakened and attributes this change to civic action, but provides no evidence.[211] A military author makes the same assumptions, writing that "the sultan [Qaboos] took great pains to win over the people of Dhofar and on the Jebel Akhdar using economic and development initiatives."[212]

Just as the caricature of Sa'id as a wicked pinchpenny has been dispelled by recent scholarship, the characterization of Sa'id as a man much hated by his people does not survive scrutiny. "Certainly on the one public occasion when I saw him among his people in Dhofar he was received with rapture," reported Purdon.[213] Similarly, the characterization of Qaboos as widely adored must be modified. Certainly his taking the throne was greeted with exultation, as any wise Omani would be sure to show appreciation for his or her new leader. Reports from British officials who spent time in Oman and Dhofar indicate dismay at the lack of popular support for the new sultan because they considered it pivotal to counterinsurgency success. In June 1971, not quite a year after Qaboos took power, Dhofaris were disillusioned with him and gloomy about their future.[214] Popular enthusiasm for Qaboos continued to decline in 1971.[215] By November, the CSAF complained, all of Oman saw the government as inefficient and corrupt.[216] In March 1975, after defeat of the insurgent threat but before its officially declared military defeat, firqats in Operation Husn refused to pursue the adversary, so SAF moved to another area but was able to make no more contact with the insurgency. "The local civilians were clearly informing them of our movements," reported SAS man Paul Sibley, who was later commissioned into SAF as a captain.[217] In December 1975, SAF found that civilians in the Eastern Area who had been the weakest supporters of the insurgency still refused to disown the remaining insurgents in their midst.[218] Popular views did not improve after the conflict: a month after Qaboos declared the insurgency defeated, a British Ministry of Defense progress report found rising Dhofari dissatisfaction over the government's inactivity and maladministration.[219]

Akehurst, the Dhofar Brigade commander at conflict's end, was a believer in the need for good governance for counterinsurgency success. Yet he notes that civilians had good reason to not support the government or SAF. "Many civilians had been forced to take cover during the war and were not too well disposed towards organizations that fired guns and dropped bombs," he writes. "It was important to make clear to them that these inconveniences were only caused by the enemy presence and that now they could see the friendly face of government." Setting up a fireworks display for Qaboos after the war, Akehurst found that civilian suspicion remained. "Some of the jebalis were convinced we were planning to decimate their homelands and there had to be much explanation, persuasion and demonstration before they would agree to clear the danger area." Often governments consider participation in projects such as weapons amnesties a sign of support for the government, but Akehurst was under no such misconception. Between August 1974 and August 1976, he writes, the government paid out nearly a million pounds to individuals, half in the first six months of 1976, right after the conflict's end. The money went to those turning in arms, ammunition, and explosives, and those turning them in had probably also hidden them in the first place.[220]

Dhofar Conclusion

In Dhofar, the government's long-term accommodation of insurgent defector and tribal elites, as in Malaya with the elites of the different ethnic communities, contributed to insurgent failure. Limited, irregular distribution of goods to various communities in the Philippines and Greece did not do so. The military defeated the insurgency on the battlefield in Dhofar thanks in part to the forceful control of civilians, which weakened insurgents' fighting capabilities and will to fight on. These findings support the predictions of the compellence theory. The case of Dhofar, along with those of Malaya, the Philippines, and Greece, strengthens the prediction of the compellence theory that success hinges on political accommodation of selected rival elites. It also shows that the use of large operations and artillery and air power, and even control and punishment of civilians, does not necessarily prevent counterinsurgent success. Indeed, it contributed to it in Dhofar. The case does show that SAF took some care, depending on individual officers' choices, to avoid civilian casualties, but SAF used brute force systematically to control civilians, as well as collective punishment, and still defeated the insurgent threat.

In Dhofar, elites of all three types saw room for gain through cooperation. All demands were limited, accommodation was less costly than reforms, and government and nongovernment elites did not see the insurgency as an existential threat. In this case, government elites accommodated nongovernment elites and insurgent elites. Both sultans saw the need for political and military capabilities provided by both other groups and recognized the nonrevolutionary interests of most insurgent elites.

High Cost Success

El Salvador

The Salvadoran civil war resonates in the United States as a military intervention that did not lead to a quagmire or to the tens of thousands of American deaths suffered in Vietnam. In the conflict, from 1979 to 1992, the United States provided the threatened government with arms, money, military training, and a small cadre of military advisers inside El Salvador to fight a powerful and popular Communist-nationalist insurgency. The repressive government defeated the insurgents as a threat to the state by 1984, but the resulting military stalemate dragged on until the powerful military elite finally agreed to a peace settlement signed in 1992.

El Salvador is a small, land-poor Central American state about two thousand miles from the Texas border. It had been ruled by the military from 1931 in a mutually beneficial arrangement with the rural oligarchy. The planters grew cotton, cattle, coffee, and sugar cane, while security forces kept the sharecropper peasants working the land and in exchange received wealth and power through running the government.[1] In 1980, the poorest 20 percent of Salvadorans earned 2 percent of the national income, less than they had ten years earlier, and the richest 20 percent earned a record high of 66 percent.[2] The landless population grew from 12 percent to 41 percent of rural families between 1961 and 1975.[3] The infant mortality rate in 1977 was 60 percent.[4]

Successive military governments oscillated between limited political reforms and violent repression through the twentieth century.[5] When the insurgency began, military elites were divided between the dominant hardliners, who saw any loosening of political control as a prelude to revolution and disaster, and younger, less powerful moderates, who believed that loosening state repression would enable regime survival.[6] Both factions believed in the need for continued military rule.[7] Civilian elites agreed, as did many better-off rural residents who supported government repression as necessary for public order.[8] About half of the rural populace was satisfied with a strong central authority while wanting an end to abuse by the security forces and the delivery of some basic services.[9] The professional class and the middle class of teachers, students, unionized workers, and others wanted a greater political voice and economic opportunity. Urban workers and the growing urban underclass that had fled rural poverty wanted the redistribution of wealth.[10] Peasants wanted land and freedom from oppressive landlords. Many Salvadorans also objected to U.S. dominance in the region.

Political participation in El Salvador was limited to elites under Spanish rule and after independence in the nineteenth century. The influence of the U.S. Alliance for Progress in the 1960s, an anti-Communism program intended to educate peasants and develop the rural economy, and the liberation theology movement of the Roman Catholic Church in the 1970s helped build civil society, especially in the countryside. The period saw an increase in church groups, student groups, political parties, and peasant organizations.[11] In the cities, the middle class pressed for political liberalization. The number of unions grew from 80 with a combined membership of just over twenty-four thousand in 1966 to 127 with a combined membership above sixty-four thousand in 1975.[12]

With landlessness and poverty also on the rise, increasing political contestation frightened the government into increased its violence against civilians. The military's party stole the 1972 election from the moderate Christian Democratic candidate, José Napoleón Duarte, who was beaten and sent into exile, shocking Salvadorans who believed that their government was democratizing. The military put down rising numbers of demonstrations and strikes until its calculated, widespread violence in the late 1970s drove many Salvadorans from political resistance to terrorism and insurgency.[13] The president who took office instead of the exiled Duarte, Col. Arturo Armondo Molina, was replaced by the conservative Gen. Carlos Humberto Romero in 1977. Under Molina, the army and security forces were linked to 37 assassinations and 69 disappearances. Under Romero, those figures rose to 461 assassinations and 131 disappearances.[14] Romero was ousted in turn by another military coup in 1979. The relatively moderate coup leaders planned structural reforms such as land redistribution and an end to corruption and repression, changes intended to quell protests while protecting military rule.[15] Further leadership changes followed as the United States attempted to create a civilian-led government and the military tried to protect its privileges.[16]

In this period of rising violence, from the late 1970s to the early 1980s, opposition swelled to insurgency while massive government violence quelled widespread popular protests in the cities.[17] The insurgency included a variety of individuals and groups, from committed Marxists to Christian Democrats and Social Democrats, intellectuals, peasants, professionals, union members, and even ex-military officers. Five insurgent groups united in 1980 under the banner of the Farabundo Marti National Liberation Front (FMLN).

Goals included the end of military dictatorship and U.S. involvement in domestic politics; democratic rights for all; nationalization of large landholdings, banks, utilities, and transport; and equal social and economic rights for women.[18]

Despite U.S. concerns about the FMLN as a tool of the Soviet bloc, external support neither created the insurgency nor explains its continued strength, though the FMLN did receive external state support throughout the war, including from U.S. allies. External support for the FMLN was primarily military at first and primarily political later. Eastern bloc support fell after 1983, but the FMLN continued to receive political advice and support from a multitude of states and organizations, including the governments of Mexico, West Germany, Sweden, Austria, and Canada.[19] Anyone wounded in an insurgent area could get free medical care in Cuba.[20] International Committee of the Red Cross refugee camps across the border in Honduras unintentionally served as a haven for insurgents.[21] According to Gen. Juan Rafael Bustillo, wartime commander of the Salvadoran Air Force, 90 percent of insurgents were Salvadoran. Bustillo regarded the small number of Cuban, Nicaraguan, and other foreign fighters as of little concern.[22] Gen. Mark Hamilton, U.S. military group commander at the end of the war, says that outside funding supported the insurgency's early growth, but that the behavior of the Salvadoran government caused the insurgency and its development.[23] An estimated one thousand Salvadoran insurgents trained in Cuba, Nicaragua, Eastern Europe, and the Soviet Union. Communist states also provided the insurgency with weapons. A U.S. military observer noted that there was little evidence of major arms and ammunition infiltration.[24] The insurgency purchased weapons on the global arms market or captured them from the military, and manufactured its own weapons as well.

The insurgency's budget was probably less than $5 million a year and costs were relatively low. It did not pay its fighters, for example.[25] It was not difficult for insurgents to meet immediate needs. Sufficient food was available year-round, insurgents faced no risk of freezing, and El Salvador's broken terrain and lush vegetation—jungle at lower altitudes and thick pasture and pine in the highlands—could hide "numberless hordes."[26] The insurgents had plenty of money from kidnapping wealthy Salvadorans early in the war, and later raised cash from land taxes in insurgent-held areas.[27]

U.S. interest in the politics of the region and in El Salvador increased with the 1980 election of President Ronald Reagan. Though President Jimmy Carter had supported the Salvadoran government, the Reagan administration was concerned that the Soviet Union was expanding its influence and military presence in the Western Hemisphere. The president warned that the Communist threat in Central America was "just two days' driving time from Harlingen, Texas."[28] The administration viewed the 1979 Sandinista revolution in Nicaragua with alarm, fearing a similar outcome in neighboring El Salvador. The president argued that the Soviet plan was to tie down U.S.

forces near home to hinder its ability to act in Western Europe, the Gulf, and East Asia.[29] The United States considered the military defeat of the Salvadoran insurgency an important national security interest from 1980 to 1988.[30] The U.S. strategy changed over time. The Reagan administration supported the military government's early attempts to violently repress its challengers. As repression intensified, members of the administration who advocated some reforms as the way to defeat the insurgency gained influence while popular and congressional opposition to U.S. support for the Salvadoran government increased. The U.S. strategy became one of helping El Salvador institute democratizing reforms that would drain support away from the insurgency, gain support for the government, and enable the military to succeed against the insurgency politically and in the field.[31]

Opposition to continued U.S. support for the Salvadoran government was based on fear that deepening U.S. involvement would lead to another costly, drawn-out war like Vietnam, and on the belief that the United States should not support repressive dictatorships.[32] The Salvadoran military's murder of Americans intensified opposition, as did the use of U.S.-supplied air power against civilian Salvadoran communities.[33]

The end of the Cold War in 1989 and the election of George H. W. Bush led to a major change in U.S. political goals in El Salvador. The new administration gave up the Reagan-era insistence on military victory, instead pushing the reluctant military leadership into peace talks and insisting that it accept the peace agreement reached under UN auspices.

The campaign provides support for the compellence model. Elite accommodation kept members of the ruling military and civilian classes united, which was the only way to keep crucial U.S. support. The military's consistent targeting of civilians throughout the war helped break the military capabilities of an insurgency deeply reliant on popular support. To the degree that reforms took place in El Salvador during the war, they were political changes that returned the state to the status quo ante bellum. The degree of political openness attained by the late 1980s was no greater than that experienced before the war began in 1979. There were no reforms benefiting the populace as a whole. The military provided food, clothing, and medical care to pro-government communities on an ad hoc basis, depending on the choices of individual battalion commanders, but it could not provide public goods in any area not already supportive of the government—had it wished to do so—because it could not hold the ground it took from insurgents. Popular support for the government, measured by rough proxies such as election participation, did not increase. The Salvadoran civil war demonstrates that uses of force against civilians do not doom a counterinsurgency campaign to failure. The military became strong enough to drive civilians out of their communities and into camps, where they were more easily controlled, or into the cities, but it never became strong or capable enough to cut the flow of resources between populace and insurgents.

In brief, the war began as a popular uprising against the government that was conjoined with military and death squad violence against civilians in 1979. The military met the formation and growth of the FMLN with increased violence in the cities and the countryside. In this period, from 1979 to 1984, the insurgency strengthened and organized itself sufficiently to begin defeating the El Salvador Armed Forces (ESAF) in conventional battle. U.S.-supplied air power broke down FMLN formations on the battlefield and ended the threat of an insurgent takeover in 1984. The United States built Salvadoran forces up to the point where the government was able to hold the insurgents to a military stalemate for the next six years, from 1984 to 1989, when the military agreed to peace talks under pressure from the United States, the United Nations, and neighboring states. The fighting continued from 1989 until the Chapultepec Accords were signed in 1992 in Mexico, though the renewal of government atrocities by hard-liners within the military threatened to derail the talks. Elite accommodation took place within the ruling elite, as in Greece, in order to keep U.S. support flowing. The military and associated militias used force throughout the war to try to control civilians and reduce the flow of resources to insurgents. The government promised reforms including free and fair elections and increased respect for human rights but did not follow through. Its reduction of political repression returned the country to the level of openness that prevailed before the war, but this level was not high. Civic group organizers and members still faced assassination. Popular support for the government did not increase.

El Salvador Analysis

INSURGENCY BROKEN BY 1984

The military defeated the insurgent revolutionary threat to topple the government in 1984, though fighting continued for years after. The date is important in this case because counterinsurgent success is usually identified as taking place with the signing of the peace agreement in 1992, after counterinsurgent gestures toward reforms. Insurgent conventional forces were smashing ESAF units in the field in 1983. But by the end of 1984, U.S.-supplied air power and ground attacks had shattered the insurgents' main-force units and destroyed many supportive communities. A mass uprising was highly unlikely by this time. Salvadorans had learned the costs of publicly challenging the government. Indeed, the insurgents' so-called Final Offensive in 1981 and another in 1989 failed to spark a popular uprising. By 1984, insurgent military victory was impossible as long as the government retained U.S. backing.

The FMLN started out training *campesinos* (peasants) in the use of arms with rifles carved out of wood. They conducted raids on military outposts and later on barracks to build their armory.[34] In the years from 1979 to 1984, the insurgency developed its army and its rear zones of control and expanded its control to 24–33 percent of national territory.[35] By 1983, the FMLN was making large battlefield gains using conventional formations of up to 1,000 fighters in pitched combat.[36] There were an estimated 4,000 insurgents in 1980.[37] In 1982, the hardcore main force had grown to an estimated 6,000–8,000, rising to 10,000–12,000 in 1983–1984.[38]

But in 1984, air and ground attacks forced the insurgency to return to small-unit operations. The insurgency could no longer face ESAF on the battlefield, but it expanded its presence to all fourteen departments (provinces) and began a terrorism campaign against state economic targets. The insurgency mounted attacks on military bases and ambushed troops in the countryside to try to grind down Salvadoran and U.S. support for the war.[39] In addition, the insurgency emphasized political development, building shadow governments in rural communities, rebuilding its networks in the cities, and offering to participate in peace talks, an offer the United States consistently rejected.[40] The FMLN sacrificed some support with its intermittent forced recruitment and its economic terrorism campaign,[41] which cut into backing from better-off Salvadorans who opposed extremely abusive state behavior to a greater degree than they supported FMLN tactics.[42] Sabotaging electrical lines affected the middle and upper classes, since few poor Salvadorans had electricity or running water.[43]

In 1985, insurgent strength was at about 9,000–11,000 fighters, reduced from their estimated strength of 10,000–12,000 in 1983–1984.[44] By 1989, the military had reduced insurgent ranks to an estimated 8,000 full-time fighters supported by 25 percent of the populace and controlling 15 percent of municipalities.[45] In 1990, the insurgency was the local government in 30 percent of El Salvador, had the sympathy of more than half a million Salvadorans, and was fielding 6,000–7,000 full-time fighters and part-time militias of up to 40,000 more.[46]

In comparison, the ESAF grew from about 10,000 men in 1979 to 40,000 in 1984 and 56,000 in 1987.[47] By war's end, the armed forces had reached a high of 63,000 troops.[48] At demobilization in December 1992, the FMLN had 12,362 troops, compared with an estimated 4,000 insurgents in 1980.[49]

U.S. Southern Command commander Gen. Maxwell Thurman told Congress early in 1990 that the government could not defeat the insurgency, but the insurgency could not seize the state either.[50] The insurgency was never able to win a majority of Salvadorans to its cause.[51] There was considerable support throughout the war, especially among better-off rural residents, for the state's right-wing repression.[52] Areas supportive of or sympathetic to the insurgents remained so throughout the war, and vice versa. "No one was in the middle in El Salvador. No neutrals," one military observer reports.[53]

ELITE ACCOMMODATION

Elite accommodation in El Salvador involved elements already within the government providing each other with benefits to keep all factions united, at least in support of continued U.S. aid, to make sure that U.S. support continued. Rather than accommodating moderates within government or in other institutions, such as the church, the government killed them. I discuss this latter aspect of the campaign in the section on targeting civilians.

One major accommodation was the military's use of entrepreneurs of violence in the form of civilian militias. The army reserve overlapped with the militia Organizacion Democratica Nationalista (National Democratic Organization), an estimated fifty thousand to one hundred thousand men.[54] Its peasant members received loans, health care, impunity, land, and fertilizer in exchange for their services, specifically uses of force against civilians to try to keep them in line.[55] The militia contributed to the government effort to separate insurgents from their sources of resources in the civilian population.

Other accommodations occurred among elites and with the United States. In an attempt to keeping U.S. congressional support flowing to an increasingly repressive military dictatorship, the military junta put a civilian face on the government in December 1980 by bringing in Duarte, previously beaten and exiled after the stolen election of 1972, as a figurehead president.[56] The United States, meanwhile, accommodated its elite allies in El Salvador by funneling them money because the administration needed the military to commit as few human rights abuses as possible. Otherwise, Congress would cut funding. U.S. aid supported the development of agribusiness, for example, benefiting the oligarchs allied with the military rather than agrarian reform programs benefiting smallholders in immediate need. The military controlled civic action funding and state economic institutions, meaning that members of the elite skimmed off much aid.[57]

In the revolutionary context of the Salvadoran civil war, in which insurgents making demands to overturn the political, economic, and social structure of the state gained significant popular support, elites also saw a zero-sum game. Indeed, they had seen one in their relationship with the peasants since the uprising of 1932 known as La Matanza.[58] Additionally, the military's belief that it was on the front line of a Cold War showdown prevented it from considering political offers to rivals.[59] Officers increasingly feared not only for the regime's survival but also for their own.[60] Further, the military's traditional attitude of entitlement, its belief in repression as the first and best tool to preserve the government and their own rule, and its scorn for and lack of comprehension of the conditions and needs of the masses all intensified its resistance to political change even in the form of limited accommodations to bring opponents on board.[61] The elites thought that any reforms at all would mean the destruction of their way of life.[62]

USES OF FORCE AGAINST CIVILIANS

Counterinsurgency authors downplay the degree to which the military's violence against civilians persisted throughout the war. One author notes, for example, that the military regularly bombed rebel-held areas from 1981 to 1986, implying that aerial attacks became at least less regular after 1986. He also plays down the effects of this use of force against civilians: "Civilians who lived in the free-fire zones quickly adapted to being the targets of aerial bombardment. They dug bomb shelters, learned to camouflage their homes, and took cover as soon as a helicopter, an A-37, or an O-2 reconnaissance aircraft was spotted."[63] Existing work also understates the high level of intentional violence against civilians throughout the campaign by emphasizing the decline from the dizzyingly high level of the 1979–1982 period rather than the persistently high level that continued through the rest of the war. Authors argue that the "idea" of focusing on all aspects of the counterinsurgency struggle—not simply the application of military force— persisted throughout the war, without providing evidence showing how this idea contributed to the war's outcome. Similarly, such authors describe one particular operation (Phoenix) as the most successful civic action campaign of the war without explaining what it achieved, in what ways it was successful, or the uses of force involved.[64] Another work appears to provide specifics without actually giving information on the degree of implementation of the program or its elements, or effects on the war effort: "In formerly guerrilla-held areas, the government implemented a civic action program that consisted of rebuilding the social and economic infrastructure and training civil defense units to protect key targets and free the military to engage in offensive operations."[65]

The counterinsurgency campaign in El Salvador began with a state crackdown intended to quickly quash public opposition. The government neutralized the early threat of revolution through terror. It then used its augmented firepower to degrade the insurgency's military capabilities through a campaign of attrition against the populace and insurgents.

The government systematically targeted civilians throughout the war because it perceived them as an existential threat. The military attacked civilians using bombing and shelling, indiscriminate capture, torture, systematic destruction of homes and crops, and forced relocation to cities and camps where civilians were easier to control.

Between 1978 and 1991, 50,000 civilians were killed out of a population of 5 million. The vast majority of those civilians, more than 42,000, were killed in 1978–1983.[66] Between October 1979 and March 1982, an estimated 1,736 civilians in politically salient groups (political activists, union activists, journalists, human rights monitors, and church people) were killed in military and paramilitary violence. There were an estimated 3,371 civilian deaths from May to September 1982; 6,639 civilian deaths and deaths attributed to the military or paramilitaries in military clashes in 1983; 4,274 in 1984; 3,036 in 1985; 1,709 in 1986; 1,434 in 1987; 1,387 in 1988; 2,875 in 1989; and 1,525 in 1990. The toll rose in 1989 and again 1990 when military hard-liners tried to derail peace talks.[67]

Assassination targets included civic group leaders, the rector of the National University, and the secretary general of a union federation. Six leaders of the Democratic Revolutionary Front party were kidnapped, shot, and strangled in 1980 ahead of a press conference at which they were to announce their desire to participate in peace talks with the junta. The same year, a death squad killed the attorney general, Mario Zamora, in his own home. The military opened fire on nonviolent vigils and protests, and sprayed the fifty thousand mourners at the 1980 funeral of the assassinated Archbishop Óscar Romero with pesticide from planes. Also in 1980, the state began targeting youths between the ages of sixteen and twenty because it assumed that all students were potential enemies of the state.[68] Death squads left the severed heads of kidnapping victims on municipal buses in San Salvador. The faces of priests and catechists and their students were skinned, their eyes and tongues cut out.[69] Warning notes were sometimes left with dumped bodies, or the name of the death squad responsible was carved into its victims' flesh. The National Police used a meatpacking plant as a murder center, beheading their victims and sometimes grinding up the bodies for easier disposal.[70] The violence was routinized. Of the death squads, military officers said, "They may commit crimes, but the victims are usually Communists."[71] Salvadorans got the message: demonstrations got smaller, and fewer individuals dared to publicly identify themselves with leftist or even civic groups.[72]

In the countryside in the spring of 1980, military activity increased dramatically. In October, the military began wiping out entire communities in areas suspected of supporting insurgents.[73] The military set up heavy artillery and mortars in the hills above villages to force everyone out and fired on communities from helicopters.[74] Cleansing operations spread fear, separating the populace from insurgents because residents afraid to return could not provide support to the insurgents.[75] Entire areas were depopulated. In December 1983, an estimated four hundred thousand people were displaced inside El Salvador, another two hundred thousand had fled to Mexico and elsewhere in Central America, including refugee camps across the border in Honduras, and an estimated half a million had entered the United States.[76]

Death squad activity against individuals and small groups of civilians declined after 1983 at U.S. insistence,[77] but U.S. augmentation of Salvadoran military power increased ESAF's targeting ability in the countryside.[78] Its primary tool was the Batallónes de Infantería de Reacción Immediata (Immediate Reaction Infantry Battalions; BIRIs). These units were the government's fighting machines.[79] The BIRIs were only moderately successful against the FMLN because they could not hold the territory they cleared, but they degraded insurgent military capabilities with search-and-destroy missions over the course of the war.

With significant U.S. training, arming, advising, and intelligence development, and despite U.S. encouragement to fight irregularly and avoid civilian casualties, the Salvadoran military fought a war of big battalions and attrition. U.S. officers were heavily involved in the campaign, but their influence was limited. There were often more U.S. officers than Salvadorans at meetings of the Joint Staff.[80] The senior member of the U.S. military's training team from 1983–1988 advised the minister of defense and the military. U.S. lieutenant colonels advised key teams at headquarters.[81] An FMLN member, Commandante Ernesto, who is known only by his nom de guerre, recalls the mismatch between U.S. goals and Salvadoran behavior. "The military targets were incongruous with the strategic and operational objectives given the damage to the population," he said.[82]

U.S. military advisers were assigned to each department. Even getting the military to fight was a struggle. Americans called it a "Monday to Friday war" for the military.[83] Troops conducted "search and avoid patrols."[84] One battalion commander, when asked why he was not ambushing FMLN supply lines, said, "If we attack them, they'll retaliate. If we leave them alone, they'll leave us alone."[85]

When troops did go out in the field, civilians suffered. "[Troops] saw an enemy in every civilian," one U.S. military adviser said. "They would stomp through a community and look into everybody's faces and see a guerrilla."[86] The military's definition of a leftist "ranged from anyone with a social conscience all the way to guerrilla supporters."[87] For Col. Sigfredo Ochoa Perez, there were no civilians in FMLN areas.[88] "I can massively bomb the red zones because only subversives live in them," he said in 1985.[89] This classification of traditional noncombatants as combatants percolated through the troops. A soldier said, "I killed children because I was told they were the subversive seeds that needed to be eliminated. And I killed their mothers because I was told the *campesino* women were factories for more guerrillas."[90]

Officers discussed the need to make an example of communities with what they called La Limpieza (The Cleansing).[91] Tactics included murder, rape, torture, and crop burning. One of the best-known examples is the El Mozote massacre, when the elite U.S.-trained Atlacatl Battalion killed more than one thousand people in six hamlets on December 11–13, 1981. Troops destroyed everything and everyone they found in the area.[92] In one community, soldiers left a graffito: "The Atlacatl Battalion will return to kill the rest."[93]

More typical in scale was an operation in October 1982, when the approximately three hundred villagers of Copapayo fled an assault by Atlacatl's sister battalion, Ramon Belloso, that included the BIRI firing 81 mm mortars into the community. Villagers returned to find their belongings and communal buildings trashed and a seventy-five-year-old man who had remained behind lying in the plaza, his shoulders dislocated and a bullet wound in his stomach. A note on his body said, "This is what happens to those who live with subversives. Ramon Belloso Battalion."[94]

The United States encouraged building specialized forces to take the offensive while poorly trained and equipped regulars handled defensive responsibilities. The 1,300-man BIRIs such as Atlacatl and Belloso were the state's fighting machines. They were offensive formations big enough to go into an area and overwhelm it, mounting search-and-destroy operations against insurgent camps and civilian communities. But it was not worth the costs to go into hardcore FMLN areas because the insurgents could hold their own. At the other end of the spectrum were the small units, such as six-man Long Range Reconnaissance Patrols developed by U.S. advisers.[95]

These big special units cleared thousands of peasants from their homes but could never hold territory.[96] Operation Phoenix demonstrates both problems. The operation began in the FMLN stronghold of the Guazapa Volcano north of San Salvador, the capital, in January 1986. The military declared victory a year later, and the FMLN moved right back in along with the displaced civilians.[97] The operation included sweeps and aerial bombing that drove out thousands of peasants.[98] Col. Leopoldo Antonio Hernandez boasted, "We were able to rescue once again 600 *masas* [the masses, FMLN supporters] and deliver them to the Red Cross and their families for relocation."[99]

Over the long term, infantry sweeps and search-and-destroy missions killed fighters and broke down the FMLN's forces into smaller bands.[100] Saturation patrolling wore insurgents out by keeping them on the move.[101] The decline in human rights abuses was in part a reflection of ESAF's earlier success in clearing communities. There were fewer civilians in areas of the countryside accessible to ESAF for the army to kill.[102]

Near war's end, the military began using ordnance in built-up areas more sparingly and sometimes refused field requests to bomb villages, but the insurgency had already been held to a stalemate. Some officers refused to fire unless they were sure their target was the enemy; comrades judged them ruined by their U.S. trainers.[103] But it was not training so much as fear that led to a reduction in atrocities, though not in uses of force against civilians. Officers realized that continued high-profile human rights abuses could cost them U.S. support in a fight that was getting tougher. With the continued strength of the insurgency, they faced "impending doom," U.S. Ambassador Thomas Pickering said. "They were beginning to stare defeat in the face."[104] Losing U.S. support meant losing to the FMLN.

Powerful Salvadoran generals argue that the populace was endangered because of the FMLN's choices, not the government's. Retired Gen. René

Emilo Ponce, the wartime defense minister and a leader within the most powerful group in the military ranks,[105] recalls that the insurgency nearly brought the state to its knees early in the war. From the government's perspective, violence was necessary to prevent revolution and chaos, he said. "The FMLN initiated its aggression towards the Salvadoran state through guerrilla warfare, with small, armed groups sabotaging the national economy and public services; they ambushed and harassed military units; they agitated the population and mobilized them; they took over embassies and other public and private establishments; they kidnapped and murdered politicians and local and foreign entrepreneurs; and they launched propaganda and disinformation campaigns aimed at tarnishing the government and the armed forces throughout the country."[106]

Gen. Alvaro Antonio Calderón Hurtado, a wartime chief of the general staff, said, "The people saw themselves affected because the subversives shielded themselves and blended into the civilian population and in certain occasions, [the civilians] ended up exposed to crossfire. Public services were attacked by the FMLN (transportation, the electrical grid, bridges, public transit, city halls . . . etc.) by performing terrorist acts and [we] had to counteract that by any means the government possessed."[107] Ponce agreed: "The armed forces planned its operations aiming to affect the civilian population as little as possible, but the FMLN used the population to hide from or evade combat, and sometimes as human shields."[108]

The military's goal was military defeat of the insurgency. Its method was to build its own strength to destroy insurgent capabilities. "The problem we faced was how to modernize and equip our forces to ensure a successful campaign against the insurgency. This was our focus and sole manner of effectively combating and resolving the economic, social, and political problems," wrote Gen. Mauricio Vargas, wartime deputy chief of the General Staff. "We needed to expand the forces, equip and train them, modernize the army, the air force, and the navy." Vargas argued that the U.S. focus on development ignored military principles: "One must neutralize the enemy on the battlefield to destroy its resistance and for it to accept the political conditions for ending the war."[109]

EL SALVADOR ALTERNATIVE EXPLANATION: THE GOVERNANCE MODEL

Had the case supported the governance approach, we should have seen reforms gaining popular support and weakening the insurgency and a reduction in the use of violence against civilians. Instead, we see a gradual return—after government success—to the level of political openness that prevailed before the war and no evident increase in popular support for the government. The government continued targeting civilians throughout the war. Intra-elite accommodation is evident here, as in the Philippines and Greece. Unlike in Dhofar, we do not see significant counterinsurgent efforts to bring rivals outside the government into an ad hoc coalition.

Reforms. The counterinsurgency literature on El Salvador identifies the campaign as a positive example for democratic great powers. Most authors focus on the liberalizing, democratizing reforms demanded by the United States, including holding free and fair elections, redistributing land, and increasing respect for and protection of human rights. This work assumes that reforms were implemented as demanded and that they caused the defeat of the insurgency but provides little evidence and rarely a causal argument.[110]

In contrast, experts on El Salvador see little in the way of reform implemented during the conflict. The peace agreement, the Chapultepec Accords of 1992, forced the military out of domestic politics—a major reform that followed the war—to begin the difficult process of democratization that continues today.[111]

Accounts of Salvadoran reforms claim that political reforms took place but rarely consider what degree of change occurred. One study, for example, says, "As a result of a series of free elections, the Salvadoran government has been awarded broad popular support and, thus, political legitimacy. To build on its legitimacy, the government implemented civic action programs to rebuild social and economic infrastructures and free the army to pursue insurgents." It adds that in El Salvador, "strong, competent, democratically elected leadership at all levels of government" was helpful in "attempting to persuade the population . . . that they will have the opportunity to improve their quality of life and the political means to express their desire for this."[112] Or, in the words of another study, "The government of El Salvador democratized and increased its legitimacy, while the military increased its competence and improved its respect for human rights."[113]

Such statements, particularly when unsupported or poorly sourced, or when they fail to consider context such as the sustainability of any counterinsurgent behavioral changes, sweep away questions about the implementation of reforms. Questions go unanswered about when and where any reforms may have been implemented and about how they might have been received (either as promised or as executed). These works also often fail to present evidence about how the promise or execution, if any, affected the behavior of other actors.

Existing work does not examine whether Salvadoran promises of reform were implemented. U.S. advisers urged ESAF "to stress pacification, civil defense, and population security rather than the destruction of guerrilla units. . . . Since support from the population was the crux of counterinsurgency, military activities were subordinate to economic, political, and psychological ones."[114] Another author similarly assumes that what the United States recommended, the Salvadorans did. "The U.S. policy," he writes, "was to emphasize land reform, political reform in the form of honest elections, economic development, and the end of human rights abuses." He notes that U.S. aid was conditional upon performance, but of implementation says only that "progress in El Salvador's internal political situation had been made since the mid-1980's after free elections and the election of a moderate reformer, Duarte, as president. Human rights abuses by the armed forces had been curbed. U.S. aid was continuing to flow," and that making U.S. aid dependent "upon a program of national land reform, fair elections, and judicial reforms . . . pushed the government to make necessary reforms."[115] Authors also sometimes claim success for specific tactics without defining any criteria for what goals they were to accomplish. One pair of authors argues that governments early in the war sought "legitimacy" through land, banking, and electoral reforms but fails to specify what was done and what came of it.[116]

The United States did press for military, political, and economic reforms it considered crucial to defeat the insurgency.[117] But government elites resisted reforms as inimical to their interests.[118] The government announced several major reforms early in the conflict, including land redistribution, elections, and civic action programs to provide immediate help to communities in need. The government executed none of the reforms fully or effectively and actively stymied some with violence. Land redistribution and free and fair elections would have cut into the heart of elite economic interests and were thus both necessary (in U.S. eyes, if popular support was to be gained) and impossible (in elite eyes). "If the reforms had functioned, the base of the FMLN would have been weakened and we would have lost the war," former FMLN commander Joaquin Villalobos said. "If there had been a real agrarian reform, the FMLN would not have been able to sustain a war whose theater of operations is fundamentally the countryside."[119]

The highest-profile reforms demanded—free and fair elections and land reform—were not fully implemented because they would have stripped government elites of power and wealth. The reforms that the government did implement merely reinstated the limited openness for civic and political activity that preceded the government violence of the late 1970s and early 1980s.

Elections were neither free nor fair.[120] They were largely "demonstration elections" necessary for the United States to show audiences at home that reforms were under way.[121] Leftist parties were not permitted to participate, the FMLN provoked attacks that deterred participation, and the military mounted operations in areas where the insurgents and military contested control, suppressing turnout.[122] Travel was difficult and dangerous, and procedures for voters were complicated and time consuming.[123] The balloting was blatantly rigged in the 1982 Assembly elections. Members of the Central Elections Council reported that 15–25 percent of votes counted were fake.[124]

The 1982 legislative elections gave the reformist Christian Democrats the most seats, but the newly formed right-wing Alianza Republicana Naciona-lista (Nationalist Republican Alliance; ARENA) allied with other rightist parties to outvote them. The rightist-controlled Assembly wrote the new constitution. Duarte was elected in 1984, but rightists controlled the Assembly until 1985, when the Christian Democrats won an absolute majority. The Right blocked what it could and cooperated only as much as necessary to retain U.S. support.[125] Rightist parties also controlled the judiciary. "As long as the right retained such power, they could block much of our Christian Democratic program for economic reforms and an effective judicial system," President Duarte writes.[126] Civilians had little faith in the electoral system. In 1990, only 19 percent of Salvadorans were confident that there would not be electoral fraud in elections, 41 percent thought there would be, and 40 percent were not sure.[127]

U.S. interference also weakened attempts to exercise democracy. The March 1982 Assembly election produced a plurality of votes for the Social Democrats,[128] but the military's party, the National Conciliation Party, in coalition with the ARENA party, prepared to name death squad leader and army officer Roberto D'Aubuisson to the presidency. U.S. Gen. Vernon Walters was dispatched to inform the military that this outcome was unacceptable. A compromise president, Dr. Álvaro Alfredo Magaña Borja, was selected, and D'Aubuisson was elected president of the Assembly.[129]

Successive governments did eventually reopen political space closed since the crackdown that began the war. The government slowly permitted regrowth of popular and civic groups, including peasant organizations, trade unions, women's groups, and neighborhood associations.[130] It continued targeting their leaders for assassination, however.[131] Elite resistance to electoral participation by centrist and center-left groups declined.[132] The military, under intense U.S. pressure, even permitted civilians to hold the presidency,[133] though these civilians reigned rather than ruled.[134]

Another major U.S. goal in El Salvador during the war was reforms leading to stable, effective, democratic civilian rule to replace the authoritarian military. The government transitioned from military rule, and eventually restored the limited degree of liberalization that it had permitted before the insurgency began, but without making the transition to democracy. Elections were competitive in theory, though in fact only some parties were allowed to compete and violence by both sides depressed turnout. The military retained its institutional autonomy while consolidating its presence in the countryside and within the government. Deals with individual civilian leaders meant the military continued to determine political choices.[135] The United States, meanwhile, needed to keep the military cooperating to keep the government's public level of human rights abuses relatively low because otherwise Congress would cut funding for the war. U.S. financial support for ESAF perpetuated the military's culture of corruption, however. Its involvement in Salvadoran politics also hindered democratization. "The oligarchy and military retained enough real power to impose severe limits on reform and perpetuate a system of widespread repression," writes one scholar. "Elections, far from democratizing El Salvador, merely rationalized increased U.S. aid to the government, thereby strengthening the armed forces and economic elites who were most implacably opposed to democracy."[136]

The junta that ousted conservative Gen. Carlos Humberto Romero as president in 1979 brought civilians into the government in December 1980 at U.S. insistence, but the military remained in control.[137] Duarte, who was installed as the civilian face of the junta in March 1980 and elected president in 1984, remained a figurehead.[138] An interim president elected in 1982, Magaña faced the same situation,[139] as did conservative ARENA president Alfredo Cristiani, elected to replace Duarte in 1989. Cristiani was initially unable to persuade the military to agree to peace talks and did not even have the power to select his own defense minister.[140] In addition, the new 1983 constitution enshrined the military's prerogatives, including responsibility for national defense and domestic law and order, compliance with the constitution and other laws, and defense of the "democratic" system of government, all as earlier constitutions had.[141]

Duarte was elected in 1984 thanks to U.S. financial backing based on hope that his reformist agenda would win the government popular support, and his party gained control of the legislature in 1985.[142] Duarte, however, remained subordinate to military preferences. He had no say in the naming of his cabinet and had no ability to implement U.S. demands for the removal of some of the worst human rights abusers in the military. As civilian junta leader during the 1982 elections, Duarte asked vice president and commander in chief of military forces Col. Jaime Abdul Gutiérrez to stop local military commanders from interfering in the voting, but "much of it was beyond his control."[143] The military's high command and the Reagan administration opposed Duarte's La Palma initiative to open peace talks with the FMLN in October 1985, constraining Duarte's options.[144] Duarte was never able to get his orders to the military about respecting human rights conveyed to local commanders, he said. Worse, his position as president was undermined by the United States when it began dealing directly with the defense minister and when it conditioned military aid on human rights improvements, he complained, because it made the U.S. ambassador more powerful than the president.[145]

Duarte was a reformer unable to implement reforms because of his political weaknesses. He was installed by the United States, he was beholden to the military for letting the United States get him elected, he faced strong military and civilian elite opposition to reforms from the military's party as well as the ARENA party, and his reform efforts were hobbled by U.S. policy choices.

The military pushed Duarte to channel U.S. development aid to the private sector (where the military would benefit through its leadership of businesses) rather than into the social provisions he had promised voters, weakening his popular appeal.[146] Moderate voices among Salvadoran elites argued that U.S. aid and advice hindered efforts to make reforms. Ricardo Ramírez Viuda, former president of the Christian Democrats and former deputy leader of the National Assembly, said during the war that successive juntas were unable to control the security services and no U.S. aid should be provided until they could.[147]

U.S. aid fed military corruption, the systemic rot that prevented the security forces from professionalizing or acting as an effective fighting force. "Everything the Left said about the air force under Gen. Bustillo—the contraband, the car thefts, the drug running—all of it was true," according to a former high-ranking air force officer. Bustillo was typical rather than an outlier. The top-to-bottom military culture of self-enrichment, which because of military rule meant a government culture of self-enrichment, is one reason why the United States made little progress in ending corruption and professionalizing the military.[148]

U.S. policymakers considered land distribution key to defeating the FMLN in a state where 1 percent of the population owned more than 70 percent of the land and more than 40 percent of the rural populace consisted of landless sharecroppers or estate laborers.[149] The junta announced a land reform plan in March 1980 under U.S. pressure. Elite intransigence severely limited execution.[150] The leading right-wing party in the legislature quickly neutered its provisions. From the U.S. perspective, it "fell far short of what everybody would like to see happen."[151] Oligarchs remained the owners of many large estates.[152] A 1992 analysis found that land reform affected 20 percent of land area and 10 percent of the population, leaving 54 percent of the workforce landless, land poor, or unemployed.[153] At peak implementation, land reform benefited 23 percent of the rural populace, and after a decade, that figure dropped to 17 percent.[154] Land redistribution, to the degree that it was enacted,[155] did little to provide greater economic opportunity.

Indeed, the brief implementation of land reform provided an opportunity for the military to target suspected challengers. It declared a state of siege to enact the program and moved into traditionally leftist areas. Its goal was to "intimidate peasants into abandoning the [new peasant] cooperatives or not applying for title to them in the first place."[156] Security forces occupied estates to prevent government expropriation.[157] In some places, troops arrived at estates, told the peasants that the land was theirs and that they could elect their own leaders to run it, then returned to kill the newly elected leaders. The military killed members of the new land co-ops when they refused to pay protection money and bribes as the former landowners had.[158] The military also ramped up operations in insurgent areas, burning crops and houses in search-and-destroy missions and firing on communities from helicopter gunships.[159] Military-linked death squads killed more than five hundred rural leaders and land reform officials in 1980 and 1981, along with two U.S. citizens advising the government on land reform.[160] The highest number of peasant deaths in 1980 was in areas affected by the first phase of the land reform program, including land reform officials and peasant union and cooperative leaders. If land reform did undermine popular support for the FMLN, it would have been evident in the countryside, one analyst argues, and it was not.[161]

The right-wing Assembly alliance controlled the agencies handling land reform, including the Ministry of Agriculture, the Salvadoran Institute for Agrarian Transformation (Instituto Salvadoreno de Transformacion Agraria), and the agrarian bank. ARENA cut training and technical assistance to the cooperatives and cut credit for new landowners. It "gutted" the second phase of the redistribution program in 1983 when the Assembly amended the 1983 constitution to take over fewer than 700 farms instead of the original 1,700, with a total acreage of about eleven thousand hectares, and to permit owners to subdivide their property into smaller parcels held by relatives. No land identified for redistribution in the second phase of the program had been distributed as of mid-1989, well after the insurgency was defeated as a threat to the government. One-third of the applicants for the third, "Land to the Tiller," phase of redistribution of property "were not working the land because they had been threatened, evicted, or had disappeared," according to a U.S. Government Accountability Office report.[162]

The United States persistently urged the government to distribute goods and services to reduce popular grievances and gain popular support through civic action. There is no indication that what efforts the government made did so. Civic action in El Salvador meant military visits to communities, including bringing in a band and "civic action gals" to drum up enthusiasm; distributing food, clothing, and medical care; giving a speech about the state's good intentions; and extending an offer to trade a local project for formation of a civil defense unit.[163] Sometimes, the populace was glad to see what the military offered.[164]

The major public goods effort in the early years of the war was the U.S. Agency for International Development–funded, military-directed National Plan. Starting in June 1983, the departments of San Vicente and Usulután were the location of a military effort to establish a government presence and gain support by meeting civilians' needs. Troops flooded in to drive out the insurgents and all civilians suspected of association with them. Military civic action teams were to follow to rebuild roads and the electrical grid, implement land reform, and provide other basic services. They were also to organize civil defense units to keep the insurgents out, and then move on. By September, the insurgents were reattacking throughout San Vicente department and the military had to bring back troops from Usulutan. The military could not hold ground long enough to build government control and had little interest in meeting popular needs. One longtime U.S. observer considers both the National Plan and the effort that followed "propaganda."[165] Worse, the civilians driven from their homes were unhappy. Aside from disliking their dispossession, they feared the military for its long history of repression.[166]

The second major civic action plan, United to Reconstruct in 1985, failed also.[167] The plan was to clear insurgents and suspect civilians from selected areas in all fourteen departments, screen the populace for loyalty, resettle them, and reconstruct communities under military control. But the military could not clear the insurgents from many areas, and its aid efforts were haphazard.[168] As with the earlier effort, civilians did not welcome the forced movement of entire communities and they feared the troops.[169] Commandante Ernesto describes the state's approach as a "chaotic application of strategies" in which the state treated peasants as insurgents while trying to provide some limited help after military operations.[170]

More ambitious efforts were equally ineffective: The United States was trying to build $15,000 clinics when hiring a nurse for a village would have sufficed. The United States wanted to provide phone lines and highways but few Salvadorans had phones or cars.[171] A 1985 rural electrification program failed because the military could not protect towers and lines from insurgent attack. Each departmental capital had electricity, as did larger towns, but villages had none and most did not get it.[172]

The single largest political change that took place during the war only occurred at the very end, with the military's agreement to negotiate with the FMLN. Moderate civilians such as Duarte had attempted peace talks in 1984, 1986, and 1987. The United States and the military opposed them, and efforts to press for talks gained no traction. The timing shows that the talks begun in 1989 did not drive counterinsurgent success. Rather, the talks were a function of continued insurgent strength and the change in power in Washington after the end of the Cold War. A June 1989 poll found 76 percent of Salvadorans favored negotiations with the FMLN.[173] But the elite had to want negotiations too.

Peace talks became possible in part because the long war had splintered the ties between the reactionary oligarchy and its allies, "tens of thousands of fiercely anticommunist peasants, petty landowners, and rural businessmen," on the one hand, and on the other hand, more moderate financiers and industrialists who wanted to get on with making money and who no longer needed the military's "protection racket state" to do so.[174] The military's role in kidnapping wealthy Salvadorans for ransom early in the war and its failure to defeat the insurgency also weakened its ties to civilian elites.[175]

As for the military, through years of war, not even reformist officers were willing to subject themselves to civilian authority.[176] But U.S. interests changed, and Salvadoran military interests were forced to follow if the military was to have any hope of continued U.S. support. With the end of the Cold War, the new Bush administration no longer insisted on a military victory over the nationalist-Marxist insurgency, and evidence of continued insurgent strength[177] and new government human rights abuses meant Washington would no longer tolerate Salvadoran military impunity.[178] A key element within the military elite came to believe it could not defeat the FMLN militarily unless it threw off U.S. constraints and fought dirty. Yet if it threw off U.S. constraints, it would lose U.S. resources and lose the war anyway. The military agreed to talks.[179]

UN-brokered negotiations began in September 1989 but only progressed after U.S. pressure followed the military's assassination of six Jesuits, their housekeeper, and her daughter in October.[180] U.S. Southern Command commander Gen. Maxwell Thurman and U.S. Ambassador William Walker told Defense Minister Gen. Ponce that the security forces must move against anyone involved in the killings; show that democratic values and professional ethics were taking hold in the military; cleanse the armed forces of human rights abusers, corrupt officers, and incompetents; meet visibly with high-level insurgent officials without conditions; and accept the insurgency as the political opposition. Otherwise, Congress would cut or condition aid; it wanted to see results for the more than $4 billion it had poured into El Salvador in the past decade. Thurman told Ponce the Jesuit killings broke the camel's back: "Business as usual is over."[181]

Once talks began in earnest, they focused on military reforms, a goal shared by the United States and the insurgency.[182] They concluded with an accord on January 16, 1992.[183] In the negotiations, the insurgency acknowledged its limited leverage, based on its inability to take over the government,[184] by giving up its goal of economic restructuring. It agreed to stop fighting in exchange for an end to the military's role in domestic politics.[185] The military was constitutionally subordinated to civilian authority, excluded from any internal security role, and replaced in that role by a new civilian police force.[186] The ruling right-wing party, ARENA, agreed to continue seeking power "by persuasion rather than force."[187] ARENA also agreed to let the insurgency become a political party. The U.S. military became the guarantor of security for both sides during demobilization.[188] All of these reforms only took place after the insurgency ended.

The most powerful officers in the army believed the peace agreement was intended to humiliate them, but they accepted it. They, like the populace, were weary of war—"beaten up."[189] Popular support for talks had always been stronger than desire for a military victory within El Salvador. One survey found that 51 percent of the electorate supported talks to end the war in 1983, and only 10 percent wanted a military victory over the insurgency.[190] The decision to accept talks and the peace agreement left one wartime military leader with a feeling of bitterness. "They [the government] accepted peace accords, followed by demobilization of the armed forces down to its *minimal* expression," former chief of the General Staff Gen. Calderón wrote in 2010. "The security forces were disbanded, the FMLN was accepted as a political party, and now the FMLN runs the government with the support of the young masses that didn't even participate in the war."[191]

Democratic reforms only gained traction after the war in El Salvador, and democratization and development remain limited. "There was no significant breakthrough toward a democratic transition until the peace accords were signed in January 1992," one pair of experts concludes.[192] A 1989 CIA memo provided a stinging assessment of the lack of progress in wartime reforms to the judicial system, a top U.S. priority. "Most Salvadorans regard the formal justice system as, at best, barely functioning," the memo stated. "Poor Salvadorans judge that the judicial process, although enshrined in a new constitution, is capricious and serves principally the interests of the rich and powerful." The conclusion was painful: "Despite improvements over the past five years, we judge that the economically and politically powerful do control the judiciary in El Salvador." The judiciary's problems included intimidation, corruption, cronyism, inadequate facilities, and archaic procedures.[193] More than twenty years later, the assessment is nearly as bleak.

After the Chapultepec Accords, the integration of the FMLN into the political party system strengthened the democratization process, though other good governance efforts, such as attempting to reduce corruption, still lag.[194] The military has mostly stayed inside its new lane, forsaking domestic politics. The new civilian police force has been "far more efficient, responsive, transparent and accountable than the old police," and judicial reforms have begun, though painfully slowly.[195] Criminal violence has risen, but political violence and human rights abuses have diminished. There is greater freedom for political activity, but economic development has primarily benefited the elites and income inequality is rising.[196] The oligarchs remain a powerful political force.[197] One scholar characterizes the changes in El Salvador after the war as moving from low-intensity conflict to low-intensity democracy.[198]

Popular Support. Along with assuming implementation of reforms, authors writing on counterinsurgency in El Salvador say that popular support rose as a result of reforms but offer little support for the claim. Overstatement is not uncommon, as with this assertion: "The massive turnout at the 1982 and 1984 elections, despite the threat of violence, could be considered a repudiation of the guerrillas' methods as well as their aims." Elsewhere, the same authors say that elections over the course of the war "delivered a government that had legitimacy and broad popular support."[199]

The United States considered voting a sign of popular support for the government. Balloting fell over the course of the war, however, undercutting claims that government popularity rose because of reforms or for any other reason. Turnout fell from 65 percent of eligible voters in 1984's presidential election to 48 percent in the 1985 midterms.[200] Turnout in the 1988 midterms was estimated at 48 percent and dropped to an estimated 40 percent in the 1989 presidential balloting. The turnout in the 1991 midterms was estimated at 44 percent. The decline in participation reflected suspicion and unrest, as well as the lack of a level playing field in elections.

Formation of community self-defense units was intended to be another indication of popular support for the government. The civil defense program of 1985 was meant to change the dynamic of resistance to the government.[201] If many individuals chose to participate in the state's armed effort by joining government-organized groups to defend their own homes and communities against insurgents, it would show that the people were on the side of the government against the insurgency.

Setting up effective units was a struggle. Usually the first volunteers were the town drunks, who used their newly bestowed authority to extort money from their neighbors to buy Tíc Táck (a Salvadoran liquor distilled from sugar cane). Others were simply "armed extortionists."[202] In many communities, if the insurgents came looking for the civil defense units, the locals would probably have given them up, one U.S. military adviser admits.[203] In a 1991 survey, 58 percent of Salvadorans said civil defense programs were not helpful.[204] These newly formed civil defense units remained "tools of oppression" without the confidence or support of other members of their communities.[205] Salvadorans saw the units as the government's traditional instrument for extortion, repression, and intimidation.[206]

Few of the estimated 240 civil defense units existing in late 1987 were in conflict zones, and only 100 were certified as minimally trained. About half were preexisting government-sponsored repressive militias.[207] There were no civil defense units in insurgent-held areas.[208]

Most people did not want to cooperate with the government by joining militias, so U.S. military advisers traded benefits such as construction of electricity lines, wells, and roads for participation. But insurgents had no trouble targeting these construction efforts. Some civil defense unit members had relatives with the insurgents, and if the community valued the project, villagers might tell insurgents not to sabotage it.[209] The units' value depended on what assets the zone commander provided and how close regular forces were in case the unit needed backup against an insurgent attack.[210]

Civil defense units made life more difficult for insurgents in some areas. Members provided information on insurgent movements. A unit's presence within a community deterred visits from insurgents who might previously have strolled into town to buy a Coke or some nails.[211] The civil defense units were not always successful in deterring insurgents, though. On one occasion insurgents took over a town by entering in the uniforms of a military band.[212]

EL SALVADOR CONCLUSION

El Salvador today is a U.S. ally and a more democratic state than it was before and during the war.[213] The FMLN candidate was elected president in 2009. The military has largely remained within its narrowed constitutional parameters. There is less political violence. Combatants have been reintegrated into civilian life. However, the civilian institutions of the state remain weak, the crime rate is extremely high, income inequality is widening, and grievances over wealth and living conditions persist.[214] Many Salvadorans rely on U.S. remittances, and the legal and justice systems barely function.[215] Figures on economic and social development are improving but still poor. In 2007 the infant mortality rate was 21 percent, the poorest 20 percent of the populace received 3.3 percent of the national income—only 1.3 percent above the 1980 figure—and 11 percent of the populace lived on less than one dollar a day.[216] If reforms and popular support had driven government success against the insurgency, path dependency suggests that we should see indications today. We do not.

In El Salvador, the primary tool in counterinsurgency success was military force targeting insurgents and civilians alike. The military failed, however, because of popular support for the insurgency and its own lack of capability, to successfully separate civilians from insurgents. These findings partially support the predictions of the compellence theory. El Salvador is the only case in this study in which the counterinsurgency succeeded in retaining power without militarily defeating the insurgency. The government did not accommodate rival elites, and it failed to cut the flow of resources between civilians and insurgents. It attained a negotiated peace rather than a military victory, suggesting that elite accommodation and control of civilians play an important role in counterinsurgency success generally.

In El Salvador, the only accommodation possible was within the government. Insurgent and popular demands, if granted, meant the end of the government as it had existed since its creation. The demands of rival elites outside the government, for less repression and more popular participation, also appeared to government elites as existential threats. Governmental elites' primary concern regarding accommodation was to keep U.S. support flowing. They knew they were likely to lose the war without it.

Contrary to the narrative of reforms in existing work on counterinsurgency in El Salvador, elite interests and state capabilities tightly constrained reforms throughout the war. While existing accounts emphasize change over time, there are significant similarities across the phases of the conflict. El Salvador was badly divided over its future. With little middle ground to meet on, there is scant evidence of accommodations of rival elites. Most accommodation took place among the elites in power—for example, between rival elements of the military and between the military and civilian elites. Soldiers' random individual acts of brutality against civilians did decline over time, as did death squad activity—until the last years of the war—but the state's systematic, intentional use of military force against civilians continued throughout the conflict.

Some might argue that it was the Salvadoran government's and military's inability to fully implement reforms that prevented the military defeat of the FMLN. It is true that the Salvadoran government's capacity was limited, particularly its administrative abilities, but there is plentiful evidence that Salvadoran elites cared little for popular interests and found the idea of trying to serve them incomprehensible. Elites' lack of will to make reforms looms large in this campaign. Many elites actively resisted the political and economic reforms pressed by the United States because they benefited from the status quo. It is this resistance to changes that would cost elites wealth and power, along with the subsidiary issue of administrative weakness, that explains the limited reforms. If the United States had succeeded in changing Salvadoran elites' beliefs about where their interests lay, reforms would have been more likely to be implemented. Furthermore, in the area where elites believed their interests lay, specifically the military's fighting ability, they successfully increased their capabilities.[217] This success suggests that elite will to reform plays an important role in increasing capabilities.

How Much Does the Compellence Theory Explain?

Turkey and the PKK

The modern Turkish state, founded by Mustafa Kemal Ataturk in 1923 from the multiethnic Ottoman Empire that was shattered in World War I, was based on a conception of citizenship as secular Turkishness. Ataturk banished ideas of religion and ethnicity as hobbles on modernization, development, and democratization.[1] Turkish belief in the so-called Kemalist state as the only way to define citizenship hardened over time, making it difficult for many Turks to grasp the concept of any other ethnic identity within Turkey.[2] Turks generally have seen the concept of a Kurdish or any other non-Turkish identity as a threat so powerful that Turkey was willing to withstand international condemnation for its war on the Partiya Karkeren Kurdistan (Kurdistan Workers' Party; PKK) despite its desire to be seen as a Western power and to join the European Union.

The government has enacted a number of policies over the years to suppress manifestations of Kurdish ethnicity. For example, expressions of Kurdish culture, such as use of either of the two main Kurdish languages, have traditionally been repressed.[3] For much of its history, and powerfully so once pro-Kurdish violence commenced, the Turkish government saw an existential threat in the issue of Kurdish identity.[4]

At the same time, the concept of Kurdishness is contested. The Kurdish homeland, broadly defined, spans parts of Turkey, Iraq, Iran, Syria, and Armenia. An estimated 20 percent of the Turkish population is Kurdish, but no one knows for sure. Many Turks of Kurdish heritage consider themselves not Kurds but Turks. Others, including those who do not know or use one of the Kurdish languages, do consider themselves Kurds.[5] "There is no single, universally agreed-upon meaning for the term 'Kurd.'"[6] More broadly, ethnic boundaries in Turkey are "porous and multifaceted" and only one factor in determining political preferences.[7]

Grievances in Turkey's southeast are real, whether identified as Kurdish or not. The Kurdish area of Turkey has traditionally been rural and under-developed compared with other regions.[8] Part of its backwardness grows from the Turkish state's decision in 1945 not to enact land redistribution in the region, a decision that was made to retain the support of large landown-ers who are Kurdish tribal chiefs, called aghas. Even businessmen from the southeast have traditionally invested elsewhere for greater returns. Many Turks of Kurdish heritage resent the neglect of the southeast. Not all hold Kurdish nationalist aims. Many flourish in mainstream parties and in Par-liament. Some are Turkish nationalists or even far-right anti-Kurdish Turk-ish nationalists, some are Kurdish nationalists, and some are Islamists. Kurd-ish voters generally did not cast their ballots based on ethnicity during the period I examine.[9]

The PKK, formed as a political party in 1978, began its violent campaign in 1984.[10] The organization grew from the leftist and Kurdish ethnic politi-cal agitation of the 1960s. Initially the PKK was a Marxist-Leninist organ-ization with an ethnic nationalist orientation. By the early 1990s its leader, Abdullah Ocalan, was only demanding political and cultural Kurdish rights within Turkey.[11] Early in the 1980s the PKK was one of many groups seek-ing popular Kurdish support. Villagers routinely turned in members to the authorities. At the same time, activist Kurds were increasingly concerned that the government had overlooked their region for generations, and they were angered by its repression and denial of Kurdish culture.[12]

The PKK was a strictly hierarchical organization, led by a charismatic per-sonality, with a coercive relationship with the populace.[13] It grew to include political, financial, media, and armed activities.[14] It violently suppressed rival organizations and killed its critics. After solidifying its position among Kurdish groups, the PKK turned to violence against the govern-ment. It targeted schoolteachers and other civil servants dispatched to the region from Ankara, the Turkish capital, but it focused mainly on attacking the military.[15]

It was the PKK's willingness to stand up to the government that gained it what popular support it had. Kurds recognized the PKK's role in raising the issue of ethnicity in the political discourse, and many with reservations about the PKK's leadership and tactics nevertheless saw the insurgents as having paid their dues. Turkish opinion, however, became more anti-Kurdish over the course of the war as military deaths rose. At the height of the violence, funerals for as many as ten soldiers a day were held at an important mosque in Ankara.[16]

The PKK's violence against civilians alienated many Kurds who saw little difference between the government and the insurgency. Ocalan's image as a ruthless, single-minded, secretive, withdrawn, suspicious, insecure, demand-ing, distant leader also alienated many Kurds, although many others adore him.[17] The general lack of enthusiasm for Marxist-Leninism since the end of the Cold War, the PKK's involvement in tribal politics, and a lack of enthusiasm for the early PKK goal of secession also limited its popular support.[18]

The PKK received significant state and nonstate support. Its longest-standing friend was Syria, which used it as a tool to bleed regional rival Turkey, with which it has border and water disputes.[19] Syria provided safe haven within its own territory and training facilities in Lebanon's Bekaa Valley, as well as military, logistical, and financial support.[20] Syria finally expelled Ocalan upon a direct military threat from Turkey in 1998. He was captured in Kenya with U.S. help in 1999. The PKK also received support at various times from entities including Greece, Iran, Greek Cyprus, and the Soviet Union and then Russia. By 1998 Syria was the PKK's only state backer.[21] The PKK received financial support from the Kurdish diaspora in Europe; extortion and protection money from Kurds and Turks within Turkey; returns on investment in small- and medium-size businesses; and ran criminal enterprises including drug trafficking, money laundering, and the smuggling of arms, people, and goods.[22] The Kurdish diaspora includes about five hundred thousand Kurds in Western Europe, including Germany, France, Sweden, Belgium, Britain, the Netherlands, and Italy.[23]

The military was traditionally the dominant political force in Turkey, seeing itself as the guardian of the Kemalist state and stepping in to take control from civilians several times over the years.[24] It was thus particularly sensitive to the threat posed by expressions of Kurdish identity, which challenged the conception of the Kemalist state. During the war against the PKK, the military stymied civilian policymakers who raised the topic of compromising on Kurdish demands. Divisions among civilian policymakers also strengthened the military's hand on the Kurdish issue.[25] Turkey's role as a NATO member, regional great power, and interlocutor for the West with the Muslim world muted international criticism of its human rights abuses in its war on the PKK. The cost of the 1984–1999 war has been estimated at $14.7 billion. Human costs were even higher. Human Rights Watch reports that 380,000 people were officially displaced in fifteen years, but Kurdish villagers report a figure closer to 1.5 million.[26]

Turkey's campaign against the PKK took fifteen years. It ended in 1999 with the capture of Ocalan and his call for fighters to leave Turkey, and a change in his goal of secession to greater Kurdish autonomy within Turkey.[27] To fight the PKK, Turkey brought big landowners and rival Kurdish groups into a coalition against the insurgency, accommodations that strengthened government military capabilities and intelligence networks. The relatively strong centralized state made few efforts to aid civilians in Kurdistan during the war.[28] Indeed, targeting civilians was a major part of the military and paramilitary effort.

To defeat the PKK, the government built its security forces and flooded the southeast with troops that targeted insurgents and civilians. In 1993, Turkey sent its newly flexible military forces out into the countryside to keep the PKK on the run, destroy its bases and safe havens, and deny it refuge and resources in communities in the mountainous southeast. The campaign included torture, targeted killing of civilians, and draconian restrictions on nonviolent political behavior. Turkey's NATO-trained and NATO-equipped military, with other security forces and militias, drove hundreds of thousands of residents of Kurdish southeastern Turkey from their homes in vast clearing operations that separated insurgents from civilians and resources.[29]

The campaign brought Turkey international condemnation for its human rights abuses, a cost the regional power was willing and able to bear, but caused relatively little stir within the democratic Turkish state.[30] Kurdish ethnic claims were incomprehensible to much of the Turkish public. The government was strong enough to seal off the Kurdish region from those who might report on the extent of the violence. Fine-grained information on the military campaign in the southeast is relatively hard to come by, but its contours are evident. The military was "the supreme authority in the southeast," and it used its power to keep the region isolated.[31] The state of emergency kept journalists out, as did a lack of interest by the Turkish media, while repression of the Kurdish media prevented reporting from within. Human rights organizations and other activists were largely denied access.[32] It is also difficult to find reliable information on the degree of popular support for the PKK; it was an extremely sensitive issue at the time, and much of the Kurdish population of the southeast was scattered by the war.

In brief, in 1984 the PKK began its violent campaign against the Turkish state and the military began striking back at insurgents and civilians in the Kurdish southeast. In April 1991 Turkey rescinded a law banning spoken and written Kurdish and use of Kurdish names, but use of Kurdish in education and broadcast remained forbidden and its use generally remains highly restricted. In October 1991, twenty-two deputies from the Kurdish People's Labor Party (Halkin Emek Partisi) were elected in national balloting. Strengthened military capabilities meant more operations against civilian communities year-round and in the mountains starting in 1993. The PKK offered a limited unilateral cease-fire in March 1993. Reform-minded President Turgut Özal died in office as the PKK extended its cease-fire in April 1993. In July 1993, the People's Labor Party was banned. In March 1994 the government stripped six Kurdish party deputies of their immunity to try them for links to the PKK. In 1997, the PKK was weakened sufficiently for the government to lift the state of emergency in three provinces in the southeast. PKK leader Ocalan was captured and returned to Turkey in 1999 for trial and imprisonment. He called on all insurgents to stop fighting.[33] This meets my definition of success as "marginalization of the insurgents to the point at which they are destroyed, co-opted, or reduced to irrelevance in numbers and capability."[34] The core elements of the campaign were elite accommodation and forceful control of civilians. Reforms limited to nonexistent and popular support for the government apparently did not rise.

Turkey Analysis

There is little in the counterinsurgency literature on Turkey and the PKK because much Western work on counterinsurgency is practitioners' efforts to determine how liberal states can more effectively support their threatened clients. These analysts consider the war on the PKK a poor model for democratic counterinsurgents because of its brutality and violence against civilians. Scholarly research on Turkey and the PKK examines a wealth of questions. There is a rising interest in the counterinsurgency campaign and increasing efforts to explain Turkish success.

The Turkey case provides support for the compellence theory of counterinsurgency success. The case includes the predicted government accommodation of elites to gain the military and information resources of domestic rivals and significant and systematic uses of force against civilians to disrupt the flow of resources to the insurgency. It is similar to Greece, the Philippines, Dhofar, and El Salvador in the government's use of irregular fighting forces against civilians. It resembles all five of the core cases in its routine use of major military operations against civilian communities. It also resembles all five in its lack of liberalizing reforms. The lack of promises of reform is due at least in part to the fact that Turkey did not have a liberal great power strongly supporting its campaign militarily inside its territory, unlike in the first five cases.[35] Finally, it resembles the first five cases in its lack of increased popular support for the government.

The case's similarity to those presented as models for democratic great powers is surprising because it is generally considered one of the nastier recent counterinsurgency campaigns. International human rights bodies, the U.S. government, and a variety of observers agree on the brutal character of Turkey's campaign. A RAND study characterizes it as "repressive and heavy handed."[36] The United States was criticized for remaining Turkey's top arms supplier without using its leverage to prevent atrocities such as attacks on civilians and other violations of human rights.[37] The *New York Times* castigated the Clinton administration for continuing to sell arms to Turkey to use in the war against the PKK.[38] Leading conflict scholar Ted Galen Carpenter accused the United States of a double standard in continuing to arm Turkey when it challenged the Bosnian Serbs and others for their human rights abuses.[39]

INSURGENCY BROKEN BY 1994–1996

The Turkish government reduced the insurgent military threat to irrelevance by 1994–1996, when insurgent attacks began dropping and insurgent casualties began rising. Özlem Kayhan Pusane sets the date at 1997, when "the PKK's terrorist acts were reduced to a controllable degree." She writes that internal insurgent correspondence also notes the decline.[40] Aysegul

Aydin and Cem Emrence also date the failure of the insurgency to the mid-1990s. They identify 1993 as the point when the government began keeping the number of insurgent attacks to a minimum.[41] By 1994–1996, with the PKK's ability to threaten the government reduced to an annoyance, the military was assessing that "radical Islamic movements pose a bigger threat today than the PKK."[42] In this case, the date of defeat is significant because the government made later gestures toward reform.

By 1991 the PKK had developed a shadow government in several provinces that included courts, police and intelligence units, and night classes.[43] In the spring of 1991, PKK strength was estimated at ten thousand.[44] In 1995, insurgent strength was about fifteen thousand, supported by seventy-five thousand part-time militias.[45] But at the same time, the PKK was losing control of major communities and roads in the region.[46] "Everyone spoke of the same problems, not enough supplies, no contact with the local people, constant attack by village guards," one insurgent was quoted as saying of the key year of 1995.[47]

PKK violence increased early in the conflict, particularly after the 1991 Gulf War weakened the Iraqi government's hold over its Kurdish areas, making the border more porous for Turkish Kurds using Iraqi Kurdistan as a safe haven. The number of terrorist incidents in Turkey grew from 521 in 1984 to 779 in 1988, 1,969 in 1989, 2,742 in 1990, 4,445 in 1991, 5,680 in 1992, and a peak of 6,956 in 1993.[48] Insurgent activities included stopping buses in the countryside to pull out and often kill soldiers, civil servants, and suspected collaborators; a firebombing attributed to the PKK at an Istanbul department store; and extension of the PKK's network of control out from bases into the countryside where shelter, intelligence, recruits, and food were available.[49] The insurgency targeted representatives of the state, including engineers, teachers, imams, banks, schools, electric power plants, pipelines, roads, tourist sites in southern Turkey, and Turkish sites abroad, such as embassies, in a bid to damage the economy. In 1996 it conducted suicide bombings in big cities but failed to rebuild its strength.[50]

The military's increased offensive capability in the countryside put the PKK on the run and quickly wore it down. The military shifted from routine patrols and ambushes, garrison duty, and convoy protection[51] to a constant war on the insurgents and often the remaining populace. The military put commandos and special forces in the field day and night hunting insurgents. Units even pressed the PKK in their famous "mountain strongholds." Equipment upgrades including night vision systems, GPS, and armored helicopters facilitated night and winter operations, longer operations, and quick-reaction operations.[52] Air power, mostly helicopters, hindered PKK movement in border areas with little cover.[53] The military continued clearing villages, particularly in mountainous areas, and pushing civilians into urban centers, where they were more easily monitored and controlled.

Finally, increased military capabilities were used for large and small operations into northern Iraq, including aerial bombing, to deny the PKK its safe havens. One large operation in March–April 1995 sent thirty-five thousand troops to push back the PKK from the border and disrupt its logistics. Another operation, in May 1997, was rumored to include fifty thousand troops.[54] The PKK's number two man, Semdin Sakik, was captured by Turkish special forces in northern Iraq in 1998. Also in 1998, Turkey used troop movements and threats to get Syria to expel Ocalan, who went on a headline-grabbing tour of European states before he was arrested by Turkish forces in Nairobi, Kenya, in early 1999 with CIA help.[55]

The PKK imposed costs on the government but could not recover and rebuild from the military's onslaught. It took terrible casualties. The Turkish military estimated up to one thousand insurgent casualties per operation.[56] Estimated insurgent deaths from 1984–1999 top thirty-five thousand.[57] With increased military capabilities, insurgent deaths reached nearly seven thousand between 1991 and 1994 alone, with half of those deaths in 1994.[58] By the summer of 1999, estimated PKK strength inside Turkey was 1,500 and falling.[59]

The PKK left Turkey in August 1999 at Ocalan's order, abandoning its armed struggle against the government. Emergency rule was officially lifted in 2002 in the final two provinces under government lockdown, but there were reports that the conditions of emergency rule continued. The estimated seventy thousand village guards set up by the government continued to pose a problem of impunity. Guards, for example, were reportedly killing returning villagers to keep land the militias had seized, but the PKK had no hope of attaining its goals militarily.[60]

ELITE ACCOMMODATION

The government provided accommodations to large landowners in the southeast whose cooperation built government force and intelligence capabilities. Turkey rewarded aghas, the landowners and tribal chiefs of the region, for providing men to serve as village militias, intelligence sources, and guides. Aghas had significant control in their territory; they determined everything from water and land allocations to contact with the outside world.[61] The PKK's anti-tribal message threatened that control, and the state seized its opportunity.[62] Payments to the aghas and smaller amounts handed down to village guards and others were a major income source in the impoverished region.[63] The government's accommodations gave the aghas independence and impunity for the major economic activity in the region, smuggling. The deal strengthened the tribal chiefs' influence. They gained a say in local decision-making and legal protection for their clan members. In return, in an area dominated by these large families, gaining even one person as an information source could provide the government with a lot of material on relatives in the PKK.[64]

The village guard system[65] inaugurated in 1985 helped the government control the civilian population of the region and target insurgents. It tapped into the kinship networks of the region, especially in the remote mountains, and particularly involved those clan leaders who had traditionally supported the government.[66] About 90 percent of village guards were in areas where the tribal system was still strong.[67] In areas where it had decayed, the state recruited socially weak villagers. Those without weapons or employment and with little land received economic and social benefits from joining the village guards.[68] Others were forced to join.[69] Criminals were encouraged to join the program in exchange for reduced sentences.[70] Some guards moved into arms trafficking.[71] Others cooperated with the PKK while retaining their position in the militia.[72] Much of the violence they participated in had little to do with the government-PKK conflict and everything to do with local rivalries. All sides used the conflict to settle scores. The village guards developed a vested interest in continued conflict.[73] Guard members were, for example, accused of seizing the land of villagers, not a difficult task in a region without property deeds or great government legibility.[74] The cost of the village guards program has been estimated at up to $135 million a year.[75] There were five thousand village guards in 1987 and one hundred thousand by 2000.[76]

The village guards program was an important component in government control of civilians, as evidenced by its response when communities declined to participate.[77] In one community in the spring of 1993, troops destroyed part of the tobacco crop and threatened to return to destroy the rest if villagers did not join the program.[78] The program expanded from an estimated six thousand members in 1987 to forty-five thousand in 1994 and sixty-seven thousand in 1995, though PKK violence against those who joined the program, and their families, sometimes hindered militia growth. Eventually the government began using the guards in offensive military operations as well as within their own villages. The guards were known for extortion, abuse of power, rape, theft, and murder.[79] Leaders of the guards and tribal chiefs also manipulated the government to gain benefits, inflating the threat they faced in exchange for support.[80]

From the start, the PKK had challenged the tribal system in Turkish Kurdistan on ideological grounds, making the tribal leaders an obvious government ally.[81] The patronage system strengthened these threatened tribal chiefs. They received arms and money for each guard member they provided, and kept back a percentage for themselves. The guards knew the area and the people, knew the trails along the borders, served as scouts for the military, and could move quickly against insurgents when necessary. Some of the first tribes recruited were the leading smugglers in the region. Their gain from cooperating with the government was a lack of interference in their main economic activity. They also received impunity for crimes, and a greater say in local decision-making.[82]

The government also accommodated right-wing religious nationalist Kurds who opposed the PKK's leftist bent. Hizbollah (no relationship to the Lebanese organization) assassinated suspected PKK members and sympathizers, particularly intellectuals and journalists. It allegedly served as a hit squad for the government until reaching a deal with the PKK in 1993, but in the lawless southeast, it was difficult to tell who was working with whom.[83] Turkey captured the PKK's second in command in 1998 after he fled from the insurgency, but imprisoned Semdin Sakik rather than cutting a deal for information and cooperation.[84] His death sentence was eventually commuted to life in prison.

The government saw the prospect of negotiations with the insurgency as an indication of weakness that would only lead to further demands.[85] It refused to meet the PKK's 1993 cease-fire, for example. Policymakers who expressed an interest in addressing Kurdish grievances, including President Süleyman Demirel and President Turgut Özal, were stymied by the military's staunch ideological opposition and the perceived aggressive attitude of activist Kurdish members of Parliament.[86]

Accommodation of political rivals was a bridge too far in Turkey. The government saw an existential threat from the PKK because of its ideological difficulty with the concept of Kurdishness compared with the Kemalist vision of Turkishness. As a heavily ideological organization, the PKK too saw a zero-sum game early in the war, though it made overtures and called cease-fires later on as it moderated its demands from independence to greater autonomy within Turkey. Much of the population of the southeast, meanwhile, knew it was caught in the middle.[87]

USES OF FORCE AGAINST CIVILIANS

The government gained military power and information to rout the PKK primarily through the use of military and allied militia forces targeting insurgents and civilians in large and small operations. These operations included the systematic, repeated, intentional targeting of civilians to cut the flow of resources to the insurgency. Turkey increased its troop numbers in the region as PKK activity increased.[88] Troop levels rose from 185,000 in the region in 1993 to more than 360,000 troops and militia members in the southeast targeting the insurgency in 1994.[89]

Turkey declared a state of emergency in its eleven southeastern provinces in 1987 after years of martial law. This step further enabled the government to censor news, ban strikes, hold suspects for extended periods, and send citizens into internal exile. The governor in the provincial capital of Diyarbakir and the regional military commander were in charge. The state of emergency regulated everything from road traffic to health care, meaning

Turkey's fight with the PKK changed daily life for civilians.[90] The military eventually drove most civilians into camps or cities, where they were easier to control than they had been in the dispersed rural communities and mountainous landscape in the southeast, with its limited communications and transport infrastructure.[91]

Government or government-affiliated killing of civilians played a role in the campaign. Kurdish party leaders, human rights activists, and journalists were among those targeted. The death toll among prominent civilians rose from 31 in 1991 to 360 in 1992 and 510 in 1993. The toll dropped to 423 in 1994 and dropped again, to 99, in 1995. The decline was due in part to the fact that there were fewer activists left to target. Many of these civilians were killed by so-called unknown actors in "mystery killings" widely believed to be committed on the instructions of or in cooperation with the government.[92] A former gendarmerie officer testified that "in the southeast one need not be a sympathizer of the [PKK] to warrant his execution. It is sufficient that he be close to its ideology."[93]

The government used indiscriminate force against civilians. In areas declared no-go zones, populated and unpopulated, "we fired artillery at anything that moved in those areas, civilian or guerrilla, it didn't matter," one former soldier said. The military conducted an urban offensive in 1992 in response to PKK provocations. It fired heavy weapons on the communities of Oirnak, Lice, and Cizre, killing at least sixty-five people, rendering some areas uninhabitable, and driving thousands of civilians from their homes. The government believed it was showing resolve: "The security forces successfully demonstrated their determination to reassert control over the cities."[94] It made similar assaults on other cities, including Cukurca and Dargecit.[95] Turkey also made its first large-scale sweep into Iraq in 1992 to destroy PKK bases and disrupt its supply lines.

The government razed villages to clear rural areas, reducing the provision of resources to the PKK and denying insurgents shelter and resources. A quarter of all rural settlements in the Kurdish southeast were emptied. In 1991, 109 villages were cleared; the figure rose to 295 in 1992 and 874 in 1993. The figure peaked at 1,531 in 1994, the year the government neutered the insurgent threat, and then fell to 243 in 1995, 68 in 1996, 23 in 1997, 30 in 1998, and 30 in 1999.[96] Officially, 378,000 people in 3,165 villages were displaced during the war, not including those who felt compelled to flee their homes by PKK or government pressure, or both.[97] By 1994, huge camps were established for displaced persons, where civilians were easier to control, but no provision was made for the many who fled to cities in the southeast and western Turkey.[98] The government's clearing operations caused a massive shift in settlement patterns. "Southeastern Turkey changed from a majority rural region to a majority urban region in only seven years."[99]

There were three conditions under which security forces destroyed villages: first, when villagers refused to join the government's village guard program;

second, in retaliation for PKK attacks on government installations in the immediate area; and third, to remove insurgents and suspected supporters from the area. Most villages destroyed were in the mountains; those on the plains and near major highways were easier to control without emptying them out. Villages were burned once their residents were driven away to deny the PKK shelter.[100] With the clearance of the countryside, it was harder for insurgents to move without being spotted and pursued, forcing them into isolated areas in the mountains and into northern Iraq, where they could be destroyed, or into urban areas, where they could be tracked down. "The evacuation of the villages really helped the state," a former PKK commander said. "The villagers provided everything for us, supplied materials and information. When the villages were emptied, all this was taken away from us."[101]

The government imposed controls on the residents of communities it did not destroy, and on the resources they needed to survive. These controls included curfews, rationing, checkpoints, and identity cards. Political activities remained suppressed also. In some areas authorities supervised consumption of food to prevent civilians from conveying anything to the insurgents.[102] The creation of maps showing the area in detail was discouraged, as was the taking of aerial photographs.[103]

In 1993 the military labeled the PKK the greatest threat the state faced, reorganized its forces from a division-based structure to a more flexible corps model, upgraded its equipment and hardware, and applied its new doctrine of "field domination" to deny the countryside to the insurgency. Turgut Özal, as prime minister and then president from 1983 to 1993, also emphasized training and modernizing the security forces' equipment and pushed for improvements in the organization of the intelligence services.[104] "The field domination strategy of the Turkish Armed Forces did not mean that the army had to be everywhere, but rather that it could be anywhere at any time," one expert wrote. It required good intelligence, good communications and infrastructure, and transport. Helicopters, armored infantry fighting vehicles, and armored personnel carriers were crucial.[105] The use of air power in particular enabled the military to bomb an area, then use helicopters to attack it at lower altitudes, and then send in special forces and finally ground troops to attack.[106]

Building security forces included forming special units. The more highly trained units treated the populace more abusively than did regular forces.[107] Special units were known for their brutality, killing, vigilantism, and flouting of authority, and "they are tolerated because they have proven to be effective against the civilian support system the PKK has established."[108] Special units included mountain commandos highly trained for close-contact fighting with insurgents and close contact with civilians suspected of supporting them, and special gendarmerie and police units that were well educated, highly trained, and mobile, including intelligence operatives and snipers.[109] These units were designed to eliminate insurgents rather than hold territory. Members were recruited from nationalistic right-wing groups for their ideological commitment to wipe out the PKK. Of the police special forces, one former officer said, "their primary motivation in life is to kill the PKK."[110] The air force provided mobility for offensives, raids on suspected PKK positions in Turkey and Iraq, aerial deforestation, and aerial bombing of massed civilians.[111] The government also focused on developing its intelligence capabilities. The National Police, for example, invested heavily in education and training to improve information sharing and develop individuals' areas of expertise; improved its data collection, storage, and searching capabilities; upgraded its technology for information sharing; and formed a special operations department.[112]

Along with the army, the regular police controlled cities while the gendarmerie (Jandarma), the rural police force, controlled the countryside and handled border control, patrolling villages and gathering intelligence through a network of police stations and outposts. The gendarmerie was largely made up of conscripts not as well trained as the police.[113] They also had "a sense of disdain and contempt for the rural population, perhaps because of that population's perceived support for the PKK and the Jandarma's relatively exposed position vis a vis PKK insurgents."[114]

TURKEY ALTERNATIVE EXPLANATION: THE GOVERNANCE MODEL

Had the Turkey campaign from 1984 to 1999 supported the predictions of the good governance approach, we should have seen reforms gaining popular support and weakening the insurgency, at least in the southeast if not nationally, and a reduction in the use of violence against civilians. Instead, reforms were limited to nonexistent, and there is little evidence of any increase in popular support for the government.

Reforms. Some systemic political and economic changes to benefit the Kurds and the southeast were introduced after the 1994–1996 defeat of the PKK threat. Most political and economic changes were only initiated after Ocalan's capture. Those development efforts benefited the large landowners who allied with the government during the war, not the populace.[115] Only a minority of Turkey's Kurdish population remains in the southeast.[116] Most rural areas remain barren, with authorities hindering villagers who want to return.[117] The Turkish government's development plans for Kurdish areas were never fully implemented, including plans to build economic centers and support entrepreneurs.[118]

The government sometimes raised the issue of reforms during the war, from economic development in the southeast to loosening of legal restrictions on expressions of Kurdish culture. But pressure from other elements within the state, including the military, prevented implementation or ensured that changes were more symbolic than substantive.[119] Each time the question of reforms arose, the idea was quashed, no steps were taken, or relatively small steps, such as loosening restrictions on the use of Kurdish, were taken and then quickly withdrawn, often accompanied by greater repression.[120] Legal pressure on and violence against members of Kurdish political parties, for example, left nationalist Kurds feeling that "merely being Kurdish was enough to invite repression."[121] In addition, from 1990 to 1998 the Turkish government formally and informally repressed pro-Kurdish political activities, including through the use of violence.

Turgut Özal, prime minister and then president from 1983 to 1993, took steps to address Kurdish feelings of cultural exclusion, such as removing the ban on public use of the Kurdish language. But the non-systemic nature of these steps is evident in the fact that they ended with his death.[122] In 1995, Prime Minister Tansu Ciller weakened the Anti-terror Law, freeing about eighty writers, publishers, activists, and others imprisoned for discussing Kurds and Kurdish demands on the government. "Yet Turkey still maintained a host of laws that were used to punish those who criticized the state's treatment of Kurds and its human rights abuses. Their use depended on the political climate," meaning they were not systemic reforms.[123] Prime Minister Necmettin Erbakan, from an Islamist party that relied less on Ataturk's concept of secular Turkishness, tried to continue secret peace talks with Ocalan but lacked support from the more nationalistic major political actors, including the military.[124] Government leaders also ignored Ocalan's change of position to autonomy or federation rather than independence.[125]

The military did signal an interest in gaining popular support in the mid-1990s, after the PKK threat was reduced to insignificance and after the height of the government's violent village clearance program, but its efforts were not broadly applied. One former soldier said the army began providing medical services for villagers after searching communities, and troops began treating civilians with greater care in village searches. "Now, they try just to find that one PKK person without hurting everyone," he said.[126] A booklet distributed in 1995, after the insurgency no longer posed a serious threat, told soldiers to "get to know the local population, to be respectful of their customs and needs, and, most important, not to abuse them physically or otherwise." The army was mindful of the international as well as domestic costs of its reputation as a massive human rights abuser.[127]

Some reforms broadening Kurdish rights came after the PKK laid down its arms. They were largely the result of Turkey's desire to join the European Union, a process that has since broken down. The incentives provided by the EU for liberalization in Turkey led to moves toward reform but not yet "genuine, substantive, and enduring changes in practice toward Kurds in Turkey."[128] The rise of Islamist parties, with their focus on religion as the key unifying factor within the state, rather than the traditional Kemalist emphasis on secular Turkishness, also played a role in Turkey's later relaxation of restrictions on Kurdish cultural expressions.[129]

Reforms were impossible when the fundamental political arbiter of policy, the military, saw a profound threat to the state in the concept of Kurdishness. The limited accommodations advanced to the aghas are an example of how interests for a specific element of elites can be identified and used to advance the campaign. The accommodation of wealthy southeastern landowners and clan leaders stands with the accommodation of ethnic elites within Malaya and defectors in Dhofar as examples of effective political targeting.

Popular Support. It is difficult to find reliable information on the degree of popular support for the PKK or the government during the war. The Turkish military estimated in 1993 that about 10 percent of the Kurdish populace in the Kurdish region was active PKK sympathizers.[130] It is not clear that the rest, or even a majority of it, supported the government. It was the PKK's ability to defy the government that gained it what support it had. Self-identified Kurds did appreciate the PKK's role in raising the issue of ethnicity in Turkey's political discourse.[131]

For many Kurds, the PKK made it easy for the government to rally anti-insurgent sentiment: "What more ideal enemy than one that has practiced massive violence, the killing of members of its own ethnic group, has espoused for long periods a Marxist-Leninist and maximalist ideological position, has alienated most other Kurdish groups, and is backed by a leader broadly seen as a megalomaniac?" write two experts.[132]

There are indications that the campaign cost the government support in the southeast. The war worsened relations between non-Kurdish Turks and Turkish Kurds; it raised Kurdish consciousness even among those who did not support the PKK; it deepened Kurds' sense of exclusion from the state; and it strained the resources of cities with large concentrations of displaced Kurds, who had few urban skills and high rates of unemployment.[133]

Conclusion

In Turkey, accommodation of armed elites was critical to counterinsurgency success. This was also the case in Malaya and in Dhofar. The Philippine and Greek governments won over some defectors but did not identify as useful an alignment of interests as the British did in Malaya and Dhofar. In El Salvador, there were several insurgent defectors, but they left Farabundo Marti National Liberation Front ranks after the government had nullified the insurgent threat. The smallest degree of accommodation—found in El Salvador—corresponds with the smallest degree of counterinsurgent success, in that the government did not defeat the insurgency on the battle-field but it did manage to retain power. This correspondence underlines the role that accommodation of elites plays in counterinsurgency success.

Accommodation of the aghas in the Kurdish region acted as a force mul-tiplier for military action against civilians. The government gained the mili-tary capacity to destroy civilian communities to prevent them from support-ing the insurgency, while it also strengthened its military ability to target the insurgency directly. Once Turkish military capacity increased, it was able to go on the offensive against insurgents, as well as civilians, throughout the southeast.

Government elites saw the need for gain through nongovernment elite ac-commodation, and specifically in the form of the provision of organized violence to support the counterinsurgency campaign. Nongovernment elites' demands were limited, and the idea of reforms meeting insurgent demands was incomprehensible to many government elites. Government and non-government elites did see an existential threat in the ideology of the insur-gency, but did not consider its capabilities as a fighting force an existential threat because of the limited cultural, political, and geographic appeal of the insurgency.

This campaign provides substantial support for the compellence theory in that the government succeeded primarily based on elite accommodation and its resultant uses of military force against the PKK and civilians, there was no evident rise in popular support for the government, and minimal re-forms largely followed government success. The Turkish use of brute force against civilians was systematic, widespread, persistent, and effective. It was similarly so in Malaya, the Philippines, Greece, and El Salvador. Uses of force against civilians in Dhofar were less massive, in part because of the small and scattered population. Again, the greatest difference is in the El Salva-dor case: the government was able to destroy communities in El Salvador, but it could not hold the land it took or prevent civilians from returning or continuing to support the insurgency. This variation in outcome, with El Sal-vador the single political but not military counterinsurgency success, em-phasizes the importance of cutting off insurgents from resources and the costs of using brute force ineffectively in attempting to control civilians.

One interesting question is why state violence destroyed, rather than fu-eled, the insurgency in Turkey. In El Salvador counterinsurgent violence failed to break the insurgency's ability to fight on, or its will to do so. In-deed, the insurgency remained strong enough to coerce a peace settlement from El Salvador and the United States. The key differences lie in the char-acteristics of the insurgencies. The PKK had a largely coercive relationship with the populace, and many Kurds did not support either its goal of seces-sion or its violent methods. Many more Turks of Kurdish extraction had little interest in the ethnicity issue. The FMLN, in contrast, had broad popular sup-port and a largely benign, even protective, relationship with its supporters and other civilians. Further, unlike the Salvadoran military in any phase of that war, in Turkey the already large, well-equipped, and relatively professional Turkish military kept a step ahead of the insurgency, pressing insurgents with large and small operations everywhere it found them.

The lack of increased popular support for the government and the lack of systemic or persistent reforms in Turkey are similar to the situations in all five counterinsurgency successes claimed as models for democratic great powers backing a client government. This finding strongly suggests that popular support and reforms are unnecessary in reducing an insurgency to an annoyance.

The PKK resumed scattered violence in 2004,[134] when the U.S. invasion of Iraq freed it from Turkey's cross-border pursuit for several years,[135] but external support beyond the safe haven found earlier and again more recently with Iraqi Kurds is not yet evident. After reducing the PKK to nuisance status by 1996, Turkey later made concessions on Kurdish cultural rights as part of its effort to join the European Union. This meant that the renascent PKK had less political traction within Turkey than it did in 1984, as long as the government's concessions stood. Furthermore, the rise of Turkish Islamist parties, who see Islam rather than Turkish ethnicity as the common bond among citizens, initially made Kurdish cultural rights a less sensitive issue for the state.[136] But the relative success of the pro-Turkish, liberal People's Democratic Party (Halkların Demokratik Partisi) in 2015 parliamentary elections threatened President Erdogan's absolute majority, and the ruling Justice and Development Party (Adalet ve Kalkınma Partisi) has increased its repression of journalists, politicians, and others considered pro-Kurdish.[137] Erdogan's concerns also include Turkish Kurdish fighters' partnerships with Kurdish fighters across the border in Syria's civil war and consolidating his power after the failed 2016 military coup against him.

The renewed conflict has waxed and waned, including with a 2013–2015 truce and a major government crackdown in 2016 that imprisoned pro-Kurdish party leaders and shuttered Kurdish media outlets. The fighting is still most intense in the southeast, but has been taking place in cities rather than the countryside. The depopulated formerly Kurdish rural southeast is no longer suited to guerrilla warfare.[138] The Turkish military has also again begun attacking PKK bases across the border in northern Iraq.[139]

The return of the PKK was supported by its previous construction of a shadow state in several southeastern provinces, including night classes, courts, local police, and intelligence units. This familiarity with the organization is likely to have contributed to its ability to return to Turkey, even though many of the residents of the Kurdish region were driven into the cities by the war, turning the PKK into an urban organization.[140] During the war, the government had reached into the lives of some villages for the first time, and not in positive ways.[141] The military state of emergency began regulating villagers' daily lives,[142] whereas PKK grassroots organizing activity had at least sometimes been altruistic. Although one goal of the clearing of Kurdish communities during the 1984–1999 war was the breakdown of social and cultural adhesion to foster Kurdish assimilation as Turks, a renewed sense of Kurdishness accompanied the return of the PKK in the 2000s. Rural Kurds driven into the big cities of western Turkey congregated in Kurdish neighborhoods, providing fertile ground for activist organizations, including the PKK and legal pro-Kurdish parties as well as more radical Kurdish groups.[143] In 2015, the military was using tanks and artillery against civilian neighborhoods in several southeastern cities, killing hundreds and driving tens of thousands from their homes. Some have fled to Istanbul, which now has the largest Kurdish population in Turkey.[144] Prospects for peace are poor.

Counterinsurgency Success

Costs High and Rising

On its face, the assumption that counterinsurgency success requires good governance, greater sensitivity to civilian interests, more restrained uses of military power, and more support for civilian state-building efforts is logical and appealing. The well-known secondary literature on a handful of successful counterinsurgency campaigns tells a story of great powers bringing more representative, distributive rule to the people of weak, repressive states; treating civilians with respect for their civil and human rights; and providing them with security against the insurgents. Typically the great power sponsor is the focus of such work. Authors identify what the intervener contributed to the counterinsurgent government's effort and what the intervener wanted the counterinsurgent government to do with its contributions. This type of work is often normative and prescriptive rather than analytical and predictive.

Beyond the secondary literature, the second- and third-hand accounts of practitioners focusing on the goals they considered appropriate for contemporary Western states as embodied in a small set of cases presented as models, the story is quite different. The documents of the time that I draw on, many of them previously unexplored in this context, show us who actually did what to whom, and what came of it militarily and politically.

My focus is on the counterinsurgent governments themselves, their interests, and their choices as the primary agents of the counterinsurgency campaign. Their own interests often diverged from those of their great power sponsors. Again and again, they chose their own path while trying to ensure continued backing from their patrons. This reorientation from intervener to counterinsurgent serves as a reminder of the limits of great power control and influence. Interveners and potential interveners must keep these constraints in mind in seeking to attain their own policy goals within conflicted states.

In these cases of successful democratic great power military intervention to support a counterinsurgent government—the Malayan Emergency, the Greek Civil War, the anti-Huk campaign in the Philippines, and the successes in Dhofar, Oman, and El Salvador—the counterinsurgent governments bargained with rival elites rather than sharing wealth and power to serve popular interests; used brute force systematically, intentionally, and directly against civilians; did not institute reforms until after defeating the insurgent threat, if at all; and gained little or no popular support. It is striking, given the belief inherent in the governance model that long-term political stability requires construction of a liberal democratic state, that all five states remain relatively stable decades after their counterinsurgency success, yet also remain illiberal or semi-democratic. In some, new insurgencies have arisen, but none have posed an existential threat to the government.

Most obvious in contemporaneous accounts of these wars are the governments' vast military clearing operations to control and destroy civilian communities and their material resources, such as crops, homes, and animals, in order to deny resources to the insurgency. The secondary literature often identifies these operations as early military errors or even erases them. My research takes them seriously and examines their political effects as part of government success—that is, "marginalization of the insurgents to the point at which they are destroyed, co-opted, or reduced to irrelevance in numbers and capability."[1]

Also noteworthy in the contemporaneous documents is that the governments made deals with rival elites, rather than sharing wealth and power with the masses, to get the cooperation, information, and military capabilities they needed to conduct the campaign. These elites—political entrepreneurs and entrepreneurs of violence—included politicians, businessmen, tribal leaders, warlords, insurgent defectors, and other individuals who wielded power or influence or had information that the counterinsurgent found useful. In several cases—the Philippines, Greece, and El Salvador—the governments were shaky enough that their accommodation efforts focused on keeping other elites within the government on board in order to keep external support flowing. In Malaya, Dhofar, and Turkey the governments co-opted rivals or potential rivals to gain their political or military contribution to the campaign.

The historical record shows that success in countering insurgency is the result of political accommodation to gain the support of other elites and the government's use of brute force against civilians. The former political efforts make the latter military efforts possible. In a civil war, the government is only one of a number of political actors using violence to attain its goals. In order to control the populace, and to gather the information and military strength necessary to target insurgents directly, the government buys off individual leaders with knowledge, military power, or influence useful for the government's campaign. It uses force against civilians, controlling their behavior, to prevent material and nonmaterial resources from flowing to the insurgents. The military campaign is one of attrition; it is not necessary to kill all the insurgents, or their political and military leaders. It is necessary to break their will to fight by showing them that they cannot attain their goals. The military campaign depends on the information and resources gained from buying off rival leaders.

In this political element of the campaign, the government provides selected elites with something of value in exchange for information and fighting power, or at the very least cooperation. The valuable thing provided may be material or nonmaterial, such as money or the opportunity to make money, or a high position, or rule over a piece of territory, for example. The interests of the populace play little role in counterinsurgency success. The role of the populace is to be forcefully controlled to prevent the provision of support to the challengers. Goods and services may reach the populace through elites, as the firqats in Dhofar, for example, controlled access to water. But accommodations do not benefit the populace as a whole; in Turkey, it was only the aghas and other elites who partnered with the government who gained money, power, prestige, and impunity.

Counterinsurgency success is about power, co-optation, building a coalition, and crushing opposition, not good governance. It requires co-opting rival elites to build a winning coalition that will overpower the opposition by cutting the flow of resources to insurgents, often through the use of brute force against civilians. Insurgent and counterinsurgent do not engage in a competition to govern with the people as the prize. They are part of a competition for power among armed groups with conflicting political interests. Because my theory is not prescriptive but explanatory, it is neutral on the type of government that emerges from the counterinsurgency campaign.

What the Cases Show

In Malaya, the British gave up their goal of a liberal pluralistic state, which they believed necessary to ensure long-term stability, in order to accommodate the interests of communal leaders within Malaya. This paradigmatic change required the British to shift the means they used to attain their long-term goal. Instead of sharing political power equally among the peninsula's ethnic communities, they ratified the continued dominance of ethnic Malays. The British succeeded in fostering a relatively stable state, though not a liberal one. Their effort included the forceful control of civilians, primarily the destruction of entire communities and the creation of scantily provisioned prison camps, to cut the flow of resources to the insurgency. Reforms that followed the successful reduction of the insurgency to a nuisance were and remain limited. Malaysia is a less than liberal society in which government support for its people varies according to ethnic community and the Malays continue their political domination over ethnic Chinese and ethnic Indians.

In Greece, the U.S.-backed government was so shaky that its accommodations amounted to the sharing of favors among government elites. This effort kept successive governments from losing U.S. support. The military effort swept clear vast areas, including through the destruction of civilian communities and the scattering or imprisonment of a significant percentage of the civilian population in squalid conditions. Government repression was widespread. Huge military operations decisively defeated the insurgency. Greece was ruled by a military dictatorship from 1967 to 1974. It is now a democracy with limited institutionalization, limited ability to serve its people, and limited tax collection ability, along with a continuing, relatively limited problem of left- and right-wing terrorism and continued domination by oligarchs and the Orthodox Church.

The Philippines, too, remains a shaky democracy. Like Greece, it suffered a dictatorship, from 1972 to 1981. It has elected a series of strongman leaders more recently, Joseph Estrada and Rodrigo Duterte. Its counterinsurgent success against the Huk included accommodation of governmental elite interests and gestures toward service to the peasants of Central Luzon. Like Malaya and Greece, the counterinsurgency campaign succeeded in part because of its militarization of the restive region, its forceful control of civilians, and its vast military operations against civilians and insurgents alike. It remains unable to keep the promises of the Magsaysay era regarding the provision of public services.

Oman, though shaken by the 2020 death of Sultan Qaboos and scattered unrest in the wake of the Arab Spring, remains a politically stable illiberal autocratic state that cooperates extensively with the Western powers. Here, as in Malaya, the British leading the counterinsurgency campaign had to sacrifice their liberal goals to achieve their practical political objective. They succeeded by accommodating potential nongovernment rivals and insurgent leaders and gaining political intelligence and military power. They also used force to control civilian communities and the movements of those within them, destroyed civilian resources from water wells to food crops, and mounted massive military operations against insurgents and civilians alike.

In El Salvador, democracy remains a work in progress, as it does in Greece and the Philippines. The counterinsurgent government's peace deal with the insurgency has held to date. The insurgency has been fully integrated into the political system; a member of the Farabundo Marti National Liberation Front's party held the presidency from 2014 to 2019. The military has honored the new constitution by staying out of domestic politics, though there is cause for concern in armed, uniformed members of the army and police joining President Nayib Bukele in Parliament in early 2020. The level of political violence has declined since the war, but criminal violence is staggeringly high in a state still suffering severe social and economic inequality. The counterinsurgency campaign consisted of accommodation within successive governments along with widespread civilian repression, including attacks on and destruction of civilian communities and vast military operations against insurgents and civilians. The government failed to defeat the insurgency militarily; the FMLN remained politically and militarily strong enough to fight the government to a standstill and ultimately coerce it into signing the peace agreement (in alignment with the U.S. shift in interests after the end of the Cold War). Yet the insurgency never gained the military or political strength it needed to overturn the government and seize the state. This case is the only one I examine in which the government failed to achieve the military defeat of the insurgency.

Finally, in Turkey, the successful counterinsurgency campaign against the Partiya Karkeren Kurdistan strongly resembles the other five cases in the use of elite accommodation to gain political and military capabilities the government lacked, and in the use of massive force against civilians and insurgents. Enormous military clearing operations reshaped the human geography of the southeastern Kurdish region of Turkey. The PKK's renaissance in 2004 with the opportunities provided by the U.S. invasion and occupation of neighboring Iraq does not lessen the force of the resemblance of this case to the earlier ones.

The five earlier cases have been lauded as models for current and future U.S. military interventions seeking creation of liberal democratic states via provision of support for good governance. Their similarity to the Turkey case underlines their lack of democratizing reforms and lack of respect for human rights. This comparative analysis sinks hopes for a better way of war, one that adheres to liberal values and attains great power liberal governance goals within other states.

My findings are likely to be controversial because they challenge the conventional wisdom on counterinsurgency success, a conventional wisdom that many analysts and pundits rely on as a professional position and even personal brand, and a conventional wisdom that carries significant emotional power. This analysis is also likely to make observers uncomfortable for its challenge to cherished beliefs about great power good intentions leading to good outcomes. It is also distressing to learn that well-intentioned interventions are likely to have painful, unintended consequences. Finally, my demonstration that government uses of force—specifically against civilians—can serve government interests is discomfiting. It challenges the normative position that uses of violence are likely to fail. It is because the use of force to control civilians in every aspect of their daily lives is so successful and so distasteful that I urge great power policymakers to avoid military intervention when the threat is quite limited, as it usually is in such cases.

In the cases here, great power backing helped the client government achieve counterinsurgent success, and all six states remain at least nominally partnered with the West on important issues. But all six campaigns also had high human and moral costs. These findings force those who support great power liberal military intervention to consider unpalatable choices about national interests. Is it better to let a smaller, weaker state valued as a partner fall to an insurgency likely to challenge the interests of the great power in some relatively minor way? Or is it better to back the repressive, illiberal client, increasing its firepower and thus its ability to attack and otherwise repress civilians and their human and civil rights, while pressing it for reforms that are unlikely to materialize because they are not in the interests of the counterinsurgent elites?

My prescription is to shun liberal military intervention as a tool intended to create greater security within smaller states and globally. The benefits to national and international security are small, the costs high. Policymakers, practitioners, and members of the public must weigh these questions for themselves. My analysis provides a theoretical and empirical foundation for their doing so.

The Great Power Role

These questions about what is to be gained provide the larger political context for counterinsurgency success: democratic great powers use military intervention to try to ensure their own security by keeping threatened governments in power. The United States and, sometimes, its partners, including Britain, France, Italy, and others, repeatedly find themselves in situations where they believe they must either defeat an insurgency or forfeit some portion of their own security and credibility. Thus the question becomes not What will succeed in counterinsurgency? but What can democratic great powers do about smaller partner states facing insurgencies when the great powers believe they must do something to protect themselves?

Democratic great powers may try to do good by fostering reforms in conflicted states, and fail at high human and moral cost. Or they may achieve their goal of long-term political stability through elite accommodation and forceful control of civilians, also at high moral cost. Support for an illiberal client means direct or indirect support for its illiberal, even brutal, policies. These difficulties suggest the need for policymakers to weigh the value of keeping client elites in power against the costs of trying to preserve their rule. Acceding to corruption and warlord rule or supporting it to gain political stability is normatively disagreeable to democratic powers. However, there is also a moral argument for ending or reducing the killing and other suffering of civil war as quickly as possible; for supporting postwar humanitarian, infrastructure, economic, and political reconstruction to the degree possible whatever the regime type; and for avoiding the increase in violence likely to follow the entrance of foreign troops into an internal conflict. No matter how well intended, military intervention may provoke a nationalistic response that extends rather than ends the suffering.

All six states I examine have thus far provided in the international realm what their great power sponsors sought in intervening to support their threatened governments: they remain at least cooperative and at best close partners with the Western powers. Turkey remains a NATO member. These states are relatively stable, responsible members of the international system (though there are increasing concerns about Turkey under Reycep Tayyip Erdogan's rule). This study shows that the democratization and development process is separate from the task of defeating an insurgent threat.[2] In successful counterinsurgency cases, state and political development slowly follows success against an insurgency over the course of many years, if at all.[3]

Implications

These findings have implications for literatures and policy choices beyond counterinsurgency and great power military intervention. They are particularly relevant to peacekeeping efforts, including UN, regional, and state-led efforts, which must defer to elite interests to have any hope of success;[4] to peacemaking efforts in considering the costs and benefits of including popular as well as elite groups in talks; to external state-building efforts, because I show that counterinsurgency and state building are two separate processes;[5] to efforts to professionalize other states' militaries, because elites are likely to serve their own interests rather than that of their sponsor;[6] and finally to all international aid-driven reform campaigns because, again, elites serve their own interests first.[7]

I underline in particular three policy lessons from my findings. First, what matters for success when a great power partners with a smaller, weaker client is the alignment of interests rather than values. Elites in the smaller state regain significant leverage over their own behavior and are more likely to act in what they consider to be their own interests than they are to obey great power orders. Great power leverage is limited by its own commitment to client survival.[8]

Second, the great power is unlikely to attain ambitious political objectives even with an alignment of interests with elites in the smaller state. The intervener is likelier to achieve its goals, and avoid the embarrassment of failure and any costs to reputation or credibility, when it sets relatively modest political objectives.[9] The power of a stronger state, even a hegemonic one, is limited. It is even more limited outside its own borders. Without permanent occupation and annexation, it is unlikely to be able to control the domestic politics of another state, while occupation and annexation are likely to drive a violent nationalist response, as after the U.S.-led invasion and occupation of Iraq and Afghanistan.

Third, policymakers, practitioners, and concerned publics bear responsibility for considering the costs as well as the benefits of a military intervention. It is easy to say this, and to criticize other's choices. But my analysis underlines the high costs of increasing the military power of repressive governments as well as the low likelihood of attaining ambitious liberal goals.

This study of how Western great powers attempt to create greater security within other states through the use of force suggests that policy choices based on belief in the power of good governance to defeat insurgency may be overambitious, extremely costly, and simply impossible to achieve. Great powers that intervene to back client states against insurgencies are more likely to succeed when they set modest goals and focus on achieving narrow interests shared with client elites. Interveners are also more likely to attain their political goals when they recognize the primacy of client elite interests in shaping outcomes. Finally, in a democracy where domestic support is considered necessary for foreign intervention, a sunny narrative about imminent counterinsurgency success that cloaks a harsher reality involving higher costs threatens the health of the polity.[10]

Notes

1. Counterinsurgency: Eating Soup with a Chainsaw

1. The statement used as this chapter's title comes from a leading U.S. Army thinker on counterinsurgency, which is often called within the army the graduate level of war. The allusion is to T. E. Lawrence, who rallied the tribes of Arabia on the side of Britain against the ruling Ottoman Empire during World War I, and in *The Seven Pillars of Wisdom* (http://gutenberg.net.au /ebooks01/0100111h.html) wrote that "war upon rebellion was messy and slow, like eating soup with a knife" (chap. 33, para. 16). This powerful statement also reveals the self-referential nature of Western practitioner work on counterinsurgency.

2. U.S. Government Interagency Counterinsurgency Initiative, *U.S. Government Counterinsurgency Guide* (Washington, DC: U.S. Government Printing Office, 2009), 4.

3. Thomas Schelling, *Arms and Influence* (New Haven, CT: Yale University Press, 1966), chap. 1.

4. Linda J. Bilmes, "Iraq and Afghanistan: The US$6 Trillion Bill for America's Longest War Is Unpaid," The Conversation, May 25, 2017, https://theconversation.com/iraq-and-afghanistan -the-us-6-trillion-bill-for-americas-longest-war-is-unpaid-78241.

5. On this debate, see, for example, William C. Wohlforth, "The Stability of a Unipolar World," *International Security* 24, no. 1 (Summer 1999): 5–41, https://doi.org/10.1162/016228899560031; and Kenneth N. Waltz, "Evaluating Theories," *American Political Science Review* 91, no. 4 (December 1997): 915–916, https://doi.org/10.2307/2952173.

6. John J. Mearsheimer, *The Great Delusion: Liberal Dreams and International Realities* (New Haven, CT: Yale University Press, 2018).

7. Alina Mungiu-Pippidi, "The Rise and Fall of Good-Governance Promotion," *Journal of Democracy* 31, no. 1 (January 2020): 88–102, https://doi.org/10.1353/jod.2020.0007, traces the development of the idea and norm of good governance and identifies the failure of efforts to intervene to encourage or impose good governance.

8. Herman Joseph S. Kraft defines political stability as constitutionalism, legitimacy, effectiveness, relative impermeability, and durability. See Kraft, "The Philippines: The Weak State and the Global War on Terror," *Kasarinlan* 18, nos. 1–2 (2003): 133–152.

9. See, for example, Alan Richards, "The Political Economy of Dilatory Reform: Egypt in the 1980s," *World Development* 19, no. 12 (1991): 1721–1730, https://doi.org/10.1016/0305-750X (91)90015-A.

10. See, for example, D. Michael Shafer, *Deadly Paradigms: The Failure of U.S. Counterinsurgency Policy* (Princeton, NJ: Princeton University Press, 1988); and Douglas J. Macdonald, *Adventures in Chaos: American Intervention for Reform in the Third World* (Cambridge, MA: Harvard University Press, 1992).

11. .See, for example, David Edelstein, *Occupational Hazards: Success and Failure in Military Occupation* (Ithaca, NY: Cornell University Press, 2008).

2. Counterinsurgency: What It Is and Is Not

1. For example, see Julian Paget, *Counter-insurgency Operations: Techniques of Guerrilla Warfare* (New York: Walker, 1967), 177; Robert Thompson, *Defeating Communist Insurgency: Experiences from Malaya and Vietnam* (London: Chatto and Windus, 1966), 50–55, 72; and Headquarters, Department of the Army, and Headquarters, Marine Corps Combat Development Command, *U.S. Army/Marine Corps Counterinsurgency Field Manual 3-24* (Washington, DC: Department of the Army, 2006), 51.

2. Stephen T. Hosmer and Sibylle O. Crane, *Counterinsurgency: A Symposium, April 16–20, 1962* (Santa Monica, CA: RAND, 1962), iv.

3. Ian F. W. Beckett, *Insurgency in Iraq: An Historical Perspective* (Carlisle, PA: U.S. Army War College Strategic Studies Institute, 2005).

4. Headquarters, Department of the Army, and Headquarters, Marine Corps Combat Development Command, *Counterinsurgency Field Manual*, xlvi, 299.

5. Peter W. Chiarelli and Patrick R. Michaelis, "Winning the Peace: The Requirement for Full-Spectrum Operations," *Military Review*, October 2006.

6. Headquarters, Department of the Army, and Headquarters, Marine Corps Combat Development Command, *Counterinsurgency Field Manual*, A-8.

7. David Galula, *Counterinsurgency Warfare: Theory and Practice* (1964; repr., New York: Prager, 2006), 5, 66; Headquarters, Department of the Army, and Headquarters, Marine Corps Combat Development Command, *Counterinsurgency Field Manual*, 300; David Petraeus, "COMISAF's Counterinsurgency Guidance," *Washington Post*, August 1, 2010, https://www.washingtonpost.com/wp-srv/hp/ssi/wpc/afghanguidance.pdf; John Nagl, "Unprepared: Review—*The Echo of Battle: The Army's Way of War*, by Brian Linn McAllister," *RUSI Journal* 153, no. 2 (April 2008): 82–89, https://doi.org/10.1080/03071840802103355.

8. For a sense of the scholarly literature, see, for example, Paul Collier and Anke Hoeffler, "Greed and Grievance in Civil War," *Oxford Economic Papers* 56 (2004): 563–595, https://doi.org/10.1093/oep/gpf064; Paul Collier et al., *Breaking the Conflict Trap: Civil War and Development Policy* (Washington, DC: World Bank; New York: Oxford University Press, 2003); Edward N. Muller and Mitchell A. Seligson, "Inequality and Insurgency," *American Political Science Review* 81, no. 2 (June 1987): 426–451, https://doi.org/10.2307/1961960; James C. Scott, *The Moral Economy of the Peasant: Rebellion and Subsistence in Southeast Asia* (New Haven, CT: Yale University Press, 1977); Samuel L. Popkin, *The Rational Peasant: The Political Economy of Rural Society in Vietnam* (Berkeley: University of California Press, 1979); Frantz Fanon, *The Wretched of the Earth* (repr., New York: Grove, 2005); Barry Posen, "The Security Dilemma and Ethnic Conflict," *Survival* 35, no. 1 (1993): 27–47, https://doi.org/10.1080/00396339308442672; and John Mueller, "The Banality of 'Ethnic War,'" *International Security* 25, no. 1 (2000): 42–70, https://doi.org/10.1162/016228800560381. One counterargument is that one side's military victory is more likely to lead to long-term peace than is a negotiated end to the conflict. See Edward N. Luttwak, "Give War a Chance," *Foreign Affairs* 78, no. 4 (July/August 1999): 36–44.

9. See Eli Berman and Aila M. Matanock, "The Empiricists' Insurgency," *Annual Review of Political Science* 18 (2015): 443–464, https://doi.org/10.1146/annurev-polisci-082312-124553.

10. For example, Berman and Matanock.

11. On regime type, see Jason Lyall, "Do Democracies Make Inferior Counterinsurgents? Reassessing Democracy's Impact on War Outcomes and Duration," *International Organization* 64, no. 1 (Winter 2010): 167–192, https://doi.org/10.1017/S0020818309990208; and Anna Getmansky, "You Can't Win If You Don't Fight: The Role of Regime Type in Counterinsurgency Out-

breaks and Outcomes," *Journal of Conflict Resolution* 57, no. 4 (August 2013): 709–724, https://doi.org/10.1177/0022002712449326. On will, see Ivan Arreguín-Toft, "How the Weak Win Wars: A Theory of Asymmetric Conflict," *International Security* 26, no. 1 (Summer 2001): 93–128, https://doi.org/10.1162/016228801753212868; and Andrew Mack, "Why Big Nations Lose Small Wars," *World Politics* 27, no. 2 (January 1975): 175–200, https://doi.org/10.2307/2009880. Neither Arreguín-Toft nor Mack addresses counterinsurgency success specifically.

12. Nadia Schadlow, *War and the Art of Governance: Consolidating Combat Success into Political Victory* (Washington, DC: Georgetown University Press, 2017), 273–277.

13. Paul D. Miller, *Armed State Building: Confronting State Failure, 1898–2012* (Ithaca, NY: Cornell University Press, 2013), 9–10.

14. Eli Berman, Joseph H. Felter, and Jacob N. Shapiro, *Small Wars, Big Data: The Information Revolution in Modern Conflict*, with Vestal McIntyre (Princeton, NJ: Princeton University Press, 2018), 16–17, 308–309, 19.

15. The focus on tactical intelligence ignores the significant problem identified by Stathis Kalyvas, that much conflict within communities during a civil war involves private interests and quarrels, making information provided in this context profoundly suspect. Stathis Kalyvas, *The Logic of Violence in Civil War* (New York: Cambridge University Press, 2006), e.g., 253.

16. Berman, Felter, and Shapiro, *Small Wars, Big Data*, 304–305.

17. Berman, Felter, and Shapiro, *Small Wars, Big Data*, 324–325. This work reflects what Helen Dexter identifies as the depoliticized "new war" in which Western military intervention is presented as a moral duty. Helen Dexter, "New War, Good War and the War on Terror: Explaining, Excusing and Creating Western Neo-interventionism," *Development and Change* 38, no. 6 (2007): 1055–1071, https://doi.org/10.1111/j.1467-7660.2007.00446.x.

18. Leading classical theorists of modernization include Walter Rostow and Talcott Parsons. Robert A. Packenham, *Liberal America and the Third World: Political Development Ideas in Foreign Aid and Social Science* (Princeton, NJ: Princeton University Press, 1973), 173, 20. For other critiques of modernization theory, see Michael Latham, *Modernization as Ideology: American Social Science and "Nation Building" in the Kennedy Era* (Chapel Hill: University of North Carolina Press, 2000); Nils Gilman, *Mandarins of the Future: Modernization Theory in Cold War America* (Baltimore: Johns Hopkins University Press, 2004); David Engerman et al., *Staging Growth: Modernization, Development, and the Global Cold War* (Amherst: University of Massachusetts Press, 2003); and David Ekbladh, *The Great American Mission: Modernization and the Construction of an American World Order* (Princeton, NJ: Princeton University Press, 2009).

19. Michael Albertus and Victor Menaldo, *Authoritarianism and the Elite Origins of Democracy* (New York: Cambridge University Press, 2018), 6.

20. See, for example, John T. Fishel and Max G. Manwaring, *Uncomfortable Wars Revisited* (Norman: University of Oklahoma Press, 2006); Headquarters, Department of the Army, and Headquarters, Marine Corps Combat Development Command, *Counterinsurgency Field Manual*; Kalev I. Sepp, "Best Practices in Counterinsurgency," *Military Review*, May/June 2005, 8–12; and David Kilcullen, *The Accidental Guerrilla* (New York: Oxford University Press, 2009).

21. See, for example, Galula, *Counterinsurgency Warfare*; Thompson, *Defeating Communist Insurgency*; John A. Nagl, *Learning to Eat Soup with a Knife: Counterinsurgency Lessons from Malaya and Vietnam* (2002; repr., Chicago: University of Chicago Press, 2005); and Andrew F. Krepinevich Jr., *The Army and Vietnam* (Baltimore: Johns Hopkins University Press, 1986).

22. See Berman and Matanock, "Empiricists' Insurgency."

23. Karl Hack, "The Malayan Emergency as Counter-insurgency Paradigm," *Journal of Strategic Studies* 32, no. 3 (June 2009): 383–414, https://doi.org/10.1080/01402390902928180, points out this problem.

24. See, for example, Galula, *Counterinsurgency Warfare*, 8–9, 53. For challenges to this view, see D. Michael Shafer, *Deadly Paradigms: The Failure of U.S. Counterinsurgency Policy* (Princeton, NJ: Princeton University Press, 1988); and Kalyvas, *Logic of Violence*.

25. See, for example, Fishel and Manwaring, *Uncomfortable Wars Revisited*; and Krepinevich, *Army and Vietnam*. On the limits of patron control over client interests, see Shafer, *Deadly Paradigms*; and Douglas J. Macdonald, *Adventures in Chaos: American Intervention for Reform in the Third World* (Cambridge, MA: Harvard University Press, 1992).

26. Caitlin Talmadge, *The Dictator's Army* (Ithaca, NY: Cornell University Press, 2015).

27. See, for example, Sepp, "Best Practices in Counterinsurgency"; and Christopher Paul, Colin P. Clarke, and Beth Grill, *Victory Has a Thousand Fathers: Sources of Success in Counterinsurgency* (Santa Monica, CA: RAND, 2010). Two leading thinkers on population-centric counterinsurgency identify the importance of controlling the populace but do not dwell on what controlling or "protecting" civilians means in terms of practical realities or human and civil rights. See, for example, Kalev I. Sepp, "Resettlement, Regroupment, Reconcentration: Deliberate Government-Directed Population Relocation in Support of Counter-insurgency Operations" (MA thesis, U.S. Army Command and General Staff College, Fort Leavenworth, KS, 1992); and David Kilcullen, "Counterinsurgency in Iraq: Theory and Practice," slideshow presentation, 2007, https://slideplayer.com/slide/10594849/. One problem with conceiving of population controls as "protection" is that civilians in a counterinsurgency campaign are more likely to need protection from the government than from the insurgents. See, for example, Shafer, *Deadly Paradigms*. Among others, David French, *The British Way in Counterinsurgency, 1945–1967* (New York: Oxford University Press, 2012); Brian Drohan, *Brutality in an Age of Human Rights: Activism and Counterinsurgency at the End of British Empire* (Ithaca, NY: Cornell University Press, 2017); and Rafael Cohen, "Beyond Hearts and Minds" (PhD diss., Georgetown University, 2014), argue that force plays a more significant role in successful counterinsurgency than is usually recognized.

28. Frank Tallett, *War and Society in Early Modern Europe, 1495–1715* (London: Routledge, 1992), 1.

29. See, for example, Fishel and Manwaring, *Uncomfortable Wars Revisited*.

30. Carl von Clausewitz, *On War*, trans. Michael Howard and Peter Paret (Oxford: Oxford University Press, 1976), 596.

31. On these points, see, for example, Jeremy Weinstein, *Inside Rebellion: The Politics of Insurgent Violence* (New York: Cambridge University Press, 2006); Shafer, *Deadly Paradigms*; Nathan Leites and Charles Wolf, *Rebellion and Authority: An Analytic Essay on Insurgent Conflicts* (Chicago: Markham, 1970); Charles Wolf Jr., *Insurgency and Counterinsurgency: New Myths and Old Realities* (Santa Monica, CA: RAND, July 1965); and Ken Dilanian, "U.S. Risks Wasting Billions More in Afghanistan Aid, Report Says," *Los Angeles Times*, June 17, 2011, http://articles.latimes.com/2011/jun/17/world/la-fg-afghan-aid-20110617.

32. Dan Slater and Joseph Wong argue that authoritarian ruling parties are primarily interested in retaining power and thus most likely to embrace democratization under three conditions: when they are relatively confident that they can win free and fair elections, when they have experienced a shock indicating that their power has begun waning, and when they can pursue new forms of legitimation of their rule. See Slater and Wong, "The Strength to Concede: Ruling Parties and Democratization in Developmental Asia," *Perspectives on Politics* 11, no. 3 (September 2013): 717–733, https://doi.org/10.1017/S1537592713002090.

33. Robert J. Art, *A Grand Strategy for America* (Ithaca, NY: Cornell University Press, 2003), 6.

34. I thank a Colombian official involved in the counterinsurgency and peacemaking effort there for sharing this insight.

35. See, for example, Edward Mansfield and Jack Snyder, "Democratization and War," *Foreign Affairs* 74, no. 3 (May–June 1995): 79–97; and Roland Paris, *At War's End: Building Peace After Civil Conflict* (Cambridge: Cambridge University Press, 2004).

36. Niel Smith and Sean MacFarland, "Anbar Awakens: The Tipping Point," *Military Review*, March–April 2008, 41–52; Rod Nordland, "Some Police Recruits Impose 'Islamic Tax' on Afghans," *New York Times*, June 12, 2011. Also see Dipali Mukhopadhyay, *Warlords, Strongman Governors, and the State in Afghanistan* (New York: Cambridge University Press, 2016).

37. U.S. Government Interagency Counterinsurgency Initiative, *U.S. Government Counterinsurgency Guide* (Washington, DC: U.S. Government Printing Office, 2009), 4.

38. There is a long history of accommodation in warfare, including in internal conflict. During the seventeenth-century Fronde in France, "nobles were bought off with gratuities, pensions and a judicious use of patronage, for the chief advantage kings in France, and monarchs generally, had over their magnates lay not in the size of their armies but in the superior size of their patronage resources." Similarly, in Brandenburg-Prussia, the government allowed the *junkers*

control of the peasantry, kept their tax rates low, and provided lucrative positions in the army and bureaucracy. Tallett, *War and Society*, 190, 192.

39. Similarly, in the early modern period, the key to successful repression of popular uprisings was using force in ways officers approved of, against opponents without widespread or elite social support, and to buttress the existing social hierarchy. Tallett, *War and Society*, 192.

40. States in a crisis bargaining situation want to coerce prudently or accommodate cheaply, or do some combination of the two. Glenn H. Snyder and Paul Diesing, *Conflict among Nations: Bargaining, Decision Making, and System Structure in International Crises* (Princeton, NJ: Princeton University Press, 1977), 207.

41. Thomas Schelling, *Arms and Influence* (New Haven, CT: Yale University Press, 1966), 173.

42. My findings do not accord with the work of Gil Merom, who argues that democracies cannot successfully defeat insurgencies because domestic political constraints prevent the use of brutality. See Merom, *How Democracies Lose Small Wars: State, Society, and the Failures of France in Algeria, Israel in Lebanon, and the United States in Vietnam* (New York: Cambridge University Press, 2003).

43. Paul Staniland, "States, Insurgents, and Wartime Political Orders," *Perspectives on Politics* 10, no. 2 (June 2012): 243–264, https://doi.org/10.1017/S1537592712000655, identifies ways in which states and insurgents may cooperate during wartime.

44. Francis Fukuyama, *Political Order and Political Decay: From the Industrial Revolution to the Globalization of Democracy* (New York: Farrar, Straus and Giroux, 2014), shows that states develop toward political order in a variety of ways, including more authoritarian and less liberal paths than that of the ideal type of liberal democracy and sometimes curiously unlike the Weberian ideal type of stateness as monopolization of the legitimate use of force within a given territory.

45. Margaret Levi, *Of Rule and Revenue* (Berkeley: University of California Press, 1988), identifies three tools of governance: force, ideology, and goods provision. In Colombia, targeting civilians believed to support the other side by driving them out of their communities serves counterinsurgent purposes by preventing these civilians from helping insurgents. It can also make the remaining residents in the community more likely to collaborate with counterinsurgents without fear of retaliation. Abbey Steele, *Democracy and Displacement in Colombia's Civil War* (Ithaca, NY: Cornell University Press, 2017), 5.

46. See, for example, Charles Tilly, *Coercion, Capital, and European States, AD 990–1992* (New York: Cambridge University Press, 1992).

47. Douglass C. North, John Joseph Wallis, and Barry R. Weingast, "Violence and the Rise of Open-Access Orders," *Journal of Democracy* 20, no. 1 (January 2009): 55–68, https://doi.org/10.1353/jod.0.0060; David A. Lake, "Anarchy, Hierarchy, and the Variety of International Relations," *International Organization* 50, no. 1 (Winter 1996): 1–33, https://doi.org/10.1017/S002081830000165X; Bruce Bueno de Mesquita et al., "Political Institutions, Political Survival, and Policy Success," in *Governing for Prosperity*, ed. Bruce Bueno de Mesquita and Hilton L. Root (New Haven, CT: Yale University Press, 2000), 59–84; Daron Acemoglu and James A. Robinson, *Why Nations Fail: The Origins of Power, Prosperity, and Poverty* (New York: Crown, 2012); Elizabeth N. Saunders, "War and the Inner Circle: Democratic Elites and the Politics of Using Force," *Security Studies* 24, no. 3 (October 2015): 466–501, https://doi.org/10.1080/09636412.2015.1070618; Stathis N. Kalyvas, "The New U.S. Army/Marine Corps Counterinsurgency Field Manual as Political Science and as Political Praxis," *Perspectives on Politics* 6 no. 2 (June 2008): 347–360, https://doi.org/10.1017/S1537592708081176; Dan Slater, *Ordering Power: Contentious Politics and Authoritarian Leviathans in Southeast Asia* (New York: Cambridge University Press, 2010), 3–5; Ronald Wintrobe, "The Tinpot and the Totalitarian: An Economic Theory of Dictatorship," *American Political Science Review* 81, no. 3 (September 1990): 849–972, https://doi.org/10.2307/1962769; Pierre Englebert and Denis M. Tull, "Postconflict Reconstruction in Africa: Flawed Ideas about Failed States," *International Security* 32, no. 4 (Spring 2008): 106–139, https://doi.org/10.1162/isec.2008.32.4.106.

48. Jason Brownlee, *Authoritarianism in an Age of Democratization* (New York: Cambridge University Press, 2007).

49. Authors considering path dependence include Daron Acemoglu and James A. Robinson, "Persistence of Power, Elites and Institutions," *American Economic Review* 98, no. 1 (2008):

267–293, https://doi.org/10.1257/aer.98.1.267; Christine Wade, *Captured Peace: Elites and Peace-building in El Salvador* (Athens: Ohio University Press, 2016); and Brownlee, *Authoritarianism.*

50. Jack Snyder, *From Voting to Violence: Democratization and Nationalist Conflict* (New York: Norton, 2000).

51. Scholars of internal conflict have long used five years as their definitional point for whether a conflict has reignited or is considered new. Astri Suhrke and Ingrid Samset, "What's in a Figure? Estimating Recurrence of Civil War," *International Peacekeeping* 14, no. 2 (2007): 195–203, https://doi.org/10.1080/13533310601150776.

52. See Robert J. Art, *A Grand Strategy for America* (Ithaca, NY: Cornell University Press, 2003), 45–46, on defining national interests.

53. Works underlining the role of political entrepreneurs and entrepreneurs of violence include Charles Tilly, *The Politics of Collective Violence* (New York: Cambridge University Press, 2003), 34; Kalyvas, *Logic of Violence*; Paul Brass, *The Production of Hindu-Muslim Violence in Contemporary India* (Seattle: University of Washington Press, 2000); Kimberly Marten, *Warlords: Strong-Arm Brokers in Weak States* (Ithaca, NY: Cornell University Press, 2012); and Steffan W. Schmidt et al., *Friends, Followers, and Factions: A Reader in Political Clientism* (Berkeley: University of California Press, 1977). In a somewhat different context, J.C. Sharman, *Empires of the Weak: The Real Story of European Expansion and the Creation of the New World Order* (Princeton, NJ: Princeton University Press, 2019), identifies the role of local allies and an alignment "between what Europeans wanted, and what locals were prepared to give" in early modern European adventures in empire building (37).

54. Kalyvas notes the role of elites as mediators between the populace and the state in "New U.S. Army/Marine Corps." In many "traditional" societies, he notes, community elites act as a communications and influence system between populace and state.

55. Tilly, *Politics of Collective Violence,* 34.

56. Kalyvas, *Logic of Violence in Civil War,* esp. 367–387.

57. Kalyvas, *Logic of Violence in Civil War,* 381–387, discusses local alliances.

58. Brass, *Production of Hindu-Muslim Violence.*

59. Jennifer Keister, "States Within States: How Rebels Rule" (PhD diss., University of California, San Diego, 2011).

60. Bruce Bueno de Mesquita et al., "Political Institutions, Policy Choice, and the Survival of Leaders," *British Journal of Political Science* 32, no. 4 (October 2002): 559–590, 561, https://doi.org/10.1017/S0007123402000236.

61. Karl Hack, a leading scholar on the Malayan Emergency, has urged consideration of explanations for the effects of violence in its multiple forms. Karl Hack, "'Devils That Suck the Blood of the Malayan People': The Case for Post-revisionist Analysis of Counter-insurgency Violence," *War in History* 25, no. 2 (2018): 202–226, https://doi.org/10.1177/0968344516671738.

62. Goran Peic, "Civilian Defense Forces, State Capacity, and Government Victory in Counterinsurgency Wars," *Studies in Conflict and Terrorism* 37, no. 2 (2014): 162–184, https://doi.org/10.1080/1057610X.2014.862904; T. David Mason, *Caught in the Crossfire: Revolution, Repression, and the Rational Peasant* (Lanham, MD: Rowman and Littlefield, 2004); Staniland, "States, Insurgents."

63. See Robert A. Pape, *Bombing to Win: Air Power and Coercion in War* (Ithaca, NY: Cornell University Press, 1996), on capability and will.

64. See Andrew Bennett, "Process Tracing and Causal Inference," in *Rethinking Social Inquiry: Diverse Tools, Shared Standards,* ed. Henry E. Brady and David Collier (Lanham, MD: Rowman and Littlefield, 2010), 209, on identifying a new role for a variable. Western norms on human rights should lead representatives of a great power intervener to play down the role of force in their success. That they do not do so in contemporaneous documents indicates that they saw force playing a useful role.

65. Schelling, *Arms and Influence.*

66. Snyder and Diesing define accommodation as demands, offers, and concessions. *Conflict among Nations,* 195.

67. Thomas Carothers, "The 'Sequencing' Fallacy," *Journal of Democracy* 18, no. 1 (January 2007): 12–27.

68. Roland Paris, *At War's End: Building Peace after Civil Conflict* (New York: Cambridge University Press, 2004), 60.

69. Karl Hack distinguishes usefully between political concessions as more costly to the state and social provisions as less costly. Hack, "Malayan Emergency."

70. See, for example, Bruce Bueno de Mesquita and Alastair Smith, *The Dictator's Handbook: Why Bad Behavior Is Almost Always Good Politics* (New York: PublicAffairs, 2011).

71. See Shafer, *Deadly Paradigms*; and Macdonald, *Adventures in Chaos*.

72. Jacqueline L. Hazelton, "The 'Hearts and Minds' Fallacy: Violence, Coercion, and Success in Counterinsurgency Warfare," *International Security* 42, no. 1 (Summer 2017): 80–113, https://doi.org/10.1162/ISEC_a_00283.

73. See, for example, Sabine C. Carey and Neil J. Mitchell, "Progovernment Militias," *Annual Review of Political Science* 20 (May 2017): 127–147, https://doi.org/10.1146/annurev-polisci-051915-045433; and Staniland, "States, Insurgents."

74. Jason Lyall, "Are Coethnics More Effective Counterinsurgents? Evidence from the Second Chechen War," *American Political Science Review* 104, no. 1 (February 2010): 1–20, https://doi.org/10.1017/S0003055409990323.

75. U.S. Government Interagency Counterinsurgency Initiative, *U.S. Government Counterinsurgency Guide*, 4.

76. Bennett, "Process Tracing and Causal Inference." See also Nina Tannenwald, "Process Tracing and Security Studies," *Security Studies* 24, no. 2 (April–June 2015): 219–217, https://doi.org/10.1080/09636412.2015.1036614.

77. U.S. Government Interagency Counterinsurgency Initiative, *U.S. Government Counterinsurgency Guide*, 4.

78. My theory is also likely to apply to insurgencies that support themselves through natural resources or external support if the counterinsurgent is able to cut their access to the resources they need. See, for example, Weinstein, *Inside Rebellion*.

79. Meredith Reid Sarkees and Frank Wayman, *Resort to War: 1816–2007* (Washington, DC: CQ, 2010).

80. See, for example, Bueno de Mesquita and Smith, *Dictator's Handbook*, for an accessible discussion of elite incentives to behave selfishly.

81. See Stephen Van Evera, *Guide to Methods for Students of Political Science* (Ithaca, NY: Cornell University Press, 1997), 77, on case selection according to intrinsic importance. This criterion resembles what Aaron Rapport calls a countervailing condition: a variable whose presence or specific value decreases the probability that the outcome posited by the theory being tested will be evident. In this study, the low level of reforms and high level of force used against civilians in Malaya make it unlikely, according to the governance theory, that the counterinsurgency campaign would succeed—and yet it did. See Aaron Rapport, "Hard Thinking about Hard and Easy Cases in Security Studies," *Security Studies* 24, no. 3 (2015): 431–465, https://doi.org/10.1080/09636412.2015.1070615. See also Alexander George and Andrew Bennett, *Case Studies and Theory Development in the Social Sciences* (Cambridge, MA: MIT Press, 2005), 121–122.

82. Van Evera, *Guide to Methods*, 47. George and Bennett, *Case Studies and Theory Development*, describe the congruence method as beginning with a theory and assessing its ability to explain or predict outcomes in specific cases through the use of process tracing (181–204). Process tracing allows the author to identify the intervening steps, or causal chains, leading to the outcome of interest (207, 212). David Collier and James Mahoney note that "no-variance design" can play a useful role in generating new information and discovering novel explanations. Collier and Mahoney, "Research Note: Insights and Pitfalls: Selection Bias in Qualitative Research," *World Politics* 49, no. 1 (1996): 56–91, https://doi.org/10.1353/wp.1996.0023.

83. George and Bennett, *Case Studies and Theory Development*, 23.

84. George and Bennett, 86.

85. William A. Barnes, "Incomplete Democracy in Central America: Polarization and Voter Turnout in Nicaragua and El Salvador," *Journal of Interamerican Studies and World Affairs* 40, no. 3 (Fall 1998): 63–101, https://doi.org/10.2307/166200.

NOTES TO PAGES 25–31

86. Scholars who consider Dhofar a governance model success include Thomas R. Mockaitis, *British Counterinsurgency in the Post-imperial Era* (Manchester: Manchester University Press, 1995); Michael Dewar, *Brush Fire Wars: Minor Campaigns of the British Army since 1945* (London: Robert Hale, 1984); John Pimlott, "The British Army: The Dhofar Campaign, 1970–1975," in *Armed Forces and Modern Counterinsurgency*, ed. Ian F. W. Beckett and John Pimlott (New York: St. Martin's, 1985), 16–45; Geraint Hughes, "A 'Model Campaign' Reappraised: The Counterinsurgency War in Dhofar, Oman, 1965–1975," *Journal of Strategic Studies* 32, no. 2 (April 2009): 271–305, https://doi.org/10.1080/01402390902743357; Walter C. Ladwig III, "Supporting Allies in Counterinsurgency: Britain and the Dhofar Rebellion," *Small Wars and Insurgencies* 19, no. 1 (March 2008): 62–88, https://doi.org/10.1080/09592310801905793; and Calvin H. Allen Jr. and W. Lynn Rigsbee II, *Oman under Qaboos: From Coup to Constitution, 1970–1996* (2000; repr., London: Frank Cass, 2001). On El Salvador, for example, the lead author on the army's 2006 counterinsurgency manual, Conrad C. Crane, says that the authors found positive models for the United States in Iraq and beyond in Malaya, El Salvador, the Philippines-Huks, Colombia, and the Civil Operations and Revolutionary Development Support program in Vietnam. Crane, email message to author, September 29, 2010. Others include Steven Metz, *Learning from Iraq: Counterinsurgency in American Strategy* (Carlisle, PA: Strategic Studies Institute, January 2007); Paul, Clarke, and Grill, *Victory*; and Angel Rabasa et al., *Money in the Bank: Lessons Learned from Past Counterinsurgency Operations*, RAND Counterinsurgency Study, Paper 4 (Santa Monica, CA: RAND, 2007). On Malaya, see also Nagl, *Learning to Eat Soup*; David W. Barno, "Fighting the 'Other War': Counterinsurgency Strategy in Afghanistan, 2003–2005," *Military Review*, September–October 2007, 32–44; Daniel Marston and Carter Malkasian, eds., *Counterinsurgency in Modern Warfare* (New York: Oxford University Press, 2008); Thomas R. Mockaitis, *Resolving Insurgencies* (Carlisle, PA: U.S. Army War College Strategic Studies Institute, 2011); and Anthony James Joes, *Resisting Rebellion: The History and Politics of Counterinsurgency* (Lexington: University Press of Kentucky, 2004), 232.

87. See, for example, Andrew Mumford, *The Counter-insurgency Myth: The British Experience of Irregular Warfare* (London: Routledge, 2012).

88. Nigar Göksel, "A New Cycle Begins in Turkey-PKK Conflict," International Crisis Group, August 11, 2015, https://www.crisisgroup.org/europe-central-asia/western-europemediterranean/turkey/new-cycle-begins-turkey-pkk-conflict.

3. Not the Wars You're Looking For: Malaya, Greece, the Philippines

1. Robert Taber, *War of the Flea: The Classic Study of Guerrilla Warfare* (1965; Dulles, VA: Brassey's, 2002), 139; Robert W. Komer, *The Malayan Emergency in Retrospect: Organization of a Successful Counterinsurgency Effort* (Santa Monica, CA: RAND, 1972), 8.

2. Komer, *Malayan Emergency in Retrospect*, 7–8.

3. Director of operations, Malaya, Review of the Emergency Situation in Malaya at the End of 1954, January 10, 1955, DEFE 11/105, National Archives of the United Kingdom (TNA); Henry Gurney, high commissioner, to Creech Jones, secretary of state for the colonies, Federation of Malaya Despatch No. 3, from King's House, Kuala Lumpur, Malaya, January 12, 1950, MSS Brit. Emp. s. 332, box 57, folder 2, A. Creech Jones Official Papers IV Asia, Bodleian Libraries, Oxford University.

4. John Newsinger, *British Counterinsurgency: From Palestine to Northern Ireland* (London: Palgrave, 2002), 37.

5. Karl Hack, *Defence and Decolonisation in Southeast Asia: Britain, Malaya and Singapore 1941–68* (Richmond, UK: Curzon, 2001), 129.

6. Julian Paget, *Counter-insurgency Operations: Techniques of Guerrilla Warfare* (New York: Walker, 1967), 75.

7. GHQ Far East Land Forces to Ministry of Defence London, telegram, November 13, 1950, FO 371/84492, TNA.

8. Director of operations, Malaya, Review of the Emergency Situation in Malaya at the End of 1954, January 10, 1955, DEFE 11/105, TNA.

9. B. Simandjuntak, *Malayan Federalism, 1945–1963: A Study of Federal Problems in a Plural Society* (London: Oxford University Press, 1969), 238. There were tensions before the war over what it meant to be Malayan, but the ethnic Chinese were not, in this period or later, clamoring for citizenship and rights equal to those of ethnic Malays. See Ariffin Oman, *Bangsa Melayu: Malay Concepts of Democracy and Community, 1945–1950* (Kuala Lumpur: Oxford University Press, 1993), 17.

10. South East Asia Department of Colonial Office, Malaya Monthly Emergency and Political Report, September 15–October 15, 1954, SEA 111/161/01, No. 57, DEFE 11/142, TNA.

11. Federation of Malaya (Sir H. Gurney) to the secretary of state for the colonies, inward telegram, January 22, 1949, DEFE 11/32, TNA.

12. Katherine McGregor, "Cold War Scripts," *South East Asia Research* 24, no. 2 (2016): 242–260, 247–248, https://doi.org/10.1177/0967828X16649310.

13. Karl Hack, "Everyone Lived in Fear: Malaya and the British Way of Counterinsurgency," *Small Wars and Insurgencies* 23, nos. 4–5 (2012):, 671–699, https://doi.org/10.1080/09592318.2012.709764.

14. Jason Brownlee, *Authoritarianism in an Age of Democratization* (New York: Cambridge University Press, 2007), 57.

15. Literature on counterinsurgency often focuses on improving the bureaucratization of the state. I do not address this aspect of campaigns for two reasons. First, effective and efficient efforts are important to the success of any military or political enterprise. Second, this administrative focus ignores the political realities of the campaigns. See Colin Jackson, "Government in a Box? Counter-insurgency, State Building, and the Technocratic Conceit," in *The New Counterinsurgency Era in a Critical Perspective*, ed. Celeste Ward Gventer and M. L. R. Smith (New York: Palgrave, 2014), , 82–110.

16. See, for example, Paget, *Counter-insurgency Operations*, 73; and the dating at "Malayan Emergency," National Army Museum, accessed May 21, 2020, https://www.nam.ac.uk/explore/malayan-emergency.

17. U.S. Government Interagency Counterinsurgency Initiative, *U.S. Government Counterinsurgency Guide* (Washington, DC: U.S. Government Printing Office, 2009), 4.

18. Commissioner general Southeast Asia to secretary of state for the colonies, inward telegram, April 20, 1949, No. 117, DEFE 11/32, TNA.

19. Federation of Malaya (Sir H. Gurney) to the secretary of state for the colonies, inward telegram, September 18, 1948, DEFE 11/32, TNA.

20. Paper on the Security Situation in the Federation of Malaya, April 5, 1949, DEFE 11/32, TNA.

21. Meeting of Prime Ministers, "The Situation in Malaya," memorandum by the United Kingdom government, P.M.M. (48) 7, October 8, 1948, DEFE 11/32, TNA; "Situation in Malaya from 19.6.48 to 12.4.49," April 5, 1949, DEFE 11/32, TNA.

22. Federation of Malaya (Sir H. Gurney) to the secretary of state for the colonies, inward telegram, March 12, 1949, DEFE 11/32, TNA.

23. Federation of Malaya Combined Appreciation of the Emergency Situation by the High Commissioner and the Director of Operations, June 4, 1951, DEFE 11/45, TNA; For a similar report, see director of operations, Progress Report on the Emergency in Malaya, October 15, 1951, DEFE 11/46, TNA.

24. Leader Chin Peng dates the high point of the insurgency to 1949–1950. He describes British ground attacks breaking down insurgent formations and the hunger that broke down the smaller bands. See, for example, *Dialogues with Chin Peng: New Light on the Malayan Communist Party*, ed. C. C. Chin and Karl Hack (Singapore: Singapore University Press, 2004), 144–147. Karl Hack also dates the breaking of the insurgency to the 1950–1952 period based on population control and the uses of force and notes the British courting of local elites. See Hack, "The Malayan Emergency as Counterinsurgency Paradigm," *Journal of Strategic Studies* 32, no. 3 (June 2009): 383–414, https://doi.org/10.1080/01402390902928180. Hack, a historian, developed his argument during the same time period that I was developing mine. His is specific to the Emergency rather than a theory of counterinsurgency success. His research is invaluable for those interested in Malaya, insurgency, counterinsurgency, and the end of empire.

25. Danny Wong Tze Ken, "View from the Other Side: The Cold War in Malaysia from the Memoirs and Writings of Former MCP Members," in *Southeast Asia and the Cold War*, ed. Albert Lau (Abingdon, Oxford, UK: Routledge, 2012), 85–100, 91–94.

26. Federation of Malaya Combined Appreciation of the Emergency Situation by the High Commissioner and the Director of Operations, June 4, 1951, DEFE 11/45, TNA.

27. Director of operations, Malaya, Review of the Emergency Situation in Malaya at the End of 1954, January 10, 1955, DEFE 11/105, TNA.

28. Director of operations, Progress Report on the Emergency in Malaya, October 15, 1951, DEFE 11/46, TNA.

29. Secretary, Chiefs of Staff Committee, Report on Visit of Dr. Cockburn's Party to Malaya, December 10, 1952, DEFE 11/49, TNA.

30. Monthly Political Intelligence Report for Period Ending 20th November 1953, dated December 29, 1953, FCO 141/7377, TNA; director of operations, Progress Report on the Emergency in Malaya, October 15, 1951, DEFE 11/46, TNA, on two-thirds of incidents taking place in the states of Johore and Perak.

31. Operational Research Section (Malaya), Memorandum No. 6/53, Statistical Survey of Activities by Security Forces in Malaya from May 1952 to April 1953, dated July 10, 1953, WO 291/1731, TNA.

32. Director of operations, Malaya, Review of the Emergency Situation in Malaya at the End of 1954, January 10, 1955, DEFE 11/105, TNA.

33. R. H. Bower, Lt. Gen., director of operations, Malaya, Review of the Emergency in Malaya from June 1948 to August 1957, September 12, 1957, WO 106/5990, TNA. On population size, see Charles Hirschman, "Demographic Trends in Peninsular Malaysia, 1947–75," *Population and Development Review* 6 no. 1 (March 1980): 103–125.

34. Director of operations, Malaya, Review of the Emergency Situation in Malaya at the End of 1954, January 10, 1955, DEFE 11/105, TNA.

35. Monthly Political Intelligence Reports from the Secretary for Chinese Affairs, Secretary for Chinese Affairs Political Report April 1956, May 2, 1956, FCO 141/7378, TNA.

36. Cabinet Malaya Committee, "The Squatter Problem in the Federation of Malaya," memorandum by the secretary of state for the colonies, April 22, 1950, DEFE 11/35, TNA. Also see, for example, S. Foster Sutton, memorandum by the officer administering the government, Federation of Malaya, in connection with General Briggs's appreciation of the military and political situation in Malaya as on 25th October, 1950, November 7, 1950, FO 371/84492, TNA, on the need to add a Malay and a Chinese "to represent planting and other commercial interests." The author continued, "I consider it of prime importance that some leading local personalities should be associated with the decisions of the War Council. There is a tendency among Asians here to regard the Emergency as 'a white man's war.'" On associating "leading Asians" with the government, see commissioner-general, South East Asia, memorandum to the secretary of state for the colonies, November 24, 1950, FO 371/84492, TNA.

37. Paper on the Security Situation in the Federation of Malaya, April 5, 1949, DEFE 11/32, TNA. On parties, see, for example, Richard Stubbs, "The United Malays National Organization, the Malayan Chinese Association, and the Early Years of the Malayan Emergency, 1948–1955," *Journal of Southeast Asian Studies* 10, no. 1 (March 1979): 77–88.

38. Taman Budiman, *Memoirs of an Unorthodox Civil Servant* (Kuala Lumpur: Heinemann Educational Books, 1979), 107.

39. Karl von Vorys, *Democracy without Consensus: Communalism and Political Stability in Malaysia* (Princeton, NJ: Princeton University Press, 1975), 255–256.

40. Simandjuntak, *Malayan Federalism*, 68, 73–74.

41. S. Foster Sutton, memorandum by the officer administering the government, Federation of Malaya, in connection with General Briggs's appreciation of the military and political situation in Malaya as on 25th October, 1950, November 7, 1950, FO 371/84492, TNA.

42. Henry Gurney, high commissioner, to Creech Jones, secretary of state for the colonies, Federation of Malaya Despatch No. 3, from King's House, Kuala Lumpur, Malaya, January 12, 1950, MSS Brit. Emp. s. 332, box 57, file 2, A. Creech Jones Official Papers IV Asia, Bodleian Libraries, Oxford University.

43. Southeast Asia Department of the Colonial Office, Malaya Monthly Emergency and Political Report, September 15–October 15, 1954, DEFE 11/142, TNA.

44. Director of operations, Malaya, Review of the Emergency Situation in Malaya at the End of 1954, January 10, 1955, DEFE 11/105, TNA.

45. Commissioner-general, Southeast Asia, to secretary of state for the colonies, inward telegram no. 117, April 20, 1949, DEFE 11/32, TNA.

46. Director of operations, Malaya, progress report on the situation in Malaya, April 26, 1951, FCO 141/15533, TNA.

47. Soh Eng Lim, "Tan Cheng Lock: His Leadership of the Malayan Chinese," *Journal of Southeast Asian History* 1, no. 1 (March 1960): 29–55, https://doi.org/10.1017/S021778110000003X.

48. Henry Gurney, high commissioner, to Creech Jones, secretary of state for the colonies, Federation of Malaya Despatch No. 3, from King's House, Kuala Lumpur, Malaya, January 12, 1950, MSS Brit. Emp. s. 332, box 57, file 2, A. Creech Jones Official Papers IV Asia, Bodleian Libraries, Oxford University.

49. A .W. D. James, ag. secretary for Chinese affairs, secretary for Chinese affairs political report, February 1956, FCO 141/7378, TNA.

50. Lee Kam Hing, "A Neglected Story: Christian Missionaries, Chinese New Villages, and Communists in the Battle for the 'Hearts and Minds' in Malaya, 1948–1960," *Modern Asian Studies* 47, no. 6 (2013): 1977–2006, https://doi.org/10.1017/S0026749X12000741, 1981.

51. Southeast Asia Department, Agrarian Policy in Malaya, "The Fight against Communist Terrorism in Malaya," June 1951, FO 371/101271, TNA.

52. K. G. Tregonning, "Tan Cheng Lock: A Malayan Nationalist," *Journal of Southeast Asian Studies* 10, no. 1 (March 1979): 25–76, 62–63, https://doi.org/10.1017/S0022463400011838.

53. Tan Siew Sin quoted in Tregonning, 65.

54. Meeting of Prime Ministers, "The Situation in Malaya," memorandum by the United Kingdom government, P.M.M. (48) 7, October 8, 1948, DEFE 11/32, TNA.

55. For example, see MAL.C. (50), eighth meeting, Cabinet Malaya Committee, minutes of a meeting held in conference room E, Ministry of Defense, Great George Street, SW1, on Monday, July 17, 1950, at 2:30 p.m., DEFE 11/37, TNA.

56. Henry Gurney to secretary of state, for Higham, May 3, 1950, DEFE 11/36, TNA.

57. Cabinet Malaya Committee, MAL.C. (50) 5, April 22, 1950, DEFE 11/35, TNA.

58. Commissioner-general, South East Asia, to secretary of state for the colonies, telegram, November 24, 1950, FO 371/84492, TNA.

59. Federation of Malaya (Sir H. Gurney) to secretary of state for the colonies, telegraph, April 27, 1950, FO 371/84490, TNA.

60. Lee, "Neglected Story," 2003.

61. Lim, "Tan Cheng Lock."

62. R. P. Bingham, Monthly Political Intelligence Reports from the Resident Commissioner, Penang, Political Intelligence Report Settlement of Penang Period March 21 to April 20, 1956, n.d., FCO 141/7529, TNA.

63. For example, Monthly Political Intelligence Reports from the Resident Commissioner, Penang, Political Intelligence Report Settlement of Penang Period February 21 to March 20, 1956, FCO 141/7529, TNA.

64. R. P. Bingham, Monthly Political Intelligence Reports from the Resident Commissioner, Penang, Political Intelligence Report Settlement of Penang Period 21 April–20 May, 1954, May 31, 1954, FCO 141/7529, TNA.

65. R. P. Bingham, Monthly Political Intelligence Reports from the Resident Commissioner, Penang, Political Intelligence Report Settlement of Penang Period March 21 to April 20, 1956, n.d., FCO 141/7529, TNA. Also see, for example, Monthly Political Intelligence Reports from the Resident Commissioner, Penang, Political Intelligence Report Settlement of Penang Period February 21 to March 20, 1956, FCO 141/7529, TNA: "The Chinese do not like colonialism more than *merdeka* [independence] but they like *merdeka* [freedom] less than the present system if it means a change from British to Malay masters."

66. Newsinger, *British Counterinsurgency*, 47–48.

67. Komer, *Malayan Emergency in Retrospect*, vi.

68. Christopher Paul et al., *Paths to Victory: Detailed Insurgency Case Studies* (Santa Monica, CA: RAND, 2013), 55–56.

69. Earlier work does note this aspect of the campaign, to a greater or lesser degree. See, for example, Newsinger, *British Counterinsurgency*, 50, 56; and Charles Townsend, *Britain's Civil Wars: Counterinsurgency in the Twentieth Century* (London: Faber and Faber, 1986), 162. More recent work, as cited, often makes an argument for these efforts as counterproductive.

70. Huw Bennett, "'A Very Salutary Effect': The Counter-terror Strategy in the Early Malayan Emergency, June 1948 to December 1949," *Journal of Strategic Studies* 32, no. 3 (2009): 415–444, https://doi.org/10.1080/01402390902928248.

71. Karl Hack, "'Iron Claws on Malaya': The Historiography of the Malayan Emergency," *Journal of Southeast Asian Studies* 30, no. 1 (March 1999): 99–125, https://doi.org/10.1017/S0022463400008043; Bennett, "'Very Salutary Effect.'"

72. Advanced Air Headquarters Malaya, Reports on Operations in Malaya, RAF Operations in Malaya during 1950, February 9, 1951, AIR 23/8443, TNA.

73. Director of operations, Malaya, Review of the Emergency Situation in Malaya at the End of 1954, January 10, 1955, DEFE 11/105, TNA.

74. Brief by Director of Operations for His Excellency, the High Commissioner on the Employment of Overseas Commonwealth Forces in the Federation after Independence, cover note directed to High Commissioner Sir Donald MacGillivray, February 26, 1957, FCO 141/7506, TNA.

75. Advanced Air Headquarters Malaya, Reports on Operations in Malaya, RAF Operations in Malaya during 1950, February 9, 1951, AIR 23/8443, TNA, on the aim of killing bandits and the RAF role as artillery.

76. Inward telegram from O.A.G., September 18, 1948, DEFE 11/32, TNA, on poor insurgent communications; Meeting of Prime Ministers, "The Situation in Malaya," memorandum by the United Kingdom government P.M.M. (48) 7, October 8, 1948, DEFE 11/32, TNA, on offensive operations causing rising insurgent casualties, a declining number of attacks, movement in smaller groups, and a growing lack of money, ammunition, food, and medical supplies, all suggesting that a coordinated national offensive is improbable; Paper on the Security Situation in the Federation of Malaya, April 5, 1949, DEFE 11/32, TNA, says operations were seriously interfering with insurgent communications and making large coordinated actions very difficult, the number of insurgents was down from an estimated 3,000–5,000 in September 1948 to an estimated 1,200 in March 1949, insurgents were pulling back into the jungle to try to regroup, the decline in insurgent activity occurred in the month (December 1948) when security forces were reaching full strength and deployment, and "the initiative has largely passed to the security forces and . . . the bandits are in considerable difficulties." Federation of Malaya (Sir H. Gurney) to the secretary of state for the colonies, inward telegram, March 12, 1949, DEFE 11/32, TNA, reports that "recently captured documents from parts of Kedah, Perak, Johore and Negri Sembilan indicate low bandit morale," with the removal of squatters and arrest of "subscription collectors" denying insurgents funds and food. Federation of Malaya (Sir H. Gurney) to the secretary of state for the colonies, inward telegram, January 22, 1949, DEFE 11/32, TNA, reports that captured documents reveal insurgent concern over resettlement and national registration, which were restricting their movements. An Appreciation of the Military and Political Situation in Malaya as on 25th October, 1950, prepared by director of operations, Malaya, on behalf of federation government, for British Defense Coordinating Committee, as Requested, November 1, 1950, FO 371/84492, TNA, reports immediate improvement in safety in areas where resettlement is complete.

77. H. R. Briggs, director of operations, Malaya, Progress Report on Situation in Malaya, April 26, 1951, FCO 141/15533, TNA, reports insurgent casualties at a record high in March 1951 and resettlement (completed in Johore and virtually completed in other priority areas by May 1, 1951) seriously hampering insurgent efforts, with regrouping of labor for greater control under way. Director of operations, Defense of and Situation in Malaya from 1.9.51 to 21.12.51, Progress Report on the Emergency in Malaya, October 15, 1951, DEFE 11/46, TNA, notes the sharp rise in major incidents was checked by the end of 1950 and the insurgency was fighting hard to survive. Director of operations, Malaya, Progress Report on Situation in Malaya, February 15,

1951, FCO 141/15533, TNA, notes that where population concentration is complete, "the Communists themselves complain of their difficulties."

78. One Time Process from FARELF to War Office Recd 20 Sept. '54 Dtg. 18043oz Sept GO/2239 Sitrep No 334, Info Received Seven Days up to 16 Sept. 54, Subject to Confirmation, DEFE 11/142, TNA. Also see, for example, Defense of Malaya against an Increased Internal Threat, Ref: DOO/PERS/302, July 23, 1954, GHQ Far East Land Forces Singapore, Subject: Additional Parachute Troops, AIR 23/8556, TNA.

79. Operational Research Section (Malaya), Technical Note No. 4/55, Some Statistics of the Emergency in Malaya from January 1954 to June 1955, August 22, 1955, WO 291/1757, TNA.

80. Operational Research Section (Malaya), Memorandum No. 7/53, A Statistical Examination of Events in Relation to Security Force and Counterterrorist Activities in Malaya (Period September 1952 to July 1953), n.d., WO 291/1732, TNA.

81. Kedah Monthly Political Intelligence Report No. 10/53 for the Period 21st September to 20th October, 1953, October 20, 1953, DEFE 11/46, TNA.

82. Director of operations, Malaya, Review of the Emergency Situation in Malaya at the End of 1954, January 10, 1955, DEFE 11/105, TNA.

83. Schelling defines brute force as the ability to take what one wants through use of the military. Thomas Schelling, *Arms and Influence* (New Haven, CT: Yale University Press, 1966), 139–140.

84. Paul Dixon, "'Hearts and Minds'? British Counterinsurgency from Malaya to Iraq," *Journal of Strategic Studies* 32, no. 3 (2009): 353–381, https://doi.org/10.1080/01402390902928172; Hack, "Everyone Lived in Fear."

85. From Federation of Malaya (Sir H. Gurney), April 27, 1950, for Higham, FO 371/84490, TNA.

86. Lee, "Neglected Story," 1998.

87. For example, H. R. Briggs, director of operations, Malaya, Progress Report on Situation in Malaya, April 26, 1951, FCO 141/15533, TNA. Karl Hack closely examines detention, deportation, and resettlement patterns in "Detention, Deportation and Resettlement: British Counterinsurgency and Malaya's Ethnic Chinese 1948–1960," *Journal of Imperial and Commonwealth History* 43, no. 4 (2015): 611–640, https://doi.org/10.1080/03086534.2015.1083218.

88. Ministry of Defense, Malaya, to prime minister, Meeting with General Briggs, November 23, 1950, FCO 141/15533, TNA; Matters Which the Director of Operations, Federation of Malaya, Wishes to Raise in the Discussion with the Prime Minister, November 23, 1950, FO 371/84492, TNA.

89. Memorandum by the Secretary of State for the Colonies, April 29, 1950, DEFE 11/35, TNA.

90. Paget, *Counter-insurgency Operations*, 59; Komer, *Malayan Emergency in Retrospect*, 54–56; Newsinger, *British Counterinsurgency*, 54.

91. Komer, *Malayan Emergency in Retrospect*, v.

92. Paget, *Counter-insurgency Operations*, 64.

93. Newsinger, *British Counterinsurgency*, 56; Townsend, *Britain's Civil Wars*, 159–160.

94. Komer, *Malayan Emergency in Retrospect*, vi, 16.

95. Komer, 54–55, 65–66.

96. Paul et al., *Paths to Victory*, 60.

97. On planning for independence, see Simon C. Smith, *British Relations with the Malay Rulers from Decentralization to Malayan Independence, 1930–1957* (Kuala Lumpur: Oxford University Press, 1995), 42–43. On all three main communities' unhappiness with British plans for a liberal multiethnic democracy, see, for example, Von Vorys, *Democracy without Consensus*, 64–70.

98. J. D. Higham to J. D. Murray, Foreign Office, Southeast Asia Department, Agrarian Policy in Malaya, minute, January 14, 1952, FO 371/101271, TNA.

99. Director of operations, Malaya, Review of the Emergency Situation in Malaya at the End of 1954, January 10, 1955, DEFE 11/105, TNA.

100. T. Q. Gaffikin, "Lecture Notes by T.Q.G. Chief Police Officer Perak, for a Series of Regular Lectures on the Police Given to Newly Joined (Mostly European) Re-settlement Officers at Their Training School, Taiping [Perak] between 1951–1953," February 4, 1967, Fed. of Malaya Police Historical Nos. 1–5, MSS. Ind. Ocn. s. 97 (1–3), Bodleian Libraries, Oxford University.

101. Simon Smith, *British Relations*, 43.

102. Smith, 43.

103. GHQ Far East Land Forces to Ministry of Defence, London, For Chiefs of Staff from British Defense Coordination Committee Far East Re Progress Report 15 October 1951 (Briggs Report), top-secret telegram, November 15, 1951, DEFE 11/46, TNA.

104. Von Vorys, *Democracy without Consensus*, 92–93.

105. Monthly Political Intelligence Reports from the Mentri Besar, Trengganu, Trengganu Monthly Political Intelligence Report for the Period Ending June 20th, 1956, June 21, 1956, FCO 141/7379, TNA. Also see, for example, Monthly Political Intelligence Reports from Mentri Besar, Negu Sembilan, Monthly Political Intelligence Report for the Month of April, 1956, n.d., FCO 141/7319, TNA: "Malay reaction to *jus soli* for the Chinese community remains unchanged, that is to say firmly opposed to it."

106. Monthly Political Intelligence Reports from the Mentri Besar, Trengganu, Trengganu Monthly Political Intelligence Report for the Period Ending May 20th, 1956, May 22, 1956, Office of the Mentri Besar, Trengganu, FCO 141/7379, TNA.

107. Monthly Political Intelligence Reports from the Mentri Besar, Trengganu, Trengganu Monthly Political Intelligence Report for the Period Ending April 20th, 1956, April 23, 1956, Office of the Mentri Besar, Trengganu, FCO 141/7379, TNA.

108. Von Vorys, *Democracy without Consensus*, 89, citing K. J. Ratnam, *Communalism and the Political Process in Malaya* (Kuala Lumpur: University of Malaya Press, 1965), 84, 92–93.

109. A. J. Stockwell, "British Imperial Policy and Decolonization in Malaya, 1942–52," *Journal of Imperial and Commonwealth History* 13, no. 1 (1984): 68–87, https://doi.org/10.1080/03086538408582679. Stockwell identifies the British liberal concerns for Malaya's constitutional developments and its ultimate realization that it must curtail its goals for a noncommunal polity by continuing to recognize Malaya political domination.

110. Tregonning, "Tan Cheng Lock," 68.

111. Malaya Monthly Emergency and Political Report, September 15–October 15, 1954, DEFE 11/142, TNA.

112. Federation of Malaya (Sir H. Gurney) to the secretary of state for the colonies, inward telegram, April 27, 1950, DEFE 11/35, TNA.

113. Lee, "Neglected Story," 1995.

114. Director of operations, Malaya, review of the Emergency in Malaya from June 1948 to August 1957, September 1957, WO 106/5990, TNA.

115. Han Suyin, *My House Has Two Doors* (London: Granta, 1982), 79–80, 82, quoted in Hack, "Everyone Lived in Fear," 685–686.

116. *Straits Times*, Singapore, July 11, 1952, quoted in Hack, "Everyone Lived in Fear, 689."

117. D. Gray, ag. resident commissioner, Penang, Monthly Political Intelligence Reports from the Resident Commissioner, Penang, Political Intelligence Report for Period February 21, 1955–March 20, 1955, March 31, 1955, FCO 141/7529, TNA.

118. R. P. Bingham, Monthly Political Intelligence Reports from the Resident Commissioner, Penang, Political Intelligence Report Settlement of Penang Period 21 April–20 May, 1954, May 31, 1954, FCO 141/7529, TNA; D. Gray, Monthly Political Intelligence Reports from the Resident Commissioner, Penang, Polintel Report, Period November 21–December 20, 1954, December 31, 1954, FCO 141/7529, TNA; R. P. Bingham, resident commissioner, Penang, Monthly Political Intelligence Reports from the Resident Commissioner, Penang, Polintel Report, Period August 21–September 20, 1954, September 29, 1954, FCO 141/7529, TNA.

119. R. P. Bingham, resident commissioner, Penang, Monthly Political Intelligence Reports from the Resident Commissioner, Penang, Political Intelligence Report Settlement of Penang Period April 21 to May 20, 1956, May 30, 1956, FCO 141/7529, TNA.

120. GHQ Far East Land Forces to Ministry of Defence, London, For Chiefs of Staff from British Defense Coordination Committee Far East, Re Progress Report 15 October 1951 (Briggs Report), top-secret telegram, November 15, 1951, DEFE 11/46, TNA.

121. R. P. Bingham, Monthly Political Intelligence Reports from the Resident Commissioner, Penang, Political Intelligence Report Settlement of Penang Period November 21 to December 20, 1955, n.d., FCO 141/7529, TNA. On MCA efforts, see Southeast Asia Department, Agrarian

Policy in Malaya, "The Fight against Communist Terrorism in Malaya," June 1951, FO 371/101271, TNA.

122. Lee, "Neglected Story," 1981, 1991, 1982, 992, 1996.

123. D. Gray, ag. resident commissioner, Penang, Monthly Political Intelligence Reports from the Resident Commissioner, Penang, Political Intelligence Report Settlement of Penang, Period April 21, 1955 to May 20, 1955, May 30, 1955, FCO 141/7529, TNA.

124. Monthly Political Intelligence Reports from the Resident Commissioner, Penang, Political Intelligence Settlement of Penang Period September 21 to November 20, 1955, December 3, 1955, FCO 141/7529, TNA.

125. Monthly Political Intelligence Reports from Mentri Besar, Perak, Monthly Political Intelligence Report for Period Ending 20th October 1955, FCO 141/7377, TNA.

126. Paul et al., *Paths to Victory*, 62; Paget, *Counter-insurgency Operations*, 59, 77; Komer, *Malayan Emergency in Retrospect*, 85.

127. Chiefs of Staff Committee, Situation in Malaya, note by the secretary, May 1949, DEFE 11/33, TNA, notes the need to gain whole-hearted Chinese support. Also see Paper on the Security Situation in the Federation of Malaya, April 5, 1949, DEFE 11/32, TNA, noting the need for public opinion generally to swing against the Communists. Gen. Sir John Harding, Commander in Chief of Far East Land Forces, underlines in 1950 that "nothing could be done to alienate the sympathies of the population," in Memorandum, Visit to Singapore of the United States Joint Defense Survey Mission (Melby Mission), cover memo dated August 15, 1950, DEFE 11/38, TNA. Also, commissioner general, South East Asia, to secretary of state for the colonies, telegram, November 24, 1950, FO 371/84492, TNA, says, "It is fundamental to successful completion of Briggs Plan [*sic*] to have the support of an overwhelming majority of the people. But it is not sufficient if that support is passive or half hearted. It must be active and enthusiastic."

128. Director of operations, Progress Report on the Emergency in Malaya, October 15, 1951, DEFE 11/46, TNA.

129. Report on Visit of Dr. Cockburn's Party to Malaya by Secretary, Chiefs of Staff Committee, December 10, 1952, DEFE 11/49, TNA.

130. South East Asia Department of Colonial Office, Malaya Monthly Emergency and Political Report, September 15–October 15, 1954, 11/142, TNA.

131. One Time Process from FARELF to War Office Recd 18th Oct '54, DEFE 11/142, TNA. Also see, for example, South East Asia Department of Colonial Office, Malaya Monthly Emergency and Political Report, September 15–October 15, 1954, DEFE 11/142, TNA.

132. R. P. Bingham, Monthly Political Intelligence Reports from the Resident Commissioner, Penang, Political Intelligence Report Settlement of Penang Period 21 April–20 May, 1954, May 31, 1954, FCO 141/7529, TNA.

133. Director of operations, Malaya, Review of the Emergency Situation in Malaya at the End of 1954, January 10, 1955, DEFE 11/105.

134. High commissioner for the Federation of Malaya to secretary of state for the colonies, Monthly Intelligence Report for November 1956, n.d., FCO 141/7306, TNA.

135. Director of operations, Malaya, Progress Report on Situation in Malaya, February 15, 1951, FCO 141/15533, TNA.

136. Monthly Political Intelligence Reports from Mentri Besar, Perak, Monthly Political Intelligence Report for Period Ending 20th March, n.d., 1955, FCO 141/7377, TNA.

137. Monthly Political Intelligence Reports from the Mentri Besar, Pahan, n.d., cover note dated August 29, 1953, FCO 141/7315, TNA; Monthly Political Intelligence Reports from the Mentri Besar, Pahan, n.d., cover note dated November 4, 1953, FCO 141/7315, TNA; Monthly Political Intelligence Reports from the Mentri Besar, Pahan, Period 21st December 1953 to 20th January 1954, cover note dated January 2, 1954, FCO 141/7315, TNA; Monthly Political Intelligence Reports from the Mentri Besar, Pahan, Period 21st April to 20th May 1956, n.d., FCO 141/7315, TNA; Monthly Political Intelligence Report for Period 21st May 1956 to 20th June 1956, n.d., FCO 141/7315, TNA. Also see Monthly Political Intelligence Reports from the Mentri Besar, Kedah, Kedah Monthly Political Intelligence Report No. 4/54 for the Period 21st March to 20th April, 1954, May 3, 1954, FCO 141/7322, TNA; Monthly Political Intelligence Reports from the Mentri Besar, Kedah, Kedah Monthly Political Intelligence Report No. 3/54 for the Period

21st February to 20th March, 1954, April 3, 1954, FCO 141/7322, TNA; Monthly Political Intelligence Reports from the Mentri Besar, Kedah, Kedah Monthly Political Intelligence Report No. 2/54, dated March 6, 1954, FCO 141/7322, TNA.

138. Meeting of Prime Ministers, "The Situation in Malaya," memorandum by the United Kingdom government, P.M.M. (48) 7, October 8, 1948, DEFE 11/32, TNA.

139. Director of operations, Malaya, Review of the Emergency Situation in Malaya at the End of 1954, January 10, 1955, DEFE 11/105, TNA.

140. Ian Hurd defines legitimacy in domestic politics as "the normative belief by an actor that a rule or an institution ought to be obeyed." "Legitimacy and Authority in International Politics," *International Organization* 53, no. 2 (Spring 1999): 379–408, 381, https://doi.org/10.1162/002081899550913.

141. Executive Secretariat John Gange to the undersecretary of state, February 25, 1947, cover note accompanying report of the committee appointed to study immediate aid to Greece and Turkey, RG 59, box 7027, U.S. National Archives, College Park, MD (NARA II).

142. Frank Smothers, William Hardy McNeill, and Elizabeth Darbishire McNeill, *Report on the Greeks: Findings of a Twentieth Century Fund Team Which Surveyed Conditions in Greece in 1947* (New York: Twentieth Century Fund, 1948), 13, 20, 24–25, 207.

143. William Hardy McNeill, *The Greek Dilemma: War and Aftermath* (Philadelphia: J. B. Lippincott, 1947), 203.

144. Dean Acheson, memorandum for the secretary, February 21, 1947, RG 59, box 7027, NARA II.

145. William G. Livesay, MG USA, commanding, to the military attaché, Athens, Greece, Monthly Historical Report, United States Army Group American Mission to Greece, on Military Operations September 1947, memo, October 10, 1947, RG 334, box 146, NARA II.

146. William G. Livesay, MG USA, commanding, to Mr. Dwight Griswold, chief, AMAG, Monthly Historical Report, United States Army Group, American Mission to Greece, August 1947, memo, September 10, 1947, RG 334, box 146, NARA II.

147. C. M. Woodhouse, *The Struggle for Greece, 1941–1949* (London: Hart-Davis, MacGibbon, 1976), 211.

148. JUSMAPG Brief History, 1 January 1948 to 31 August 1949, n.d., RG 334, box 146, NARA II.

149. There is little scholarly disagreement on the timing of the insurgent failure. See, for example, Stathis Kalyvas, *The Logic of Violence in Civil War* (New York: Cambridge University Press, 2006), 266.

150. On harrying, see William G. Livesay, MG USA, commanding, to the military attaché, Athens, Greece, Subject: Monthly Historical Report, United States Army Group American Mission to Greece, on Military Operations September 1947, memo, October 10, 1947, RG 334, box 146, NARA II. Also see Monthly Historical Report, United States Army Group American Mission to Greece, March 1948, RG 334, box 147, NARA II.

151. Lincoln MacVeagh to secretary of state, July 28, 1947, RG 59, box 7031, NARA II.

152. On food shortages, see Raleigh A. Gibson, American consul general, Salonika, to secretary of state, Subject: Transmitting Memorandum of Conversation: Col. Frondistis, Intelligence Officer, C Army Corps, Regarding Conditions in Northern Greece, cover note dated August 14, 1947, memo dated August 8, 1947, RG 59, box 7031, NARA II. Also see JUSMAPG Operations Report No. 22, July 16, 1948, RG 334, box 154, NARA II.

153. JUSMAPG Report No. 21, Period 30 June–6 July 48 Inclusive, July 8, 1948, RG 334, Box 154, NARA II.

154. William G. Livesay, MG USA, commanding, to director, Plans and Operations Division, United States Army General Staff, Washington, DC, Subject: Monthly Historical Report, memo, November 6, 1947, RG 334, box 146, NARA II.

155. Rankin to secretary of state, Events since Mytel, no. 2155, December 16, Not Otherwise Reported, January 8, 1948, RG 59, box 7036, NARA II.

156. Monthly Historical Report, United States Army Group American Mission to Greece, May 1948, RG 334, box 147, NARA II.

157. Lawrence S. Wittner, *American Intervention in Greece, 1943–1949* (New York: Columbia University Press, 1982), 119–124.

158. Joint U.S. Military Advisory and Planning Group, Subject: Report on Military Conferences in "A" and "B" Corps Areas to: Director, JUSMAPG B Corps Conference, June 10, 1949, RG 334, box 51, NARA II.

159. Quoted in Smothers, McNeill, and McNeill, *Report on the Greeks*, 33.

160. Minutes of a conference held in the JUSMAPG conference room, 3 p.m., January 11, 1949, JUSMAPG, BMM, RAF DEL, RG 334, box 51, NARA II.

161. JUSMAPG Brief History, 1 January 1948 to 31 August 1949, n.d., RG 334, box 146, NARA II.

162. William G. Livesay, MG USA, commanding, to director, Plans and Operations Division, United States Army General Staff, Washington, DC, Subject: Monthly Historical Report, memo, November 6, 1947, RG 334, Box 146, NARA II.

163. Wittner, *American Intervention in Greece*, 253.

164. USAGG Monthly Historical Reports, August thru December 1947, n.d., RG 334, Entry 155, box 146, NARA II; JUSMAPG Brief History, 1 January 1948 to 31 August 1949, n.d., RG 334, box 146, NARA II.

165. USAGG Monthly Historical Reports, August thru December 1947, n.d., JUSMAPG History, 25 March 1949–30 June 1950, RG 334, box 146, NARA II.

166. David H. Close, "The Reconstruction of a Right-Wing State," in *The Greek Civil War, 1943–1950: Studies of Polarization*, ed. David H. Close (London: Routledge, 1993), 156–157.

167. Gibson Salonika to secretary of state, September 27 1947, RG 59, box 7033; William G. Livesay, MG USA, commanding, to the military attaché, Athens, Greece, Subject: Monthly Historical Report, memo, October 10, 1947, RG 334, box 146, NARA II. Events Otherwise Unreported October 13–28, 1947, n.d., RG 59, box 7034, NARA II, says the Greek government reports that more than three thousand insurgents had surrendered in the first month of the fall 1947 amnesty. Gibson Salonika to secretary of state, Transmitting Memorandum of Conversation with Major Verros, C Corps Intelligence Officer, Concerning Conditions in Northern Greece, October 16, 1947, RG 59, box 7033, NARA II.

168. Close, "Reconstruction," 158.

169. Close, 158–159, 160.

170. Close, 158.

171. David H. Close, "The Legacy," in Close, *Greek Civil War*, 214–234, 214.

172. Close, "Reconstruction," 165–166, 168, 170.

173. Wittner, *American Intervention in Greece*, 113, 152.

174. Jon V. Kofas, *Intervention and Underdevelopment: Greece during the Cold War* (University Park: Pennsylvania State University Press, 1989), 97.

175. Quoted in Wittner, *American Intervention in Greece*, 108.

176. John O. Iatrides, "The Doomed Revolution," in *Stopping the Killing: How Civil Wars End*, ed. Roy Licklider (New York: New York University Press, 1993), 205–235, 230.

177. Wittner, *American Intervention in Greece*, 129–131, 132–134.

178. David H. Close and Thanos Veremis, "The Military Struggle, 1945–1949," in Close, *Greek Civil War*, 97–128, 115–117.

179. Close and Veremis, 106; Iatrides, "Doomed Revolution," 211.

180. William G. Livesay, MG USA, commanding, to Mr. Dwight Griswold, chief, AMAG, Subject: Monthly Historical Report, United States Army Group, memo, September 10, 1947, RG 334, box 146, NARA II.

181. Meeting in office of minister of war, present: Minister of War Stratos, General Van Fleet, and Mr. Berry, memo, September 30, 1948, RG 334, box 51, NARA II.

182. William G. Livesay, MG USA, commanding, to Mr. Dwight Griswold, chief, AMAG, Subject: Monthly Historical Report, United States Army Group, memo, September 10, 1947, RG 334, box 146, NARA II.

183. JUSMAPG Brief History, 1 January 1948 to 31 August 1949, n.d., RG 334, box 146, NARA II.

184. To Baxter From Howard: Department of State Division of Near Eastern Affairs to NE—Mr. Baxter from DRN—Mr. Howard, Subject: Points for Consideration in Investigating and Evaluating the Leftist Opposition in Greece and the Border Situation, January 8, 1947, RG 59, box 7027, NARA II.

185. Much of the counterinsurgency literature also considers Yugoslavia's closing of its border with Greece to have dealt the National Popular Liberation Army its death blow. Work on Greece beyond the counterinsurgency literature, however, indicates that while the insurgency had rear areas in Yugoslavia, Bulgaria, and Albania, its most important base areas were in Albania and Bulgaria, which did not close their borders to the insurgents. For work emphasizing the importance of the closure of the Yugoslav border, see, for example, Paul et al., *Paths to Victory*: "While the Albanian border areas were still open to the DSE [Democratic Army of Greece], they were a poor alternative to the safe havens the group had previously enjoyed in Yugoslavia. . . . The role of safe havens is distinctive in this case, because the insurgents relied almost exclusively on external support they received from Greece's communist neighbors and lacked any significant sources of internal support. As a result, the insurgents were particularly vulnerable to the loss of Yugoslavia's support" (19, 21); and Cloyd Smith: "Although they still received limited support from Albania and Bulgaria, this support was insufficient for the Communist guerillas to continue against an increasingly powerful Greek military funded and equipped by the United States." Cloyd A. Smith Jr., "Greece and Oman: Successful Anglo/American Counterinsurgencies Viewed from Current American Counterinsurgency Doctrine" (MA thesis, U.S. Army Command and Staff College, 2009), 47. This argument is unconvincing because the insurgents relied more heavily on rear areas in Bulgaria and Albania than they did on Yugoslavia. The insurgents, Sir Reginald Leeper wrote in 1950, fought "with the help mainly of Bulgaria, always the most bitter foe of Greece." Reginald Leeper, *When Greek Meets Greek* (London: Chatto and Windus, 1950), xviii. In 1948, a top British official reported that government operations have not succeeded "largely owing to Albanian assistance" to the insurgents. The official continued, "The reports of the UNSCOB [United Nations Special Committee on the Balkans] confirm continuing aid from Albania, Bulgaria, and to a lesser degree Yugoslavia to the Markos rebels." Quoted in Elisabeth Barker, "Yugoslav Policy towards Greece 1947–1949," in *Studies in the History of the Greek Civil War, 1945–1949*, ed. Lars Baerentzen, John O. Iatrides, and Ole L. Smith (Copenhagen: Museum Tusculanum Press, 1987), 283. On the question of Stalin's and Tito's support for the National Popular Liberation Army, there is evidence of Tito's support, including use of Yugoslav territory, but not of Stalin's. The Soviet leader opposed the insurgency as having no prospect of success, predicting that the United States would never let the insurgents break Western lines of communication in the Mediterranean (Barker, "Yugoslav Policy," 273). Stalin saw the insurgency and Greece as peripheral to the interests of the USSR (266). Greek insurgent and Communist leader Nikos Zachariadis met with Stalin in 1946 and 1947, pressing for support in the form of everything from shoes to stationary, but Stalin appears to have strung him along, telling him to focus on political struggle rather than fighting, and providing no aid. Haris Vlavianos, *Greece, 1941–1949: From Resistance to Civil War: The Strategy of the Greek Communist Party* (New York: St. Martin's, 1992), 226, 240, 258. Also on Stalin's lack of support for the Greek insurgency, see Woodhouse, *Struggle for Greece*, 231. Amikam Nachmani, in *International Intervention in the Greek Civil War: The United Nations Special Committee on the Balkans, 1947–1952* (New York: Praeger, 1990), provides a comprehensive analysis of the UN committee's effort to determine the degree of external support to the insurgency.

186. Paul et al., *Paths to Victory*, 19–20.

187. Paul et al., 21.

188. Howard Jones, *A New Kind of War: America's Global Strategy and the Truman Doctrine in Greece* (New York: Oxford University Press, 1989), 4.

189. Paul et al., *Paths to Victory*, 19–20.

190. Smith, "Greece and Oman," 39, 48.

191. Frank J. Abbott, *The Greek Civil War, 1947–1949: Lessons for the Operational Artist in Foreign Internal Defense* (Fort Leavenworth, KS: U.S. Army School of Advanced Military Studies, 1994). For example, see 11, 19–20. Abbott does note mass arrests helping the campaign (30).

192. Woodhouse, *Struggle for Greece*, 215–216.

193. Angeliki E. Laiou, "Population Movements in the Greek Countryside during the Civil War," in Baerentzen, Iatrides, and Smith, *Studies in the History*, 63, 64, 69.

194. Keeley in Athens to secretary of state, April 10, 1947, RG 59, box 7029, NARA II.

195. Laiou, "Population Movements," 68, 85.

196. On withholding UN supplies and other foodstuffs from large areas "to isolate the Leftist bands," also see Smothers, McNeill, and McNeill, *Report on the Greeks*, 42.

197. Laiou, "Population Movements," 64.

198. Close and Veremis, "Military Struggle," 118.

199. Kofas, *Intervention and Underdevelopment*, 95.

200. Leeper, *When Greek Meets Greek*, 213.

201. Laiou, "Population Movements," 62.

202. Minutes of a conference held in the JUSMAPG conference room, 3 p.m., January 11, 1949, JUSMAPG, BMM, RAF DEL, RG 334, box 51, NARA II.

203. Dwight Griswold to secretary of state, October 27, 1947, RG 59, box 7034, NARA II.

204. Dwight Griswold to secretary of state, October 23, 1947, transmitting a copy of letter to the prime minister concerning the return of evacuees to their villages, RG 59, box 7034, NARA II.

205. Laiou, "Population Movements," 75, 78.

206. Smothers, McNeill, and McNeill, *Report on the Greeks*, 42.

207. Smothers, McNeill, and McNeill, 186.

208. On food controls, see Lincoln MacVeagh, Athens embassy, to secretary of state, Re: Political Exiles in Cyclades Islands, November 27, 1946, RG 59, box 7027, NARA II. On mass arrests, see Lincoln MacVeagh to secretary of state, July 10, 1947, RG 59, box 7030, NARA II. On mass deportations, see Lincoln MacVeagh to secretary of state, incoming telegram, March 7, 1947, RG 59, box 7027, NARA II. On families held hostage, see Howard to Baxter: Department of State Division of Near Eastern Affairs to NE—Mr. Baxter from DRN—Mr. Howard, Subject: Points for Consideration in Investigating and Evaluating the Leftist Opposition in Greece and the Border Situation, January 8, 1947, RG 59, box 7027, NARA II.

209. JUSMAPG Operations Report No. 3, February 26, 1948, RG 334, box 147, NARA II.

210. Headquarters U.S. Army Group, Greece, JUSMAPG Operations Report No. 24, July 30, 1948, RG 334, box 154, NARA II; JUSMAPG Operations Report No. 23, July 23, 1948, RG 334, box 154, NARA II.

211. Woodhouse, *Struggle for Greece*, 209.

212. Bickham Sweet-Escott, *Greece: A Political and Economic Survey, 1939–1953* (London: Royal Institute of International Affairs, 1954), 73.

213. Wittner, *American Intervention in Greece*, 145–148.

214. William G. Livesay, MG USA, commanding, to the military attaché, Athens, Greece, Subject: Monthly Historical Report, memo, January 13, 1948, RG 334, box 146, NARA II.

215. Lincoln MacVeagh to secretary of state, July 24, 1947, RG 59, box 7031, NARA II.

216. William G. Livesay, MG USA, commanding, to Mr. Dwight Griswold, chief, AMAG, Subject: Monthly Historical Report, memo, September 10, 1947, RG 334, box 146, NARA II.

217. Smothers, McNeill, and McNeill, *Report on the Greeks*, 32.

218. Lincoln MacVeagh, Athens embassy, to secretary of state, Re: Political Exiles in Cyclades Islands, November 27, 1946, RG 59, Box 7027, NARA II.

219. Quoted in Close, "Reconstruction," 174.

220. Dwight Griswold, Athens, to secretary of state, November 13, 1947, RG 59, box 7034, NARA II.

221. Laiou, "Population Movements," 83.

222. Spyridon Plakoudas, "Population Transfers in Counterinsurgency: A Recipe for Success?," *Small Wars and Insurgencies* 27 no. 4 (2016): 681–701, 686, 688, https://doi.org/10.1080/09592318.2016.1189542. This author argues that population control was necessary in this case to defeat the insurgency but can alienate the population and should be "approached with caution" (695).

223. See, for example, Konstantina E. Botsiou, "New Policies, Old Politics: American Concepts of Reform in Marshall Plan Greece," *Journal of Modern Greek Studies* 27 (2009): 209–240, https://doi.org/10.1353/mgs.0.0063; and Stelios Zachariou, "Implementing the Marshall Plan

in Greece: Balancing Reconstruction and Geopolitical Security," *Journal of Modern Greek Studies* 27 (2009): 303–318, https://doi.org/10.1353/mgs.0.0072.

224. Joseph Marion Jones, *The Fifteen Weeks (February 21–June 5, 1947)* (New York: Harcourt, Brace, and World, 1955), 77.

225. Quoted in Jones, 156.

226. For those who argue that liberalization and development should prevent insurgency, a leading analysis of conditions in post–World War II Greece notes that before the war, "a spirit of reform and modernization took hold of the country. Greece experienced more basic reform under the Venizelos republic than at any other time in its modern history. A new and ultraliberal constitution was adopted in 1927; roads were built; extensive improvements in water control, drainage and irrigation were undertaken; the large estates were nearly all broken up and the land redistributed among the peasants." Smothers, McNeill, and McNeill, *Report on the Greeks*, 17.

227. Smothers, McNeill, and McNeill, *Report on the Greeks*, describes the Greek government as "notoriously weak and inefficient in administration. Its machinery included an overloaded bureaucracy, of poor morale and shot through with corruption. A large degree of the corruption arose from the fact that civil servants received salaries so miserable that for some men the temptation to accept bribes was irresistible" (33–34).

228. Report of the Committee Appointed to Study Immediate Aid to Greece and Turkey, cover note from Executive Secretariat John Gange to the undersecretary, February 25, 1947, RG 59, box 7027, NARA II.

229. George Marshall to Lincoln MacVeagh, May 13, 1947, RG 59, box 7029, NARA II.

230. George Marshall to Lincoln MacVeagh for prime minister of Greece, May 28, 1947, RG 59, box 7029, NARA II.

231. George Marshall to Dwight Griswold and embassy, outgoing telegram, January 8, 1948, RG 59, box 7036, NARA II

232. Henderson, Near East Affairs, Instruction from the Secretary to Mr. Griswold Containing Certain Suggestions Relating to the Conduct of Mr. Griswold's Mission, cover letter, July 10, 1947, RG 59, box 7030, NARA II.

233. Keith Legg, "Musical Chairs in Athens: Analyzing Political Instability 1946–1952," in Baerentzen, Iatrides, and Smith, *Studies in the History*, 21.

234. George Marshall to Athens embassy, July 3, 1947, RG 59, box 7030, NARA II; George Marshall to Athens embassy, March 9, 1948, RG 59, box 7038, NARA II.

235. Dean Acheson, Department of State, to Athens embassy, outgoing telegram, October 10, 1946, RG 59, box 7027, NARA II.

236. Lincoln MacVeagh to secretary of state, incoming telegram, March 7, 1947, RG 59, box 7027, NARA II. Other concerns about upholding democracy also referenced the need for the United States to be seen as supporting a democratic rather than a reactionary government. See, for example, Keeley in Athens to secretary of state, April 10, 1947, RG 59, box 7029, NARA II, where Keeley wrote that security agencies and rightists are defeating their own purposes. There is a "need for strict observance in act as well as word of democratic safeguards in course of suppressing communist threat to constituted authority. . . . Right wing excesses might vitiate entire U.S. program and eventually place us in position of supporting reaction as critics now contend." Also see Dean Acheson to Athens embassy, outgoing telegram, April 11, 1947, RG 59, box 7029, NARA II; and Keeley in Athens to secretary of state, April 14, 1947, RG 59, box 7029, NARA II.

237. Division of Near Eastern Affairs, Department of State, memorandum regarding Greece, October 21, 1946, RG 59, box 7027, NARA II.

238. Dwight Griswold to secretary of state, April 8, 1948, RG 59, box 7040, NARA II.

239. Quoted in Wittner, *American Intervention in Greece*, 175.

240. Quoted in Wittner, 116.

241. Quoted in Wittner, 116–117.

242. Wittner, 155–160.

243. Wittner, 249.

244. Yiannis P. Roubatis, *Tangled Webs: The U.S. in Greece, 1947–1967* (New York: Pella, 1987), 66, 30.

245. Christos Hadziiossif, "Economic Stabilization and Political Unrest: Greece 1944–1947," in Baerentzen, Iatrides, and Smith, *Studies in the History*, 25.

246. Vlavianos, *Greece*, 5.

247. See, for example, deputy chief, American Mission, to George C. Mcghee, coordinator for aid to Greece and Turkey, Department of State, February 9, 1948, RG 59, box 7037, NARA II.

248. Smothers, McNeill, and McNeill, *Report on the Greeks*, 74, 75.

249. Keeley in Athens to secretary of state, April 10, 1947, RG 59, box 7029, NARA II.

250. Gibson Salonika to secretary of state, Transmitting Memorandum of Conversation with Major Verros, C Corps Intelligence Officer, Concerning Conditions in Northern Greece, October 16, 1947, RG 59, box 7033, NARA II; Dwight Griswold to secretary of state, transmitting a copy of letter to the prime minister concerning the return of evacuees to their villages, October 23, 1947, RG 59, box 7034, NARA II; Raleigh A. Gibson, American consul general, Salonika, to secretary of state, August 4, 1947, RG 59, box 7031, NARA II; meeting in office of minister of war, present: Minister of War Stratos, General Van Fleet, and Mr. Berry, September 30, 1948, RG 334, box 51, NARA II.

251. Lincoln MacVeagh to secretary of state, July 24, 1947, RG 59, box 7031, NARA II.

252. Smothers, McNeill, and McNeill, *Report on the Greeks*, 44.

253. The insurgency took the name of the Hukbong Mapagpalaya Ng Bayan, or People's Liberation Army, a peasant organization from the 1920s that fought the Japanese during the occupation and became the nucleus of the insurgency. Its name changed several times over the years from Japanese occupation to counterinsurgency success. See Bernard J. Kerkvliet, *The Huk Rebellion: A Study of Peasant Revolt in the Philippines* (Berkeley: University of California Press, 1977), xv–xvi, 157. The Huk sang the national anthem at the beginning of meetings, underlining their belief in the government rather than in revolution. See William J. Pomeroy, *The Forest: A Personal Record of the Huk Guerrilla Struggle in the Philippines* (New York: International, 1963), 17.

254. Kerkvliet provides an excellent, extensive discussion of the breakdown in landlord-tenant relations in *Huk Rebellion*.

255. Douglas S. Blaufarb, *The Counterinsurgency Era* (New York: Free Press, 1977), 24.

256. Kerkvliet, *Huk Rebellion*, 164, 171–172, 249–260, 159–160; D. Michael Shafer, *Deadly Paradigms: The Failure of U.S. Counterinsurgency Policy* (Princeton, NJ: Princeton University Press, 1988), 211.

257. Shafer, *Deadly Paradigms*, 219.

258. Shafer, 212–213.

259. Kerkvliet, *Huk Rebellion*, traces the personal and ideological relationships in great detail.

260. Shafer, *Deadly Paradigms*, 211. During the Japanese occupation, the elite had allied with the Japanese and the peasants had resisted, but after the war the United States left the collaborators in power despite popular opposition. The elite sought U.S. support against the restless peasantry, which it called Communists. The United States paid, armed, and supplied security forces in Central Luzon and backed collaborator Roxas for the presidency, choices that alienated the Huk from their own government and from the United States. Roxas pardoned all collaborators while ignoring the role of the anti-Japanese resistance, further angering the Huk. See Shafer, 209–212.

261. Shafer, 208; Lawrence M. Greenberg, *The Hukbalahap Insurrection: A Case Study of a Successful Anti-insurgency Operation in the Philippines, 1946–1955* (Washington, DC: U.S. Army Center of Military History, 1987), http://purl.access.gpo.gov/GPO/LPS32792.

262. Kerkvliet, *Huk Rebellion*, 164, 177, 168, 171–172.

263. JCS to SecDef, in Shafer, *Deadly Paradigms*, 220.

264. Andrew J. Birtle, *U.S. Army Counterinsurgency and Contingency Operations Doctrine, 1942–1976* (Washington, DC: Center for Military History, 1998), 58, 328, 58–59.

265. Birtle, 58.

266. Greenberg, *Hukbalahap Insurrection*, 138–140.

267. Luis Taruc, *He Who Rides the Tiger: The Story of an Asian Guerrilla Leader* (New York: Praeger, 1967), 67.

268. Douglas J. Macdonald, *Adventures in Chaos: American Intervention for Reform in the Third World* (Cambridge, MA: Harvard University Press, 1992), 153.

269. Birtle, *U.S. Army Counterinsurgency*, 58.

270. Greenberg, *Hukbalahap Insurrection*, 115–116.

271. Pomeroy, *Forest*, 89–91.

272. Kerkvliet, *Huk Rebellion*, 208–210.

273. Birtle, *U.S. Army Counterinsurgency*, 66.

274. Pomeroy, *Forest*, 161, 169.

275. Pomeroy, 156–157.

276. Kerkvliet, *Huk Rebellion*, 246.

277. Pomeroy, *Forest*, 168.

278. Taruc, *He Who Rides the Tiger*, 158.

279. Pomeroy, *Forest*, 131, 156–157, 168.

280. Greenberg, *Hukbalahap Insurrection*, 134, 130. However, U.S. advisers were still complaining about lack of training and aggressiveness and terrorization of the populace. See Birtle, *U.S. Army Counterinsurgency*, 65.

281. Greenberg, *Hukbalahap Insurrection*, 133–137.

282. Memorandum by the Under Secretary of State (Smith) to the Executive Secretary of the National Security Council (Lay), July 16, 1953, Third Progress Report on NSC 84/2, The Position of the United States with Respect to the Philippines, No. 335 S/P-NSC files, lot 61 D 167, NSC 84 Series, in United States Department of State, *Foreign Relations of the United States, 1952–1954, East Asia and the Pacific (in Two Parts)* (Washington, DC: U.S. Government Printing Office, 1952–1954), vol. 12, pt. 2, 542, http://digital.library.wisc.edu/1711.dl/FRUS.FRUS195254v12p2.

283. Memorandum of Conversation, by the Chief of the Division of Philippine Affairs (Ely), Subject: Matters Taken Up on the Occasion of President Quirino's Call on President Truman on August 9, 1949, 896.00/8-949, August 9, 1949, in United States Department of State, *Foreign Relations of the United States, 1949: The Far East and Australasia (in Two Parts)* (Washington, DC: U.S. Government Printing Office, 1975), vol. 7, pt. 1, 598, http://digital.library.wisc.edu/1711.dl/FRUS.FRUS1949v07p1.

284. J. H. Burns, office of the secretary of defense, to Dean Rusk, assistant secretary of state, June 13, 1950, RG 59, box 4323, NARA II.

285. R. J. Marshall to Dean Rusk, assistant secretary of state, on the reestablishment and maintenance of peace and order in the Philippines, memo, September 7, 1950, RG 59, box 4315, NARA II.

286. National Security Council Staff Study, "The Position of the United States with Respect to the Philippines," NSC 84/2, November 9, 1950, in United States Department of State, *Foreign Relations of the United States, 1950: East Asia and the Pacific* (Washington, DC: U.S. Government Printing Office, 1950), 6:1517, http://digital.library.wisc.edu/1711.dl/FRUS.FRUS1950v06.

287. Shafer, *Deadly Paradigms*, 231.

288. Ambassador in the Philippines (Spruance) to the Department of State, Manila, telegram, March 6, 1953, No. 329, 796.00/653, in United States Department of State, *Foreign Relations of the United States, 1952–1954*, vol. 12, pt. 2, 530.

289. Ambassador in the Philippines (Spruance) to the Department of State, telegram, November 24, 1953, No. 345, 796.00/11-2453, in United States Department of State, *Foreign Relations of the United States, 1952–1954*, vol. 12, pt. 2, 565–566.

290. Memorandum Prepared by the Department of State for the National Security Council Planning Board, Current Situation in the Philippines, No. 351, January 14, 1954, S/P-NSC files, lot 61 D 167, NSC 84 Series, in United States Department of State, *Foreign Relations of the United States, 1952–1954*, vol. 12, pt. 2, 577.

291. Kerkvliet, *Huk Rebellion*, mentions, among other things, gestures toward agrarian reform (198–199); the government-violated amnesty of 1948 and the lack of political control over military behavior (200–201); and the few new agrarian courts, government-paid lawyers to help tenants, government-sponsored credit facilities, and promises to reduce sharecropper rents (240). A recent assessment credits Edward Lansdale, Magsaysay's CIA/U.S. Air Force adviser, with much of Magsaysay's success. See Max Boot, *The Road Not Taken: Edward Lansdale and the American Tragedy in Vietnam* (New York: Norton, 2018). Crediting Lansdale denies Magsaysay credit for his own agency and political acumen.

292. Macdonald, *Adventures in Chaos*, 180, 132.
293. Macdonald, 183; Shafer, *Deadly Paradigms*, 234–236.
294. Macdonald, *Adventures in Chaos*, 180.
295. Like Napolean D. Valeriano and Charles T. R. Bohannan, *Counter-guerrilla Operations: The Philippine Experience* (1962; Westport, CT: Praeger Security International, 2006), Kerkvliet finds the symbolism of the changes more significant than their extent or degree of implementation. The goal was co-optation of the Huk slogan, "Land for the Landless." Kerkvliet, *Huk Rebellion*, 239–240.
296. Macdonald, *Adventures in Chaos*, 146; Shafer, *Deadly Paradigms*, 237.
297. Taruc, *He Who Rides the Tiger*, 97.
298. Birtle, *U.S. Army Counterinsurgency*, 53–65.
299. Shafer, *Deadly Paradigms*, 236; Kerkvliet, *Huk Rebellion*, 241.
300. Birtle, *U.S. Army Counterinsurgency*, 62–63.
301. Macdonald, *Adventures in Chaos*, 148.
302. Greenberg, *Hukbalahap Insurrection*, 120–121, 115–116.
303. Valeriano and Bohannan, *Counter-guerrilla Operations*, 22.
304. Kerkvliet, *Huk Rebellion*, 160, 189–190.
305. Shafer, *Deadly Paradigms*, 207.
306. Kerkvliet, *Huk Rebellion*, 158–159, 160.
307. Birtle, *U.S. Army Counterinsurgency*, 56.
308. Greenberg, *Hukbalahap Insurrection*, 76–77, 73–74.
309. Birtle, *U.S. Army Counterinsurgency*, 56; Greenberg, *Hukbalahap Insurrection*, 76–77.
310. Greenberg, *Hukbalahap Insurrection*, 76–77, 69.
311. Luis Taruc, *Born of the People* (Bombay: People's Publishing House, 1953), 216–219.
312. Valeriano and Bohannan, *Counter-guerrilla Operations*, 155, 165.
313. Taber, *War of the Flea*, 137.
314. Kerkvliet, *Huk Rebellion*, 240–241, 189.
315. Birtle, *U.S. Army Counterinsurgency*, 66.
316. Ambassador Myron Cowan to Department of State, Subject: Peace and Order—the Philippines Armed Forces and the Hukbong Mapagpalaya Ng Bayan (HMB), July 7, 1950, RG 59, box 4315, NARA II.
317. Taruc, *He Who Rides the Tiger*, 121.
318. Birtle, *U.S. Army Counterinsurgency*, 57.
319. Birtle, 57; Greenberg, *Hukbalahap Insurrection*, 68–69; Kerkvliet, *Huk Rebellion*, 189–196.
320. Greenberg, *Hukbalahap Insurrection*, 75–76.
321. Valeriano and Bohannan, *Counter-guerrilla Operations*, 107, 155.
322. Greenberg, *Hukbalahap Insurrection*, 75–76; Birtle, *U.S. Army Counterinsurgency*, 57.
323. Valeriano and Bohannan, *Counter-guerrilla Operations*, 79.
324. Kerkvliet, *Huk Rebellion*, 160.
325. Birtle, *U.S. Army Counterinsurgency*, 66; Pomeroy, *Forest*, 166–169, 210.
326. Greenberg, *Hukbalahap Insurrection*, 133.
327. Kerkvliet, *Huk Rebellion*, 189–196.
328. Greenberg, *Hukbalahap Insurrection*, 133.
329. Greenberg, 55–56, 76–77, 115–116.
330. Macdonald, *Adventures in Chaos*, 153.
331. Greenberg, *Hukbalahap Insurrection*, 130–131, 118.
332. Blaufarb, *Counterinsurgency Era*, 28; Birtle, *U.S. Army Counterinsurgency*, 61.
333. Macdonald, *Adventures in Chaos*, 146.
334. Greenberg, *Hukbalahap Insurrection*, 112.
335. Kerkvliet, *Huk Rebellion*, 240–242.
336. Macdonald, *Adventures in Chaos*, 153.
337. Birtle, *U.S. Army Counterinsurgency*, 65; Macdonald, *Adventures in Chaos*, 151.
338. Greenberg, *Hukbalahap Insurrection*, 129–130.
339. Macdonald, *Adventures in Chaos*, 149; Shafer, *Deadly Paradigms*, 232.
340. Birtle, *U.S. Army Counterinsurgency*, 64.

341. Greenberg, *Hukbalahap Insurrection*, 122–123, 125.

342. Greenberg, 122–123, 113–114.

343. Greenburg, 119–121.

344. Pomeroy, *Forest*, 160.

345. Greenberg, *Hukbalahap Insurrection*, 118–119.

346. Greenberg, 70–72.

347. Pomeroy, *Forest*, 206, 210.

348. The lead author on the army's counterinsurgency manual identifies the Huk campaign under Ramon Magsaysay as one of the key positive examples of successful counterinsurgency identified by the authors. Conrad Crane, email message to author, October 19, 2010. A typical example of the usual emphasis on the primacy of political reforms in the Huk case: Magsaysay "forced the government to reform land management, created civic action improvement programs, and encouraged popular participation in government. By addressing the peasants' needs and offering a better future than that promised by the Huk, he undercut the popular support the insurgents required." Robert J. Molinari, "Carrots and Sticks: Lessons for COCOMS Who Must Leverage National Power in Counterinsurgency Warfare" (paper, U.S. Naval War College, 2004). James S. Corum and Wray R. Johnson note that the campaign is widely described as "a model counterinsurgency effort" based on socioeconomic reforms, including taking civic action, befriending the peasants, reducing corruption, and enacting "systemic reform." Corum and Johnson, *Airpower in Small Wars: Fighting Insurgents and Terrorists* (Lawrence: University Press of Kansas, 2003), 120–122, 138. Robert Taber, in *War of the Flea*, emphasizes the transformational role of reforms in marginalizing the insurgency (137–139). Also see Wray R. Johnson and Paul J. Dimech, "Foreign Internal Defense and the Hukbalahap: A Model Counterinsurgency," *Small Wars and Insurgencies* 4, no. 3 (1993): 29–52, https://doi.org/10.1080/095923 19308423036. There is praise for reforms in Kalev Sepp, "Resettlement, Regroupment, Reconcentration: Deliberate Government-Directed Population Relocations in Support of Counterinsurgency Operations" (MA thesis, U.S. Army Command and General Staff College, Fort Leavenworth, KS, 1992).

349. Boot, *Road Not Taken*.

350. Greenberg, *Hukbalahap Insurrection*, 146.

351. Taber, *War of the Flea*, 137.

352. Valeriano and Bohannan, *Counter-guerrilla Operations*, 174.

353. Greenberg, *Hukbalahap Insurrection*, 2.

354. Kerkvliet, *Huk Rebellion*, 240.

355. Taruc, *Born of the People*, 235.

356. Shafer, *Deadly Paradigms*, 220, 227, 220–221, 230.

357. Magsaysay was appointed because of pressure from the United States, and its recognition of increasing intraelite competition as an opportunity worth seizing. Magsaysay was an honest politician from a modest background who was popular within the ruling Liberal Party (Macdonald, *Adventures in Chaos*, 140–144), and he provided a way for the United States to pressure and then remove President Quirino, whom the United States considered intransigent on reforms. Ambassador Myron Cowan described Quirino as "incompetent, vain, stubborn, and unwilling to listen to his close advisors." Macdonald, 139.

358. Draft Paper Prepared in the Department of State for Consideration by National Security Council Staff, "The Situation in the Philippines," June 20, 1950, Executive Secretariat Files: Lot 61D167: File NSC 84 Series, in United States Department of State, *Foreign Relations of the United States, 1950*, 6:1463.

359. Draft Memorandum by the Secretary of State to the President, Washington, Subject: Recent Developments in the Philippine Situation, April 20, 1950, 896.00/4-1450, in United States Department of State, *Foreign Relations of the United States, 1950*, 6:1442.

360. Memorandum of Agreement, Between the Administrator of the Economic Cooperation Administration (Foster) and the President of the Philippine Republic, 896.00/11-1750, November 14, 1950, in United States Department of State, *Foreign Relations of the United States, 1950*, 6:1522.

361. Memorandum by the Under Secretary of State (Smith) to the Executive Secretary of the National Security Council (Lay), Third Progress Report on NSC 84/2, "The Position of the United States with Respect to the Philippines," July 16, 1953, No. 335 S/P-NSC files, lot 61 D 167, NSC 84 Series, in United States Department of State, *Foreign Relations of the United States, 1952–1954*, vol. 12, pt. 2, 544.

362. Draft Memorandum by the Secretary of State to the President, Washington, Subject: Recent Developments in the Philippine Situation, April 20, 1950, 896.00/4-1450, in United States Department of State, *Foreign Relations of the United States, 1950*, 6:1442.

363. Chargé in the Philippines (Chapin) to the secretary of state, Manila, April 7, 1950, No. 432, 796.5 MAP/4-750, despatch, in United States Department of State, *Foreign Relations of the United States, 1950*, 6:1435. This report does not support assertions that changes made to the constabulary constituted reforms or that they gained popular support.

364. Chargé in the Philippines (Chapin) to the secretary of state, Manila, 1436.

365. Birtle, *U.S. Army Counterinsurgency*, 63–65.

366. Programs such as land redistribution and vocational training were not intended "to make a significant contribution to the economic or social welfare of the country," according to Napolean Valeriano, a Philippine army officer and death squad leader, and U.S. Army officer Charles Bohannan. "They helped a few people, perhaps all told a thousand families were benefitted directly by their assistance. . . . Their real value—and it was tremendous—was as dramatic proof of the intentions and desires of the government, proof that lent itself to publicity, to propaganda." Valeriano and Bohannan, *Counter-guerrilla Operations*, 180.

367. Birtle, *U.S. Army Counterinsurgency*, 63–64; Shafer, *Deadly Paradigms*, 236.

368. Macdonald, *Adventures in Chaos*, 156–157.

369. Birtle, *U.S. Army Counterinsurgency*, 63–64.

370. Shafer, *Deadly Paradigms*, 236.

371. Macdonald, *Adventures in Chaos*, 157.

372. Macdonald, 168–179.

373. Macdonald, 138.

374. Shafer, *Deadly Paradigms*, 222, 224.

375. Quoted in Valeriano and Bohannan, *Counter-guerrilla Operations*, 86.

376. Ramon Magsaysay, First State of the Nation Address, January 25, 1954, https://www.officialgazette.gov.ph/1954/01/25/ramon-magsaysay-first-state-of-the-nation-address-january-25-1954/. It is noteworthy that it was charities providing clean water to communities, not the government, underlining the degree to which reforms remained unimplemented.

377. Quoted in Shafer, *Deadly Paradigms*, 227.

378. Bureau of Far Eastern Affairs analyst Carlton Ogburn to Dean Rusk, assistant secretary of state for Far Eastern affairs, January 15, 1951, quoted in Shafer, *Deadly Paradigms*, 225–226.

379. Macdonald, *Adventures in Chaos*, 147.

380. Dean Acheson to George Marshall, secretary of defense, [stamped] January 18, 1951, RG 59, box 4324, NARA II.

381. Raymond Spruance, Manila, to secretary of state, Department of State, incoming telegram, No. 2035, January 10, 1953, RG 59, box 4324, NARA II.

382. Memorandum by the Under Secretary of State (Smith) to the Executive Secretary of the National Security Council (Lay), Third Progress Report on NSC 84/2, "The Position of the United States with Respect to the Philippines," July 16, 1953, No. 335 S/P-NSC files, lot 61 D 167, NSC 84 Series, in United States Department of State, *Foreign Relations of the United States, 1952–1954*, vol. 12, pt. 2, 524.

383. National Security Council Staff Study [NSC 84/2], "The Position of the United States with Respect to the Philippines," November 9, 1950, in United States Department of State, *Foreign Relations of the United States, 1950*, 6:1519.

384. Memorandum by the Assistant Secretary of State for Far Eastern Affairs (Rusk) to the Acting Secretary of State (Webb), Subject: The Situation in the Philippines, 796.00/5.1750, May 17, 1950, in United States Department of State, *Foreign Relations of the United States, 1950*, 6:1450.

385. Memorandum for the Assistant Secretary of State for Far Eastern Affairs (Allison), Subject: Report, Dated December 15, 1952, on Current Political Situation in the Republic of the Philippines, December 16, 1952, 796.00/12-1652, in United States Department of State, *Foreign Relations of the United States, 1952–1954*, vol. 12, pt. 2, 524.

386. Memorandum Prepared for the Ambassador to the Philippines (Spruance), Subject: Philippines Situation, October 3, 1953, No. 338, 796.00/10-853, in United States Department of State, *Foreign Relations of the United States, 1952–1954*, vol. 12, pt. 2, 551.

387. Kerkvliet, *Huk Rebellion*, 208, 238, 240.

388. Birtle, *U.S. Army Counterinsurgency*, 64.

389. Taruc discusses insurgent willingness to compromise with the government in *Born of the People*, 206, 221.

4. A New Laboratory: Dhofar, Oman

1. John Townsend, *Oman: The Making of the Modern State* (London: Croom Helm, 1977), 35.

2. Uzi Rabi, *The Emergence of States in a Tribal Society: Oman under Sa'id bin Taymur, 1932–1970* (2006; repr., Eastbourne, UK: Sussex Academic Press, 2007), 190; Brig. John Akehurst, commander, Dhofar Brigade, 1974–1976, interview, October 14, 1992, Imperial War Museum (IWM) sound recording, catalog number 11156/5, reel 2.

3. Calvin H. Allen Jr. and W. Lynn Rigsbee II, *Oman under Qaboos: From Coup to Constitution, 1970–1996* (2000; repr., London: Frank Cass, 2001), 21–22.

4. David Smiley, *Arabian Assignment*, with Peter Kemp (London: Leo Cooper, 1975), 40–41.

5. Townsend, *Oman*, 103.

6. Foreign and Commonwealth Office, The Sultanate of Muscat and Oman, draft, research memorandum, January 13, 1970, FCO 51/138, National Archives of the United Kingdom (TNA).

7. Rabi, *Emergence of States*, 16.

8. Rabi, 16.

9. Rabi, 16; John Akehurst, *We Won a War: The Campaign in Oman, 1965–1975* (Salisbury, Wiltshire, UK: Michael Russell, 1982), 6–7, 11.

10. Fred Halliday, *Arabia without Sultans* (New York: Vintage Books, 1975), 286–287.

11. David Holdren, *Farewell to Arabia* (New York: Walker, 1966), 236.

12. Ministry of Defense to prime minister, British Military Assistance in Oman, memo, December 4, 1973, DEFE 25/312, TNA.

13. Tony Jeapes, *SAS: Operation Oman* (London, William Kimber, 1980), 74, 122, 129.

14. Abdel Razzak Takriti, *Monsoon Revolution: Republicans, Sultans, and Empires in Oman, 1965–1976* (Oxford: Oxford University Press, 2012), 103–104, 108 on training in China, 130–131, 147.

15. Maj. Gen. Ken Perkins, SAF commander, 1975–1977, interview by author, May 20, 2009, Great Bedwyn, Marlborough, Wiltshire.

16. James Fromson and Steven Simon, "Visions of Omani Reform," *Survival* 64, no. 1 (2019): 99–116, https://doi.org/10.1080/00396338.2019.1637117.

17. Sultan Sa'id survived an insurgent challenge in northern Oman in 1958–1959 by agreeing to accept British military and financial assistance, reorganize his armed forces under British supervision, and begin a civil development program, also under British supervision. Allen and Rigsbee, *Oman under Qaboos*, 19–22. Sa'id also had an arrangement with Pakistan that included loan service officers and recruiting rights in Gwadur, Pakistani territory formerly owned by Oman. See Consul General D. C. Carden, annual report 1965, January 2, 1966, FO 1016/765, TNA.

18. Consul General D. C. Carden to Sir Stewart Crawford, British resident in the Persian Gulf, October 8, 1966, FO 1016/766, TNA.

19. Lt. Col. Peter Thwaites, commander, Muscat Regiment, 1967–1970, Dhofar 1967–1970, MSS lecture, n.d., Peter Thwaites Collection, box 2, folder 2, King's College London, Liddell-Hart Center for Military Archives (LHCMA).

20. Brief, Muscat and Oman—Dhofar, cover letter dated February 12, 1970, FCO 8/1415, TNA.

21. John Graham, *Ponder Anew: Reflections on the Twentieth Century* (published privately on behalf of the author in a limited edition of three hundred copies, Staplehurst, Kent, UK: Spellmount, 1999), 316, John Graham Collection, Oman Archive, Middle East Center, St. Antony's College, Oxford (OA). Sa'id, not unreasonably given the recent imamate rebellion, insisted on keeping some troops in the north in case of another uprising. Corran Purdon, *List the Bugle: Reminiscences of an Irish Soldier* (Antrim, Northern Ireland: Greystone Books, 1993), 244.

22. Consul General D. G. Crawford, Sultanate Balance Sheet—3rd Quarter 1969, October 13, 1969, FO 1016/791, TNA; Ken Nutting, MOD, to D. J. S. Murray, FO, October 18, 1968, FCO 8/1091, TNA.

23. Peter Thwaites, *Muscat Command* (London: Leo Cooper, 1995), 85; Purdon, *List the Bugle*, 191–192; Ian Gordon, major in the Muscat Regiment, email message to author, November 27, 2009.

24. Thwaites, *Muscat Command*, 70; Purdon, *List the Bugle*, 241, 245, 253–254.

25. Thwaites, *Muscat Command*, 39.

26. Purdon, *List the Bugle*, 305.

27. Consul General D. C. Carden, Sultanate Balance Sheet—Third Quarter 1968, October 22, 1969, FO 1016/790, TNA; Consul General D. G. Crawford, Annual Review—1969, December 30, 1969, FO 1016/791, TNA; Purdon to Thwaites, September 26, 1969, Thwaites Collection, box 1, folder 3, LHCMA.

28. Purdon, *List the Bugle*, 221, 277, 221, 257, 244, 294.

29. On counterinsurgency and military capability, see Daniel Byman, "Friends like These: Counterinsurgency and the War on Terrorism," *International Security* 31, no. 2 (Fall 2006): 79–115, https://doi.org/10.1162/isec.2006.31.2.79. On the capability of Arab armies, see Kenneth Pollack, *Arabs at War: Military Effectiveness, 1948–1991* (Lincoln: University of Nebraska Press, 2002).

30. CSAF Maj. Gen. Ken Perkins, Report Commander Sultan's Armed Forces to Chiefs of Staff 28 December 1975, December 28, 1975, DEFE 11/899, TNA.

31. Training Guide, n.d. but context of folder suggests post-March 1972, Graham Collection, box 2, folder 2, OA. Previously, the CSAF had directed the campaign from his base in northern Oman in conjunction with the regimental commander on roulement in Dhofar.

32. Brig. John Akehurst, commander, Dhofar Brigade, 1974–1976, interview, October 14, 1992, IWM sound recording, catalog number 11156/5, reel 2.

33. Ministry of Defense Chiefs of Staff Committee, The Principles Governing British Military Assistance to Oman, COS 13/74, May 1974, DEFE 24/574, TNA.

34. Ken Perkins, *A Fortunate Soldier* (London: Brassey's, 1988), 154.

35. Graham diary, October 2, 1972, Graham Collection, box 4, folder 1, OA; Perkins, *Fortunate Soldier*, 130, 139. The Jordanians, like the Iranians, displayed a heavy hand with the populace. They relied on heavy firepower and fear, mounting search-and-destroy missions that included setting villages afire in order to kill insurgents. Perkins, interview by author.

36. Townsend, *Oman*, 110; Akehurst, *We Won a War*, 175.

37. Ian Gardiner, *In the Service of the Sultan: A First Hand Account of the Dhofar Insurgency* (2006; repr., Barnsley, South Yorkshire, UK: Pen and Sword Military, 2008), 148, 154; Perkins, *Fortunate Soldier*, 148.

38. Akehurst, *We Won a War*, 30.

39. Graham, *Ponder Anew*, 347.

40. Deputy Chief of the Defense Staff (Intelligence), The Threat to Oman, May 20, 1971, DEFE 24/1868, TNA; Chiefs of Staff Committee Defense Operational Planning Staff, The Military Facilities Likely to Be Required in Oman in the Immediate Future, received July 21, 1971, DEFE 24/1835, TNA; Oman Defense Secretary Col. Hugh Oldman, The Dhofar Rebellion, July 1971, FCO 8/1667, TNA. These contemporaneous accounts estimate a significantly smaller number of insurgents, from four hundred to one thousand hardcore fighters and one thousand militia members.

41. CSAF Maj. Gen. Tim Creasey, untitled review after ten days as CSAF, September 28, 1972, DEFE 24/1831, TNA.

42. Graham, *Ponder Anew*, 347–348; SAF activity report, January 22, 1971, FCO 8/1667, TNA; Sitrep, March 23, 1971, FCO 8/1667, TNA; Sitrep, April 4, 1971, FCO 8/1667, TNA; Sitrep,

April 13, 1971, FCO 8/1667, TNA; Sitrep, April 20, 1971, FCO 8/1667, TNA; Sitrep, April 27, 1971, FCO 8/1667, TNA; Sitrep, May 4, 1971, FCO 8/1667, TNA; Sitrep, May 11, 1971, FCO 8/1667, TNA; BT to FMHQBF Gulf, CAB, FCO, MODUK, etc., weekly report [to May 17, 1971], May 1971, FCO 8/1667, TNA; Sitrep, May 25, 1971, FCO 8/1667, TNA; Directive Commander Dhofar for August–September 1972, August 5, 1972, Graham Collection, box 2, folder 3, OA; Commander SAF Maj. Gen. Ken Perkins, Record of Audience 1700 Hours Monday 10 February 1975, February 16, 1975, DEFE 24/1869, TNA.

43. Graham diary, November 3, 1971, Graham Collection, box 4, folder 1, OA.

44. Directive Commander Dhofar for August–September 1972, August 5, 1972, Graham Collection, box 2, folder 3, OA.

45. Report by the Directors of Defense Policy, Principles Governing British Assistance to Oman, May 14, 1974, DEFE 25/315, TNA.

46. CSAF Maj. Gen. Ken Perkins, Record of Audience 1700 Hours Monday 10 February 1975, February 16, 1975, DEFE 24/1869, TNA.

47. Situation Assessment, February 1971, Graham Collection, box 2, folder 1, OA.

48. Situation in Dhofar, June 21, 1971, FCO 8/1667, TNA.

49. The Dhofar Rebellion—An Evaluation by the Defense Secretary of the Sultanate of Oman, Colonel H.R.D. Oldman, OBE, MC, August 1971, FCO 8/1667, TNA.

50. Diplomatic Report #428/71 Muscat Ambassador Hawley to Secretary of State for FCA, August 5, 1971, DEFE 24/1837, TNA; Record of Meeting Dhofar, August 7, 1971, FCO 8/1667, TNA.

51. CSAF Maj. Gen. Tim Creasey, untitled brief for Sultan Qaboos, September 28, 1972, DEFE 4/1831, TNA.

52. A SAF battalion plus sixty to seventy firqats and one or two SAS troops, backed with artillery and air support, would take the targeted territory, then the base would be wired and the perimeter mined. The defenses would come down as security improved. Maj. Gen. Tony Jeapes, in Dhofar as SAS squadron leader in 1971, 22nd SAS regimental commander in 1974–1976, interview by author, May 15, 2009, Warminster, Wiltshire, UK.

53. Jeapes, SAS, 164.

54. SAF Sitrep, November 2, 1971, TFCO 8/1668, TNA.

55. CSAF Brig. John Graham, CSAF's Assessment of the Military Situation in Dhofar as at 14 February 1972, February 17, 1972, DEFE 25/293, TNA.

56. SAF Sitrep, January 16, 1972, FCO 8/1846, TNA. This pocket again required military attention as late as May 1979. Ian Gordon, major in the Muscat Regiment during the second half of the conflict, email message to author, November 27, 2009.

57. CSAF Brig. John Graham, CSAF's Assessment of the Military Situation in Dhofar as of 14 February 1972, February 17, 1972, DEFE 25/293, TNA.

58. Gardiner, In the Service, 140–141; Col. W. J. Reed, Notes on Visit to Oman by Col GS MO2 20–24 January 1974, January 30, 1974, DEFE 25/312, TNA; Akehurst, We Won a War, 77.

59. Jeapes, SAS, 190–191.

60. Jeapes, SAS, 196, 202–203.

61. John H. McKeown, "Britain and Oman: The Dhofar War and Its Significance" (MPhil diss., University of Cambridge, 1981, reproduced by U.S. Army Command and Staff College, Fort Leavenworth, KS), 89; Perkins, Fortunate Soldier, 130.

62. Perkins, Fortunate Soldier, 126; Chiefs of Staff Committee Defense Operational Planning Staff, The Progress of Operations in Dhofar, DOP Note 733/74, February 17, 1975, DEFE 24/1869, TNA.

63. Perkins, Fortunate Soldier, 146.

64. Akehurst, We Won a War, 77.

65. Ministry of Defence Chiefs of Staff Committee, Principles Governing British Military Assistance to Oman, Note by the Secretary, copy stamped May 29, 1974, DEFE 24/574, TNA; Col. W. J. Reed, Notes on Visit to Oman by Col GS MO2 20–24 January 1974, January 30, 1974, DEFE 25/312, TNA; Ministry of Defense Chiefs of Staff Committee, The Principles Governing British Military Assistance to Oman, Annex A to COS 13/74, received May 29, 1974, DEFE 24/574,

TNA; Maj. Gen. W. M. R. Scotter, director of military operations, DMO's Visit to Oman 19–22 Feb 1975, received February 26, 1975, DEFE 24/1869, TNA.

66. Jeapes, *SAS*, 190–191.

67. Edward Ashley to John Graham, August 16, 1975, Edward Ashley Collection, box 3, folder 2/4, OA; Sitrep, January 27, 1976, DEFE 24/1874, TNA.

68. In light of research on ethnic conflict, it is interesting that despite the ethnic differences between Omanis and Dhofaris, Dhofaris had no apparent problem switching sides over the course of the conflict. See Chaim Kaufmann, "Possible and Impossible Solutions to Ethnic Civil Wars," *International Security* 20, no. 4 (Spring 1996): 136–175, https://doi.org/10.2307/2539045; Stephen Biddle, "Seeing Baghdad, Thinking Saigon," *Foreign Affairs* 85, no. 2 (March–April 2006): 2–10; and Stathis Kalyvas, "Ethnic Defection in Civil War," *Comparative Political Studies* 41, no. 8 (August 2008): 1043–1068, https://doi.org/10.1177/0010414008317949.

69. Oman Military Secretary Pat Waterfield to Peter Thwaites, May 25, 1969, Thwaites Collection, box 1, folder 3, LHCMA; Consul General D. G. Crawford, Muscat, to British Residency, Bahrain, February 7, 1970, FCO 8/1415, TNA.

70. Takriti, *Monsoon Revolution*, 35. Important recent work includes that of Takriti; James Worrall, *Statebuilding and Counterinsurgency in Oman: Political, Military and Diplomatic Relations at the End of Empire* (London: I. B. Tauris, 2014); and Marc Valeri, *Politics and Society in the Qaboos State* (2009; London: Hurst, 2017), but none focuses specifically on Sa'id's political choices regarding the insurgency.

71. Valeri, *Politics and Society*, 102, 108.

72. Valeri, 75.

73. H. G. Balfour-Paul, political resident, Bahrain, to J. F. Ford, Joint Research Department, Foreign Office, December 6, 1967, FCO 51/41, TNA.

74. Consul General D. C. Carden, annual report 1965, FO 1016/765, TNA.

75. Takriti, *Monsoon Revolution*, 267–268.

76. In Dhofar, *civic action* referred to meeting immediate popular needs by drilling wells and providing medical care and food. *Civil development* referred to longer-term projects to build the economy, such as constructing ports and paved roads. Ken Perkins, "Oman: Year of Decision," *Journal of the Royal United Services Institute* 124, no. 1 (March 1979): 38–45.

77. Jeapes, *SAS*, 33–34, 40.

78. Jeapes, 101; Graham diary, February 24, 1971, Graham Collection, box 4, folder 1, OA.

79. Jeapes, *SAS*, 33–34.

80. Akehurst, *We Won a War*, 68, reports that the policy of installing firqats in their own areas got under way in October 1974.

81. Jeapes, *SAS*, 28.

82. Tony Geraghty, *Who Dares Wins: The Special Air Service, 1950 to the Gulf War*, 3rd ed. (London: Little, Brown, 1992), 185.

83. Akehurst, *We Won a War*, 19.

84. Jeapes, *SAS*, 227.

85. Perkins, interview by author; Jeapes, *SAS*, 78.

86. Gardiner, *In the Service*, 159; Jeapes, *SAS*, 231; Akehurst, *We Won a War*, 96.

87. Jeapes, *SAS*, 123, 48.

88. Jeapes, interview by author.

89. Jeapes, interview by author; Perkins, interview by author.

90. Gardiner, *In the Service*, 159; Jeapes, *SAS*, 231; Akehurst, *We Won a War*, 96.

91. Jeapes, *SAS*, 64–65.

92. Perkins, interview by author; Jeapes, *SAS*, 78.

93. Akehurst, IWM interview, August 13, 2004, IWM sound recording, catalog number 27184, reel 24.

94. Akehurst, *We Won a War*, 178.

95. Jeapes, *SAS*, 163.

96. Akehurst, *We Won a War*, 177, 81.

97. Graham diary, May 21, 1972, Graham Collection, box 4, folder 1, OA.

98. Gardiner, *In the Service*, 40.

99. .Walter C. Ladwig III, "Supporting Allies in Counterinsurgency: Britain and the Dhofar Rebellion," *Small Wars and Insurgencies* 19, no. 1 (March 2008), 62–88, 78, doi.org/10.1080/09592310801905793.

100. Ladwig, "Supporting Allies in Counterinsurgency," 72.

101. Geraint Hughes, "A 'Model Campaign' Reappraised: The Counterinsurgency War in Dhofar, Oman, 1965–1975," *Journal of Strategic Studies* 32, no. 2 (April 2009): 271–305, 290, 276, https://doi.org/10.1080/01402390902743357.

102. Hughes, 290.

103. Perkins, "Oman," 38–39.

104. Townsend, *Oman*, 99.

105. British Army Capt. C. F. Hepworth, seconded to the Northern Frontier Regiment in 1968, found that all the jebalis and most of the coastal Dhofaris supported the insurgency. Hepworth, "The Unknown War," *White Horse and the Fleur de Lys* Vol. 6, no. 6 (Winter 1970), held by Tameside Local Studies and Archives Center, Ashton-under-Lyne, UK.

106. First Night Contact Report, April 11, 1969, Thwaites Collection, box 2, folder 4, LHCMA. Also see, for example, Corran Purdon to Peter Thwaites, February 26, 1969, Thwaites Collection, box 1, folder 3; MR Gp Op Instr No. 3 Op Lance Confirmatory Notes of Verbal Orders, May 20, 1969, Thwaites Collection, box 2, folder 3, LHCMA; Ops Dhofar Outline of Future Intentions, June 10, 1969, Thwaites Collection, box 1, folder 3, LHCMA; Dhofar Ops (as of Jan 70), n.d., Thwaites Collection, box 1, folder 2, LHCM; Purdon, *List the Bugle*, 272.

107. Thwaites, *Muscat Command*, 1–8, 12.

108. Gardiner, *In the Service*, 140–141; Col. W. J. Reed, Notes on Visit to Oman by Col GS MO2 20–24 January 1974, January 30, 1974, DEFE 25/312, TNA; Akehurst, *We Won a War*, 77; Jeapes, *SAS*, 190–191, on battalion-strength operations.

109. Purdon, *List the Bugle*, 199.

110. Peter Thwaites, for example, often discusses in his memoirs and correspondence his concerns about the harm done by rough treatment of civilians. Thwaites, *Muscat Command*, 7–8, 54, 58. Other officers, including CSAF Corran Purdon, believed in the efficacy of a more forceful approach. See, for example, Purdon to Thwaites, letter, February 26, 1969, and Purdon to Thwaites, letter, May 11, 1969, box 1, file 3, Peter Thwaites Papers, LHCMA. Also see David C. Arkless, *The Secret War: Dhofar 1971/1972* (London: William Kimber, 1988), 173.

111. Purdon, *List the Bugle*, 200, 291.

112. Purdon, 269. The population of Salalah stood at 35,000 in 1977, up from 7,500 in 1970. Takriti, *Monsoon Revolution*, 38.

113. Purdon, *List the Bugle*, 269.

114. Rabi, *Emergence of States*, 202.

115. Purdon to Thwaites, September 22, 1969, Thwaites Collection, box 1, folder 3, LHCMA.

116. Jeapes, *SAS*, 35.

117. Gordon, email message to author, November 27, 2009.

118. Captured Enemy Documents—Third National Congress of Rakyut June 1971, December 15, 1971, Graham Collection, box 2, folder 5, OA.

119. Jeapes, *SAS*, 130–131.

120. CSAF Brig. John Graham, CSAF's Assessment of the Military Situation in Dhofar as at 14 February 1972, February 17, 1972, DEFE 25/293, TNA.

121. Directive for Commander Dhofar for 1972, Update, March 3, 1972, Graham Collection, box 2, folder 3, OA. Also see Fred Halliday, *Mercenaries: "Counter-insurgency" in the Gulf* (Nottingham, UK: Bertrand Russell Peace Foundation, 1977), 53.

122. Halliday, *Mercenaries*, 53–54.

123. Directive for Commander Dhofar for 1972, Update, March 3, 1972, Graham Collection, box 2, folder 3, OA.

124. Arkless, *Secret War*, 81.

125. Perkins, interview by author. By 1974, SAF was removing tracer from its general purpose machine gun links in the dry season whenever there was a threat of grass fires. Gordon, email message to author, November 27, 2009.

126. Perkins, interview by author.

127. Ranulph Fiennes, *Where Soldiers Fear to Tread* (London: Hodder and Stoughton, 1975), 62–63.

128. Purdon, *List the Bugle*, 287, 290.

129. Marbat Incident Jul 1972, March 5, 1975, DEFE 24/1869, TNA; Arkless, *Secret War*, 211. Interestingly, the bodies of insurgents killed during Operation Jaguar were not put on display. See Graham diary, October 6, 1971, Graham Collection, box 4, folder 1, OA.

130. Graham diary, February 13, 1971, Graham Collection, box 4, folder 1, OA.

131. Directive for Commander Dhofar for 1972 Update, March 3, 1972, Graham Collection, box 2, folder 3, OA.

132. Fiennes, *Where Soldiers Fear to Tread*, 237.

133. Graham diary, February 12, 1971, Graham Collection, box 4, folder 1, OA.

134. Graham diary, June 10, 1972, Graham Collection, box 4, folder 1, OA.

135. Record of a Conversation between the Prime Minister and the Sultan of Oman at 5:15 P.M. on 11 September 1973 at No. 10, DEFE 25/370, TNA. Yet Qaboos recognized the political importance of seeming to protect the populace. He is quoted in a translation of an interview with a Lebanese newspaper as saying that he does not permit the aerial bombing of villages in order to protect the innocent. April 26, 1972, DEFE 24/1837, TNA.

136. Purdon, *List the Bugle*, 265.

137. Col. Mike Harvey was replaced as commander of Dhofar by Col. Jack Fletcher on July 31, 1972. Graham diary, July 31, 1972, Graham Collection, box 4, folder 1, OA. The CSAF's first directive to Fletcher included a concept of operations focused on offensive operations, interdiction, and causing enemy losses, rather than on reprisals. See Directive Commander Dhofar for August–September 1972, August 5, 1972, Graham Collection, box 2, folder 3, OA.

138. Chiefs of Staff Committee Defense Operational Planning Staff, The Military Facilities Likely to Be Required in Oman in the Immediate Future, DOP 530/71 final, July 20, 1971, DEFE 24/1835, TNA.

139. Halliday, *Mercenaries*, 50.

140. Halliday, *Arabia without Sultans*, 54.

141. Jeapes, *SAS*, 212, 225–226.

142. This attitude became inculcated deeply enough that one example of SAF humor, focusing on the increasing problem of antipersonnel mines laid by the DLF, noted that goat troops could be used to locate the mines, but the employment of livestock in this manner was not likely to enhance SAF's relationship with the goats' owners. See Goat Troop—Dhofar Gendarmerie Annex A to OP5/D/20, September 14, 1971, Ashley Collection, box 2, folder 2/1, OA.

143. Arkless, *Secret War*, 173.

144. Operational Instructions for Move to Central Area, January 1975, Ashley Collection, box 2, folder 2/3, OA.

145. Anti-guerrilla Operations in Dhofar Training Guide, n.d., context suggests post-March 1972, Graham Collection, box 2, folder 2, OA.

146. Akehurst, *We Won a War*, 68–69, 36.

147. Thwaites, *Muscat Command*, 49, 50.

148. Consul General D. C. Carden, Annual Review 1967, January 5, 1968, FO 1016/790, TNA.

149. Purdon to Thwaites, September 26, 1969, Thwaites Collection, box 1, folder 3, LHCMA; McKeown, "Britain and Oman," 39–40.

150. Perkins notes the strategic importance of the thinly populated Western Area. Interview by author.

151. Review of the Military Situation in Oman, November 26, 1973, DEFE 25/312 TNA; CSAF Maj. Gen. Tim Creasey, Review of the Military Situation since the 10th December 1973 for National Defense Council meeting on 23rd January 1974, n.d., cover memo 21st January refers to them as talking points, DEFE 25/312, TNA; Col. W. J. Reed, Notes on Visit to Oman by Col GS MO2 20–24 January 1974, January 30, 197, DEFE 25/312, TNA; Perkins, *Fortunate Soldier*, 126; Chiefs of Staff Committee Defense Operational Planning Staff, The Progress of Operations in Dhofar, DOP Note 733/74, February 17, 1975, DEFE 24/1869, TNA.

152. Akehurst, *We Won a War*, 20–21.

153. Chief of the Defense Staff, Situation in Dhofar, brief for secretary of state, December 15, 1971, DEFE 25/187, TNA.

154. CSAF Brig. John Graham, "CSAF's Assessment of the Military Situation in Dhofar as at 14 February 1972," February 17, 1972, DEFE 25/293, TNA.

155. Deputy Chief of the Defense staff (intelligence), The Outlook for Oman—JIC (A)(72):1, March 10, 1972, DEFE 24/1837, TNA.

156. CSAF Maj. Gen. Tim Creasey, Review of the Military Situation since the 10th December 1973 for National Defense Council meeting on 23rd January 1974, n.d., cover memo 21st January refers to them as talking points, DEFE 25/312, TNA; Col. W. J. Reed, Notes on Visit to Oman by Col GS MO2 20–24 January 1974, January 30, 1974, DEFE 25/312, TNA.

157. Perkins, *Fortunate Soldier*, 126; Chiefs of Staff Committee Defense Operational Planning Staff, The Progress of Operations in Dhofar, DOP Note 733/74, February 17, 1975, DEFE 24/1869, TNA.

158. Perkins, *Fortunate Soldier*, 146.

159. Col. W. J. Reed, Notes on Visit to Oman by Col GS MO2 20–24 January 1974, January 30, 1974, DEFE 25/312, TNA.

160. Jeapes, *SAS*, 224–225.

161. See, for example, Thomas R. Mockaitis, *British Counterinsurgency in the Post-imperial Era* (Manchester: Manchester University Press, 1995); John Newsinger, *British Counterinsurgency: From Palestine to Northern Ireland* (London: Palgrave, 2002); Ian F. W. Beckett, *Modern Insurgencies and Counter-insurgencies: Guerrillas and Their Opponents since 1750* (London: Routledge, 2001); Michael Dewar, *Brush Fire Wars: Minor Campaigns of the British Army since 1945* (London: Robert Hale, 1984); Hughes, "'Model Campaign' Reappraised"; Bard E. O'Neill, "Revolutionary War in Oman," in *Insurgency in the Modern World*, ed. Bard E. O'Neill, William R. Heaton, and Donald J. Alberts (Boulder, CO: Westview, 1980), 212–233; John Pimlott, "The British Army: The Dhofar Campaign, 1970–1975," in *Armed Forces and Modern Counterinsurgency*, ed. Ian F. W. Beckett and John Pimlott (New York: St. Martin's, 1985), 16–45; and Ladwig, "Supporting Allies in Counterinsurgency."

162. One interesting new project to fill this lacuna is by Naghmeh Sohrabi, "Where the Small Things Are: Thoughts on Writing Revolutions and their Histories," *Jadaliyya*, May 21, 2020, https://www.jadaliyya.com/Details/41154/Where-the-Small-Things-Are-Thoughts-on-Writing-Revolutions-and-their-Histories.

163. Joshua Rovner, "The Heroes of COIN," *Orbis* 56, no. 2 (Spring 2012): 215–232, https://doi.org/10.1016/j.orbis.2012.01.005.

164. Nathan Ray Springer, "Stabilizing the Debate between Population and Enemy-Centric Counterinsurgency: Success Demands a Balanced Approach" (Combat Studies Institute, Fort Leavenworth, KS, 2012), 66, 78.

165. James S. Corum and Wray R. Johnson, *Airpower in Small Wars: Fighting Insurgents and Terrorists* (Lawrence: University Press of Kansas, 2003), 211.

166. Dewar, *Brush Fire Wars*, 167.

167. Michael Noonan, "A Mile Deep and an Inch Wide: Foreign Internal Defense Campaigning in Dhofar, Oman, and El Salvador," in *The US Army and the Interagency Process: Historical Perspectives: The Proceedings of the Combat Studies Institute 2008 Military History Symposium*, ed. Kendall D. Gott and Michael G. Brooks (Fort Leavenworth, KS: Combat Studies Institute Press, 2008), 199–210.

168. Noonan, 204.

169. Ladwig, "Supporting Allies in Counterinsurgency," 72.

170. Hughes, "'A 'Model Campaign,'" 290.

171. O'Neill, "Revolutionary War in Oman," 228.

172. Perkins, interview by author.

173. Jeapes, *SAS*, 162–164, 209, 228; Akehurst, *We Won a War*, 78–79. On long-term development efforts, see Jeapes, interview by author; CSAF Maj. Gen. Ken Perkins, Report Commander Sultan's Armed Forces to Chiefs of Staff 28 December 1975, December 28, 1975, DEFE 11/899, TNA; Chief of Defense Staff, Notes on a Visit to Oman 19–22 January 1976, January 30, 1976, DEFE 25/371, TNA; and CSAF Maj. Gen. Tim Creasey, Review of the Military Situation since

the 10th December 1973 for National Defense Council meeting on 23rd January 1974, n.d.; cover memo dated 21st January refers to this as talking points, DEFE 25/312, TNA.

174. Takriti, *Monsoon Revolution*, 6, 194–229.

175. Record of Meeting Dhofar, August 7, 1971, FCO 8/1667, TNA.

176. Richard Lloyd Jones, Head DS11, Factors in Oman, November 6, 1972, DEFE 24/831, TNA; Defense Assistance to the Sultanate of Oman, draft, November 17, 1972, DEFE 25/294, TNA.

177. CSAF Maj. Gen. Tim Creasey, Review of the Situation by Major General T. M. Creasey OBE Commander the Sultan's Armed Forces December 1973–May 1974, June 9, 1974, DEFE 24/574, TNA.

178. Chief of Defense, Notes on a Visit to Oman 19–22 January 1976, January 30, 1976, DEFE 25/371, TNA; Chiefs of Staff Committee Defense Operational Planning Staff, Progress Report on Oman, draft, January 26, 1976, DEFE 25/371, TNA.

179. Purdon, *List the Bugle*, 305.

180. Rabi, *Emergence of States*, 210, 51–53, 54.

181. Worrall, *Statebuilding and Counterinsurgency*, 62, 55, 65.

182. Takriti, *Monsoon Revolution*, 161–162.

183. Purdon, *List the Bugle*, 243.

184. Rabi, *Emergence of States*, 208.

185. Valeri, *Politics and Society*, 66.

186. Rabi, *Emergence of States*, 209.

187. Valeri, *Politics and Society in the Qaboos State*, 67, 68.

188. Allan and Rigsbee, *Oman under Qaboos*, 24–25.

189. Worrall, *Statebuilding and Counterinsurgency*, 52–53.

190. Draft letter, July 1969, Thwaites Collection, box 1, folder 3, LHCMA; Thwaites, *Muscat Command*, 133–134.

191. Purdon to Thwaites, September 26, 1968, Thwaites Collection, box 2, folder 3, LHCMA.

192. Thwaites, *Muscat Command*, 81.

193. Thwaites, 122; MR GP Contact Report Nos 26 & 27, August 9, 1969, Thwaites Collection, box 2, folder 4, LHCMA.

194. Purdon, *List the Bugle*, 266, 291; Fiennes, *Where Soldiers Fear to Tread*, 225.

195. Consul General D. G. Crawford, Sultanate Balance Sheet—Third Quarter 1969, October 13, 1969, FO 1016/791, TNA.

196. Record of Meeting Dhofar, August 7, 1971, FCO 8/1667, TNA.

197. Graham diary June 11, 1972, Graham Collection, box 4, folder 1, OA.

198. CSAF Maj. Gen. Tim Creasey, Review of the Situation by Major General T. M. Creasey OBE Commander the Sultan's Armed Forces December 1973–May 1974, June 9, 1974, DEFE 24/574, TNA.

199. Ian Skeet, *Oman: Politics and Development* (Basingstoke, Hampshire, UK: Palgrave, 1992), 16.

200. Akehurst, *We Won a War*, 63, 75.

201. CSAF Maj. Gen. Tim Creasey, Review of the Military Situation since the 10th December 1973 for National Defense Council meeting on 23rd January 1974, n.d.; cover memo dated 21st January refers to this as talking points, DEFE 25/312, TNA.

202. Chiefs of Staff Committee, Future United Kingdom Defense Activity in Oman, COS 46/73, January 3, 1974, DEFE 25/312, TNA.

203. J. E. Petersen, *Oman's Insurgencies: The Sultanate's Struggle for Supremacy* (London: Saqi, 2008), 393.

204. For example, Visit by DSAS to the Oman 3–10 November 1975, November 19, 1975, DEFE 24/1838, TNA; Chief of Defense Staff, Progress Report on Oman, Annex D to DOP Note 722/75, February 1976, DEFE 25/371, TNA.

205. CSAF Maj. Gen. Ken Perkins, Half Yearly Report on the Armed Forces A Review of the Period 1st May 1975–31st October 1975, December 18, 1975, DEFE 25/371, TNA.

206. CSAF Maj. Gen. Ken Perkins, Report Commander Sultan's Armed Forces to Chiefs of Staff 28 December 1975, December 28, 1975, DEFE 11/899, TNA.

207. Chief of Defense, Notes on a Visit to Oman 19–22 January 1976, January 30, 1976, DEFE 25/371, TNA; Chiefs of Staff Committee Defense Operational Planning Staff, Progress Report on Oman, draft, January 26, 1976, DEFE 25/371, TNA.

208. Chief of Defense Staff, report on visit, January 19–22, 1976, DEFE 24/1874, TNA.

209. Hughes, "'Model Campaign' Reappraised," 276.

210. Dewar, *Brush Fire Wars*, 168.

211. Ladwig, "Supporting Allies in Counterinsurgency," 77.

212. Springer, "Stabilizing the Debate," 75. This source mistakenly locates Jebel Akhdar in Dhofar rather than in northern Oman. It was the location of an earlier uprising against Sultan Sa'id, one based on central-periphery tensions as Sa'id centralized his control over the state.

213. Purdon, *List the Bugle*, 305.

214. Consul General D. G. Crawford to Wright Bahrain, April 18, 1971, FCO 8/1667, TNA; Sir Geoffrey Arthur, political resident, Bahrain, to Muscat, June 11, 1971, FCO 8/1667, TNA.

215. Ambassador D. F. Hawley, "Impressions of Oman: The First and the Last," August 5, 1971, DEFE 24/1837, TNA; Record of Points Made by Colonel Oldman, Defense Secretary to the Sultan, at a Meeting in Sir William Luce's Office on 17 August 1971, FCO 8/1667, TNA.

216. Graham diary, November 14, 1971, Graham Collection, box 4, folder 1, OA.

217. Paul Sibley, *A Monk in the SAS* (Oxford: Trafford, 2006), 171, 164.

218. CSAF Maj. Gen. Ken Perkins, Report Commander Sultan's Armed Forces to Chiefs of Staff 28 December 1975, December 28, 1975, DEFE 25/371, TNA.

219. Chief of Defense, Notes on a Visit to Oman 19–22 January 1976, January 30, 1976, DEFE 25/371, TNA; Chiefs of Staff Committee Defense Operational Planning Staff, Progress Report on Oman, draft, January 26, 1976, DEFE 25/371, TNA.

220. Akehurst, *We Won a War*, 176–179.

5. High Cost Success: El Salvador

1. William Stanley, *The Protection Racket State: Elite Politics, Military Extortion, and Civil War in El Salvador* (Philadelphia: Temple University Press, 1996).

2. Hugh Byrne, *El Salvador's Civil War: A Study of Revolution* (Boulder, CO: Lynne Rienner, 1996), 20.

3. Philip J. Williams and Knut Walter, *Militarization and Demilitarization in El Salvador's Transition to Democracy* (Pittsburg: University of Pittsburg Press, 1997), 88.

4. Tommie Sue Montgomery, *Revolution in El Salvador: From Civil Strife to Civil Peace* (1982; repr., Boulder, CO: Westview, 1995), 24.

5. Jeffery M. Paige, *Coffee and Power: Revolution and the Rise of Democracy in Central America* (Cambridge, MA: Harvard University Press, 1997), 319; Cynthia McClintock, *Revolutionary Movements in Latin America: El Salvador's FMLN and Peru's Shining Path* (Washington, DC: U.S. Institute of Peace, 1998), 104; Williams and Walter, *Militarization and Demilitarization*, 9–10, 21.

6. Elisabeth Jean Wood, *Forging Democracy from Below: Insurgent Transitions in South Africa and El Salvador* (New York: Cambridge University Press, 2000), 33.

7. Williams and Walter, *Militarization and Demilitarization*, 100–101.

8. Thomas Pickering, ambassador to El Salvador, 1983–1985, interview by Max Manwaring for Small Wars Operational Requirements Division, SOUTHCOM, conducted in Tel Aviv, Israel, August 28, 1987, Vol. 1, Research Data, Oral History of the Conflict in El Salvador 1979–present, U.S. Army Military History Institute, Army Heritage Education Center, Carlisle, PA (MHI), 48, 50.

9. Jeff Cole, email message to author, April 4, 2010. Cole, a retired U.S. Marine, was an adviser in Usulután in 1985–1986 and served as military attaché in San Salvador in 1990–1992.

10. Col. Lyman C. Duryea, USA, defense and army attaché in El Salvador, November 1983–October 1985, Project 86-9 El Salvador, interview by Lt. Col. Emil R. Bedard, USMC, and Lt. Col. L. R. Vasquez, USA, March 4, 1986, for the AWC/MHI 1986 El Salvador Oral History Project, MHI, 85.

11. Wood, *Forging Democracy from Below*, 88–89.

12. Williams and Walter, *Militarization and Demilitarization*, 89.

13. McClintock, *Revolutionary Movements*, 104–105.

14. Williams and Walter, *Militarization and Demilitarization*, 91; William M. LeoGrande, *Our Own Backyard: The United States in El Salvador, 1977–1992* (Chapel Hill: University of North Carolina Press, 1998), 40.

15. Williams and Walter, *Militarization and Demilitarization*, 100–101.

16. LeoGrande, *Our Own Backyard*, 41.

17. Stanley, *Protection Racket State*, 110; McClintock, *Revolutionary Movements*, 259, 267.

18. "Platform of the Revolutionary Democratic Government," issued February 27, 1980, in Marvin E. Gettleman et al., eds., *El Salvador: Central America in the New Cold War* (New York: Grove, 1981), 122–123.

19. Leamon Ratterree, email message to author, April 2, 2010. Ratterree, a retired U.S. Army officer, was involved in intelligence and training in El Salvador beginning in 1979 and served on the ground in 1984 and 1985–1986.

20. Charles Clements, interview by author, April 13, 2010, Cambridge, MA. Clements, a U.S. physician, worked in the FMLN-held Guazapa Volcano area in 1982–1983.

21. Duryea, interview by Bedard and Vasquez, 241.

22. Referenced by Col. John D. Waghelstein, USA, interview by Col. Charles A. Carlton Jr., USA, January 21, 1985, El Salvador Papers, Oral History, Gonzalez-Waghelstein, box 1 of 6, file: John D. Waghelstein, Senior Officers Oral History Program, Project 85-7, El Salvador, MHI, 23.

23. Maj. Gen. Mark Hamilton, U.S. military group leader at the time of the successful peace talks, phone interview by author, April 13, 2010.

24. Duryea, interview by Bedard and Vasquez, 234.

25. McClintock, *Revolutionary Movements*, 61–63.

26. Duryea, interview by Bedard and Vasquez, 51–53.

27. McClintock, *Revolutionary Movements*, 62.

28. Eleanor Clift, "With Rebel Leader at His Side, Reagan Presses for Contra Aid," *Los Angeles Times*, March 4, 1986. https://www.latimes.com/archives/la-xpm-1986-03-04-mn-15033-story.html.

29. Ronald Reagan, "Remarks on Central America and El Salvador at the Annual Meeting of the National Association of Manufacturers," March 10, 1983, American Presidency Project, https://www.presidency.ucsb.edu/node/262935.

30. Terry Lynn Karl, "El Salvador's Negotiated Revolution," *Foreign Affairs* 71, no. 2 (Spring 1992): 147–164. See also Wood, *Forging Democracy from Below*, 221, identifying El Salvador as the fifth-largest recipient of U.S. aid worldwide in the 1980s.

31. McClintock, *Revolutionary Movements*, 223; Wood, *Forging Democracy from Below*, 233.

32. Karl, "El Salvador's Negotiated Revolution."

33. Susan Burgerman argues that diplomatic pressure for reform is only likely to succeed if domestic elites are willing and able to cooperate. See Burgerman, "First Do No Harm: U.S. Foreign Policy and Respect for Human Rights in El Salvador and Guatemala, 1980–1996," in *Implementing U.S. Human Rights Policy: Agendas, Policies, and Practices*, ed. Debra Liang-Fenton (Washington, DC: U.S. Institute of Peace, 2004), 267–297.

34. Wendy Shaull, *Tortillas, Beans, and M-16s: A Year with the Guerrillas in El Salvador* (London: Pluto, 1990), 19; Clements, interview by author. In 1980, the FMLN had Israeli and U.S. assault rifles, grenade launchers, U.S. machine guns and mortars, Chinese rocket launchers, and commercial radios, some bought at Radio Shack in the United States. Clements, interview by author; Kevin Higgins, U.S. military adviser in El Salvador in 1983–1984 and 1986–1988, email interview with author, March 16, 2010.

35. McClintock, *Revolutionary Movements*, 83, 80; Stanley, *Protection Racket State*, 227.

36. Williams and Walter, *Militarization and Demilitarization*, 132; Pickering, interview by Manwaring, 6.

37. Brian J. Bosch, *The Salvadoran Officer Corps and the Final Offensive of 1981* (Jefferson, NC: McFarland, 1999), 61–63.

38. Waghelstein, interview by Carlton, 64–64.

39. Leigh Binford, *The El Mozote Massacre: Anthropology and Human Rights* (Tucson: University of Arizona Press, 1996), 148, 232; Stanley, *Protection Racket State*, 227; McClintock, *Revolutionary Movements*, 83.

40. McClintock, *Revolutionary Movements*, 84.

41. McClintock, 77; Hamilton, interview by author. Hamilton judges that FMLN support declined because of war weariness throughout the last half to one-third of the war, approximately from 1985 or 1988. Hamilton notes that the military too was war weary.

42. Chalmers Johnson argues that "the willingness of the population to support the guerrillas depends upon the intensity of its hostility to the guerrillas' enemies; it is not necessarily related to the ultimate goals of the guerrilla leadership." Johnson, "Civilian Loyalties and Guerrilla Conflict," *World Politics* 14, no. 4 (July 1962): 646–661, https://doi.org/10.2307/2009313.

43. Charles Clements, *Witness to War: An American Doctor in El Salvador* (New York: Bantam, 1984), 220.

44. Bosch, *Salvadoran Officer Corps*, 112; Waghelstein, interview by Carlton.

45. McClintock, *Revolutionary Movements*, 73, 77, 80.

46. Benjamin C. Schwarz, *American Counterinsurgency Doctrine and El Salvador: The Frustrations of Reform and the Illusions of Nation Building* (Santa Monica, CA: RAND, 1991), 78.

47. McClintock, *Revolutionary Movements*, 230.

48. "U.S. Relations with El Salvador," U.S. Department of State, December 30, 2016, http://www.state.gov/r/pa/ei/bgn/2033.htm.

49. Cynthia Arnson and Dinorah Azpuru, "From Peace to Democratization: Lessons from Central America," in *Contemporary Peacemaking: Conflict, Violence and Peace Processes*, ed. John Darby and Roger MacGinty (New York: Palgrave Macmillan, 2003), 197–211; Bosch, *Salvadoran Officer Corps*, 61–63.

50. Bosch, 121.

51. During the period of stalemate, "neither side was able to make inroads upon the core of its opponent's strength." Timothy P. Wickham-Crowley, *Guerrillas and Revolution in Latin America: A Comparative Study of Insurgents and Regimes since 1956* (Princeton, NJ: Princeton University Press, 1992), 211.

52. Pickering, interview by Manwaring, 48, 50.

53. Jeff Cole, email message to author, April 4, 2010.

54. Cynthia Arnson, "The Frente's Opposition: The Security Forces of El Salvador," in Gettleman et al., *El Salvador*, 126–138.

55. Wood, *Forging Democracy from Below*, 40.

56. Wood, 45–46. Duarte writes that one powerful military officer, Carlos Eugenio Vides Casanova, asked him to accept the presidency of the junta in December 1980 because the military owed Duarte for stealing the election from him in 1972. José Napoléon Duarte, *My Story*, with Diana Page (New York: G. P. Putnam's Sons, 1986), 131.

57. McClintock, *Revolutionary Movements*, 234.

58. The elite's formative thinking about reform and revolution developed from a peasant massacre in 1932. La Matanza (The Massacre) had also followed a brief period of democratic opening, economic crisis, and popular unrest. La Matanza occurred in 1932, when up to a few hundred peasants armed with sticks and machetes attacked wealthy families and government representatives in western El Salvador. After putting down the uprising, the military spent approximately two weeks killing ten thousand to thirty thousand peasants. The elite remembered the massacre as an example of what Communism could accomplish: those massacred, in the memory of the elite, were their forefathers, not their laborers. See Hector Lindo-Fuentes, Erik Ching, and Rafael Lara-Martinez, *Remembering a Massacre in El Salvador: The Insurrection of 1932, Roque Dalton, and the Politics of Historical Memory* (Albuquerque: University of New Mexico Press, 2007), 79–81, 28–43; and Wood, *Forging Democracy from Below*, 32.

59. Mark Danner, *The Massacre at El Mozote* (New York: Vintage, 1993), 42.

60. Francisco Pedrozo, email message to author, March 29, 2010. Pedrozo, a retired U.S. Army officer, trained the first group of Salvadoran cadets at Fort Benning, Georgia, in 1982; served as military adviser in San Vicente in 1985–1986; and served as training officer, operations adviser, and deputy commander of the U.S. military group in San Salvador in 1989–1992.

61. Salvadoran politicians did not understand the conditions under which most Salvadorans lived any more than the U.S. politicians did, one trainer argues. "Neither had a clue about what the campesino [peasant] thought, needed or wanted." Francisco Pedrozo, email message to author, April 5, 2010. The rich were oblivious to conditions in the countryside, according to Capt. Emilio Gonzalez, USA, interview by Col. Hershel Webb, USA, November 3, 1987, El Salvador Papers, Oral History, Gonzalez-Waghelstein, box 1 of 6, Proj. 88-1, MHI. Gonzalez was the assistant army attaché at the embassy from January to December 1984.

62. Wood, *Forging Democracy from Below*, 32.

63. James Corum, "The Air War in El Salvador," *Air Power Journal*, Summer 1998, 27–44, 40.

64. John T. Fishel and Max G. Manwaring, *Uncomfortable Wars Revisited* (Norman: University of Oklahoma Press, 2006), 111–112, 114.

65. Angel Rabasa et al., *Money in the Bank: Lessons Learned from Past Counterinsurgency (COIN) Operations* (Santa Monica, CA: RAND, 2007), 45.

66. Stanley, *Protection Racket State*, 3.

67. McClintock, *Revolutionary Movements*, 114, 117.

68. Stanley, *Protection Racket State*, 210, 198.

69. Mario Menendez Rodriguez, *Voices from El Salvador* (San Francisco: Solidarity, 1983), 83. Members of the clergy were targeted because a reformist element within the church, led by Archbishop Romero until his assassination, called for an end to the violence and greater social justice.

70. Stanley, *Protection Racket State*, 1, 20.

71. Duarte, *My Story*, 161.

72. Stanley, *Protection Racket State*, 178.

73. Stanley, 210.

74. Gerry E. Studds, *Central America 1981: Report to the Committee on Foreign Affairs, U.S. House of Representatives* (Washington, DC: U.S. Government Printing Office, 1981), 26–29.

75. Danner, *Massacre at El Mozote*, 108; Binford, *El Mozote Massacre*, 151–152.

76. Commission on the Truth for El Salvador, *From Madness to Hope: The 12-Year War in El Salvador—Report of the Commission on the Truth for El Salvador* (Washington, DC: U.S. Institute of Peace, March 15, 1993), 26–27, https://www.usip.org/publications/1992/07/truth-commission-el-salvador.

77. Max Manwaring, interview by author, March 11, 2010, Carlisle, PA. Manwaring, a retired U.S. Army officer, served at U.S. Southern Command during the war and has conducted extensive research and interviews on El Salvador for the army.

78. Terry Karl, "Imposing Consent? Electoralism vs. Democratization in El Salvador," in *Elections and Democratization in Latin America, 1980–1985*, ed. Paul W. Drake and Eduardo Silva (San Diego: Center for Iberian and Latin American Studies, University of California, San Diego, 1986), 9–36; Stanley, *Protection Racket State*, 229–230; Manwaring, interview by author.

79. Hamilton, interview by author.

80. Gonzalez, interview by Webb.

81. Luis Orlando Rodriguez, phone interview by author, April 21, 2010. Rodriguez spent most of the 1980s working on El Salvador for the U.S. government.

82. Ernesto, email message to author, April 21, 2010, translated, as are all emails with Salvadoran officials and insurgents, by Rodrigo Javier Massi.

83. Rodriguez, interview by author.

84. Andrew J. Bacevich et al., *American Military Policy in Small Wars: The Case of El Salvador* (Washington, DC: Pergamon-Brassey's, 1988), 27–28, 37.

85. Ratterree, email message to author.

86. Rodriguez, interview by author.

87. Duarte, *My Story*, 161.

88. Williams and Walter, *Militarization and Demilitarization*, 130–131.

89. Montgomery, *Revolution in El Salvador*, 152, citing Carlos Ramos, "Puedo bombardear zonas donde hay subversivos," *La Jornada* (Mexico), January 19, 1985.

90. Clements, *Witness to War*, 218.

91. Danner, *Massacre at El Mozote*, 44, 52.

92. Binford, *El Mozote Massacre*, 22–24.

93. Raymond Bonner, *Weakness and Deceit: U.S. Policy and El Salvador* (New York: Times Books, 1984), 339.

94. Clements, *Witness to War*, 1–6, 194–195.

95. Henry Ramirez, interview by author, May 17, 2010, Fort Bragg, NC. Ramirez, a retired U.S. Army officer, trained Salvadoran forces in Panama in 1982, trained the first Patrullas de Reconocimiento de Alcance Largo [Long Range Reconnaissance Patrols, PRALs] in 1982–1983, and was a military adviser in Chalatenango in 1987–1988.

96. Francisco Pedrozo, email interview with author, April 1, 2010; Arie Bogaard, U.S. military advisory group commander at time of interview, phone interview by author, March 24, 2010.

97. Byrne, *El Salvador's Civil War*, 157.

98. Randolph Harrison, "Salvador Rebels Lose Advantage, Government Improves Battle Tactics, Air Force," *Orlando Sentinel*, May 7, 1986, https://www.orlandosentinel.com/news/os-xpm-1986-05-07-0220130229-story.html.

99. Col. Leopoldo Antonio Hernandez, "Civil Military Operations El Salvador," SWORD paper, February 17, 1988, Small Wars Operations Requirements Division J-5 Directorate, USSOUTHCOM, MHI, 10–12.

100. Manwaring, interview by author.

101. Waghelstein, interview by Carlton, 113.

102. Williams and Walter, *Militarization and Demilitarization*, 144.

103. Rodriguez, interview by author.

104. Pickering, interview by Manwaring.

105. The so-called big *tanda*, or cohort, from the military academy.

106. Gen. René Emilio Ponce, former defense minister, email message to author, April 20, 2010.

107. Gen. Alvaro Antonio Calderón Hurtado, email message to author, April 18, 2010. Calderón, a former chief of the General Staff, notes that counterinsurgency requires the use of small units, and under such conditions, control of troops is more difficult and thus excessive force may be more likely to occur.

108. Ponce, email message to author.

109. Gen. Mauricio Vargas, former deputy chief of the General Staff, email message to author, April 17, 2010.

110. On El Salvador as a model, see, for example, Conrad C. Crane, the lead author of the U.S. Army's 2006 counterinsurgency manual, email to author, September 29, 2010; Steven Metz, *Learning from Iraq: Counterinsurgency in American Strategy* (Carlisle, PA: Strategic Studies Institute, January 2007); Christopher Paul, Colin P. Clarke, and Beth Grill, *Victory Has a Thousand Fathers: Sources of Success in Counterinsurgency* (Santa Monica, CA: RAND, 2010); and Rabasa et al., *Money in the Bank*.

111. See, for example, Williams and Walter, *Militarization and Demilitarization*; Karl, "Imposing Consent?"; Bianca Vaz Mondo, "Transitions to Good Governance: The Case of El Salvador" (ERCAS Working Paper No. 24, European Research Center for Anti-corruption and State-Building, Berlin, January 2001), https://www.againstcorruption.eu/publications/transitions-to-good-governance-the-case-of-el-salvador/; William Deane Stanley, "El Salvador: State-Building before and after Democratization, 1980–1995," *Third World Quarterly* 27, no. 1 (2006): 101–114, https://doi.org/10.1080/01436590500369311; Margaret Popkin, *Peace without Justice: Obstacles to Building the Rule of Law in El Salvador* (University Park: Pennsylvania State University Press, 2000), x; Roland Paris, *At War's End: Building Peace after Civil Conflict* (Cambridge: Cambridge University Press, 2004); and Paige, *Coffee and Power*.

112. Rabasa et al., *Money in the Bank*, xii, xv.

113. Paul, Clarke, and Grill, *Victory*, 13.

114. Metz, *Learning from Iraq*, 10.

115. Corum, "Air War in El Salvador," 30, 35–36, 38.

116. Fishel and Manwaring, *Uncomfortable Wars Revisited*, 111.

117. William M. LeoGrande, "A Splendid Little War: Drawing the Line in El Salvador," *International Security* 6, no. 1 (Summer 1981): 27–52.

118. T. David Mason and Dale A. Krane, "The Political Economy of Death Squads: Toward a Theory of the Impact of State-Sanctioned Terror," *International Studies Quarterly* 33, no. 2 (June 1989): 175–198, https://doi.org/10.2307/2600536; Burgerman, "First Do No Harm"; Mark Peceny and William D. Stanley, "Counterinsurgency in El Salvador," *Politics and Society* 38, no. 1 (2010): 67–94; Timothy Wickham-Crowley, "Understanding Failed Revolution in El Salvador: A Comparative Analysis of Regime Types and Social Structures," *Politics and Society* 17, no. 4 (1989): 511–537, https://doi.org/10.1177/003232928901700404.

119. Byrne, *El Salvador's Civil War*, 157, quoting Marta Harnecker, "La propuesta del FMLN: Un desafío a la estrategia contrainsurgente," entrevista a Joaquin Villalobos (25 de Febrero de 1989), *Estudios Centroamericanos* 485 (March 1989): 213.

120. Karl, "Imposing Consent?"; McClintock, *Revolutionary Movements*, 120–128; Enrique Baloyra, "Elections, Civil War, and Transition in El Salvador, 1982–1994: A Preliminary Evaluation," in *Elections and Democracy in Central America, Revisited*, ed. Mitchell A. Seligson and John A. Booth (Chapel Hill: University of North Carolina Press, 1995), 45–65, 59.

121. Karl argues that "'demonstration' elections can . . . ratify existing power arrangements." "Imposing Consent?," 9.

122. McClintock, *Revolutionary Movements*, 128. Karl, "Imposing Consent?," argues that enduring political democracy rests on "agreements regarding the permanent rules governing the competition for public office; the resolution of conflict; the reproduction of capital; and the appropriate role of the state, particularly the military and the bureaucracy," 10. None of these conditions was present in El Salvador throughout the war, though Karl argues that the 1982 Assembly elections, the 1984 presidential elections, and the 1985 legislative elections did evolve into something more than "demonstration" exercises but less than examples of durable democratization.

123. Baloyra, "Elections," 59; McClintock, *Revolutionary Movements*, 120–125.

124. McClintock, *Revolutionary Movements*, 124–125.

125. Schwarz, *American Counterinsurgency Doctrine*, 59.

126. Duarte, *My Story*, 231.

127. McClintock, *Revolutionary Movements*, 112.

128. Support for ARENA and the military party, the National Conciliation Party, was strongest in areas under military control. Karl, "Imposing Consent?"

129. Stanley, *Protection Racket State*, 232–233.

130. Williams and Walter, *Militarization and Demilitarization*, 121.

131. Wood, *Forging Democracy from Below*, 49. Elisabeth Jean Wood, *Insurgent Collective Action and Civil War in El Salvador* (New York: Cambridge University Press, 2003), analyzes this phenomenon in detail.

132. McClintock, *Revolutionary Movements*, 95.

133. Wood, *Forging Democracy from Below*, 45–46.

134. Duarte, *My Story*, 132. See Daron Acemoglu and James A. Robinson, "Persistence of Power, Elites, and Institutions," *American Economic Review* 98, no. 1 (2008): 267–293, on the concept of captured democracy.

135. Williams and Walter, *Militarization and Demilitarization*, 114–115.

136. Richard Stahler-Sholk, "El Salvador's Negotiated Transition: From Low-Intensity Conflict to Low-Intensity Democracy," *Journal of Interamerican Studies and World Affairs* 36, no. 4 (Winter, 1994): 1–59, 3, https://doi.org/10.2307/166318.

137. Wood, *Forging Democracy from Below*, 45–46.

138. Duarte, *My Story*, 132.

139. "President Magaña was consulted but President Magaña, in my opinion, did not rule." Gonzalez, interview by Webb, 14.

140. McClintock, *Revolutionary Movements*, 153.

141. Williams and Walter, *Militarization and Demilitarization*, 118.

142. Stanley, *Protection Racket State*, 283; Schwarz, *American Counterinsurgency Doctrine*, 59.

143. Duarte, *My Story*, 132, 180.

144. Terry Karl, "Exporting Democracy: U.S. Electoral Policy in El Salvador," in *Crisis in Central America: Regional Dynamics and U.S. Policy in the 1980s* , ed. Nora Hamilton et al. (Boulder, CO: Westview Press, 1988), 173–192; Williams and Walter, *Militarization and Demilitarization*, 139.

145. Duarte, *My Story*, 171–172.

146. Karl, "Imposing Consent?"

147. Studds, *Central America 1981*, 23.

148. Williams and Walter, *Militarization and Demilitarization*, 147.

149. Schwarz, *American Counterinsurgency Doctrine*, 44.

150. Alberto Vargas, *El Salvador Country Brief: Property Rights and Land Markets* (Madison: Land Tenure Center, University of Wisconsin–Madison, March 2003); Peter Shiras, "The False Promise—and Real Violence—of Land Reform in El Salvador," in Gettleman et al., *El Salvador*, 63–70, 163–167; Williams and Walter, *Militarization and Demilitarization*, 106; Schwarz, *American Counterinsurgency Doctrine*, 47–48; Duryea, interview by Bedard and Vasquez, 66–67.

151. Pickering, interview by Manwaring, 60. Mitchell A. Seligson, in "Thirty Years of Transformation in the Agrarian Structure of El Salvador," *Latin American Research Review* 30, no. 3 (1995): 43–74, https://www.jstor.org/stable/2503979, argues that land reform during the war did provide popular benefits. This point is inarguable. For the purpose of this analysis, the question is to what degree land reform may have driven counterinsurgent success. Because peasants continued supporting the insurgency, more so than any other class, throughout the war, it is difficult to argue that land reform as enacted or as a promise for the future helped gain support for the government.

152. McClintock, *Revolutionary Movements*, 175; Leonel Gomez, "El Salvador's Land Reform: A Real Promise, but a Final Failure," in Gettleman et al., *El Salvador*, 178–181; Schwarz, *American Counterinsurgency Doctrine*, 48.

153. William C. Thiesenhusen, *Trends in Land Tenure Issues in Latin America: Experiences and Recommendations for Development Cooperation* (Eschborn, Germany: Deutsche Gesellschaft für Technische Zusammenarbeit, 1996), cited in Vargas, *El Salvador Country Brief*, 10.

154. Schwarz, *American Counterinsurgency Doctrine*, 48, citing a UN study.

155. The land reform plan announced in March 1980 was to take place in three stages: In Phase I, the state would take over all holdings of 500 hectares (1,235 acres, 5 square kilometers) or more to form agricultural cooperatives. This phase included about 16 percent of all agricultural land. In Phase II, holdings between 150 hectares (370 acres, 1.5 square kilometers) and 500 hectares would be taken over for co-ops. This represented 23 percent of agricultural land. In Phase III, the "land to the tiller" phase, farmers of rented and sharecropped plots up to 7 hectares (17 acres, 0.07 square kilometers) would be allowed to apply to purchase the land. Landholders were to be compensated with cash and bonds. But in May 1980, the Right ended Phase I appropriations and suspended Phase II. It was the second phase of the plan that would have broken up most of El Salvador's coffee farms, the heart of the oligarchy's agricultural wealth. Phase I lands were mostly used for cotton, cane, and cattle, and up to 60 percent of them were fallow or unusable for anything but grazing. See Shiras, "False Promise," 163–167; and Williams and Walter, *Militarization and Demilitarization*, 106.

156. Schwarz, *American Counterinsurgency Doctrine*, 45–46.

157. Williams and Walter, *Militarization and Demilitarization*, 106.

158. Gomez, "El Salvador's Land Reform," 178–181.

159. Shiras, "False Promise," 169.

160. McClintock, *Revolutionary Movements*, 176.

161. Schwarz, *American Counterinsurgency Doctrine*, 45–46, 79–80.

162. Cited in Schwartz, 47.

163. Jeffrey Cole, email message to author, April 4, 2010; Ramirez, interview by author. Cole, a retired U.S. Marine, was an adviser in Usulután in 1985–1986 and served as military attaché in San Salvador in 1990–1992.

164. Bogaard, interview by author.

165. Manwaring, interview by author.

166. Kalev Sepp, "The Evolution of United States Military Strategy in Central America, 1979–1991" (PhD diss., Harvard University History Department, February 2002), 50; Williams and Walter, *Militarization and Demilitarization*, 118–119.

167. Sepp, "Evolution," 134.

168. Williams and Walter, *Militarization and Demilitarization*, 119–120.

169. Gonzalez, interview by Webb, 42.

170. Ernesto, email message to author.

171. Gonzalez, interview by Webb, 115.

172. Bogaard, interview by author. Even today, while most towns have electricity and there are some paved roads, there is little infrastructure or health care and education is mostly only through sixth grade.

173. Montgomery, *Revolution in El Salvador*, 215.

174. Schwarz, *American Counterinsurgency Doctrine*, 47; Stanley, "El Salvador."

175. Stanley, *Protection Racket State*, 234–240; Charles D. Brockett, *Political Movements and Violence in Central America* (New York: Cambridge University Press, 2005), 249.

176. Williams and Walter, *Militarization and Demilitarization*, 9–10.

177. McClintock, *Revolutionary Movements*, 85. In the FMLN's November Final Offensive, it attacked multiple sites inside the capital and other cities, helping convince the United States and the Salvadoran military that they could not achieve a battlefield victory. The offensive required smuggling more than one thousand fighters and their materiel into San Salvador. "There was a torrent of arms and ammunition into the capital. That couldn't have taken place had not a lot of people helped, or at the minimum, kept quiet," one U.S. administration official said. Schwarz, *American Counterinsurgency Doctrine*, 13n24, quoting Ricardo Chivera, "The Sheraton Siege," *Time*, December 12, 1989, 51.

178. McClintock, *Revolutionary Movements*, 154, 150.

179. Hamilton, interview by author.

180. McClintock, *Revolutionary Movements*, 154.

181. Sepp, "Evolution," 188, 189.

182. Williams and Walter, *Militarization and Demilitarization*, 151.

183. McClintock, *Revolutionary Movements*, 154.

184. Hamilton, interview by author. Álvaro de Soto, mediator of the peace talks, argues that by 1989 the FMLN was no longer fighting to take power but rather was fighting to leverage political change. See de Soto, "Ending Violent Conflict in El Salvador," in *Herding Cats: Multiparty Mediation in a Complex World*, ed. Chester A. Crocker, Fen Osler Hampson, and Pamela Aall (Washington, DC: U.S. Institute of Peace, 1999), 345–386.

185. Stanley, *Protection Racket State*, 7; Stanley, "El Salvador."

186. Stanley, *Protection Racket State*, 218. Up to 20 percent of this new force was to come from the FMLN, 20 percent from former National Police agents who could pass admission tests and screening for abuses, and 60 percent from civilians who had played no role in the war. Responsibility for domestic intelligence was taken over by a new civilian agency. Military officers with a record of brutality or corruption were to be purged and a UN Truth Commission and human rights ombudsman were to investigate abuses. Ultimately, 103 senior officers were purged.

187. Stanley, *Protection Racket State*, 220.

188. Sepp, "Evolution," 224.

189. Hamilton, interview by author.

190. Karl, "Imposing Consent?," 27, citing a 1983 study.

191. Calderón, email message to author; emphasis in original.

192. Williams and Walter, *Militarization and Demilitarization*, 115.

193. Memorandum, Subject: Assessing the Judicial Process in El Salvador, December 18, 1989, "CIA Doc's [*sic*] Vol. 1," box 24, unpublished material on El Salvador, El Salvador 2 Collection, National Security Archive, Washington, DC.

194. Vaz Mondo, "Transitions to Good Governance."

195. Stanley, "El Salvador," 111; Popkin, *Peace without Justice*, x.

196. Paris, *At War's End*, 122–128.

197. Paige, *Coffee and Power*, 13.

198. Stahler-Sholk, "El Salvador's Negotiated Transition."

199. Rabasa et al., *Money in the Bank*, 43, 44–45.

200. Karl, "Imposing Consent?"

201. Hy Rothstein, phone interview by author, April 14, 2010. Rothstein, a retired U.S. Army officer, was senior military adviser in San Miguel in 1987–1989 and served in El Salvador in the mid-1980s and in 1991–1992.

202. Waghelstein, interview by Carlton, 77.

203. James Roach, phone interview by author, March 24, 2010. Roach, a retired army colonel, was U.S. military chief of operational planning and training teams from 1984 to 1986.

204. McClintock, *Revolutionary Movements*, 231n183. The author notes that it is remarkable for 139 of 621 respondents to openly criticize soldiers to an interviewer in the wartime atmosphere of 1991.

205. Pickering, interview by Manwaring, 8.

206. Williams and Walter, *Militarization and Demilitarization*, 121.

207. Williams and Walter, 120; Col. Leopoldo Antonio Hernandez, "Civil Military Operations El Salvador," SWORD paper, February 17, 1988, Small Wars Operations Requirements Division J-5 Directorate, USSOUTHCOM, Military History Institute, Carlisle, PA, 16, reports an estimated sixty thousand men in civil defense units, about half of them certified by U.S. advisers.

208. Bogaard, interview by author.

209. Roach, interview by author.

210. Waghelstein, interview by Carlton, 77.

211. Higgins, interview by author.

212. Francisco Pedrozo, email message to author, April 6, 2010.

213. The increase in popular participation in politics grew from the organizational efforts of, first, the liberation theology priests and laypeople who helped peasants build community organizations in the countryside in the 1970s, and second, the local shadow governments formed in FMLN-controlled territory during the conflict. It is also interesting that throughout the war the Salvadoran military and the FMLN were both quite democratic in their internal deliberations. Both groups held long meetings to debate courses of action and sought consensus on decisions. See Montgomery, *Revolution in El Salvador*, 86–99, 120–123; Shaull, *Tortillas, Beans, and M-16s*, 13, 23–25; McClintock, *Revolutionary Movements*, 56; and Duarte, *My Story*, 257–258. Commanders and officers "were only able to rule by consensus, each depending on the other and on subordinates for support. The system survived because junior officers lent their support to the system with the hope that when their time came they would get theirs." Francisco Pedrozo, email message to author, April 3, 2010.

214. Paris, *At War's End*, 122–128.

215. U.S. military officer with years of experience in El Salvador, phone interview with author. William Deane Stanley notes that El Salvador's justice system is equal to or better than those of its neighbors in terms of effectiveness, accountability, and transparency. Stanley, "El Salvador," 111–112.

216. United Nations, Millennium Development Goals Indicators, accessed January 20, 2010, http://mdgs.un.org/unsd/mdg/Data.aspx.

217. Jacqueline L. Hazelton, "Take the Money and Run" (Discussion Paper 2017-03, International Security Program, Belfer Center for Science and International Affairs, Harvard Kennedy School, September 2017), https://www.belfercenter.org/publication/take-money-and-run.

6. How Much Does the Compellence Theory Explain? Turkey and the PKK

1. The Kemalist state did retain control over the official practice of Islam through the Directorate of Religious Affairs.

2. Henri J. Barkey and Graham E. Fuller, *Turkey's Kurdish Question* (New York: Rowman and Littlefield, 1998), 142. In the period after that which I examine, the role of Islam in private and public life has taken on greater salience with the rise of Islamist parties.

3. Barkey and Fuller, 14–16, 61–64.

4. Henri J. Barkey, "Turkey and the PKK: A Pyrrhic Victory?," in *Democracy and Counterterrorism: Lessons from the Past*, edited by Robert J. Art and Louise Richardson, (Washington, DC: U.S. Institute of, 2007), 343–382, 354; Evren Balta, "Causes and Consequences of the Vil-

lage Guard System in Turkey" (unpublished manuscript, December 2004); Ahmet Sozen, "Terrorism and the Politics of Anti-terrorism in Turkey," in *National Counter-terrorism Strategies*, ed. R. W. Orttung and A. Makarychev (Amsterdam: IOS, 2006), 131–144. Gülistan Gürbey identifies constraints on minority identities, illiberal aspects of Turkish law relating to Kurdish identity, and the role of the military in national politics in "The Development of the Kurdish Nationalism Movement in Turkey since the 1980s," in *The Kurdish National Movement in the 1990s: Its Impact on Turkey and the Middle East*, ed. Robert W. Olsen (Lexington: University Press of Kentucky, 1996), 9–37.

5. Barkey and Fuller, *Turkey's Kurdish Question*, 62–63.

6. Paul J. White, *Primitive Rebels or Revolutionary Modernizers? The Kurdish National Movement in Turkey* (New York: Zed Books, 2000), 43.

7. Matthew Kocher, "The Decline of the PKK and the Viability of a One-State Solution in Turkey," *International Journal on Multicultural Societies* 4, no. 1 (2002): 1–20, 2.

8. Svante E. Cornell, "The Kurdish Question in Turkish Politics," *Orbis* 45, no. 1 (Winter 2001): 31–46, 37, https://doi.org/10.1016/S0030-4387(00)00056-9.

9. Barkey and Fuller, *Turkey's Kurdish Question*, 190, 14, 71, 73, 101, 103, 194.

10. White, *Primitive Rebels?*, 135.

11. Michael M. Gunter, "The Continuing Kurdish Problem in Turkey after Ocalan's Capture," *Third World Quarterly* 21, no. 5 (October 2000): 849–869, 853, https://doi.org/10.1080/713701074.

12. Barkey and Fuller, *Turkey's Kurdish Question*, 15.

13. Barkey and Fuller, 23; Gokhan Bacik and Bezen Balamir Coskun, "The PKK Problem: Explaining Turkey's Failure to Develop a Political Solution," *Studies in Conflict and Terrorism* 34, no. 3 (February 2011): 248–265, 251, https://doi.org/10.1080/1057610X.2011.545938.

14. Zuhal Ay Hamdan, "The Governmental Policies and Military Methods against the PKK in the 1990s" (MS thesis, Middle East Studies, Graduate School of Social Sciences, Middle East Technical University, December 2009), 19.

15. Barkey and Fuller, *Turkey's Kurdish Question*, 28.

16. Barkey and Fuller, 28, 47, 116.

17. Barkey and Fuller, *Turkey's Kurdish Question*, 40.

18. Cornell, " Kurdish Question in Turkish Politics," 40.

19. Cornell, 41.

20. Michael P. Roth and Murat Sever, "The Kurdish Workers Party (PKK) as Criminal Syndicate: Funding Terrorism through Organized Crime, a Case Study," *Studies in Conflict and Terrorism* 30, no. 10 (2007): 901–920, 906, https://doi.org/10.1080/10576100701558620.

21. Cornell, " Kurdish Question in Turkish Politics," 42.

22. Barkey and Fuller, *Turkey's Kurdish Question*, 30.

23. Michael M. Gunter, "Transnational Sources of Support for the Kurdish Insurgency in Turkey," *Conflict Quarterly*, Spring 1991, 7–29, 12.

24. Barkey and Fuller, *Turkey's Kurdish Question*, 133. Also see, for example, David Romano, "Iraqi Kurdistan and Turkey: Temporary Marriage?," *Middle East Policy* 22, no. 1 (Spring 2015): 89–101, https://mepc.org/iraqi-kurdistan-and-turkey-temporary-marriage, for the more recent power shift from the Kemalist military toward Prime Minister and now President Reycep Tayyip Erdogon and his Justice and Development Party.

25. Barkey and Fuller, *Turkey's Kurdish Question*, 143–145, 188, 113, 134–139.

26. Hamdan, "Governmental Policies," 21, 222–223.

27. I code the war as ending in 1999 with Ocalan's capture. The renewed violence after 2004 and then 2007 involves splinters and realignments within the PKK, as well as the opening of the Turkey-Iraq border after the U.S. and partner invasion of Iraq in 2003. The PKK officially renewed its struggle in 2004. The best estimated death toll dropped dramatically from 1,399 in 1999 to 174 in 2000, stayed in the double digits until 2004, then began rising precipitously again in 2007. See Uppsala Conflict Data Project, Government of Turkey-PKK dyad data, accessed May 29, 2020, https://ucdp.uu.se/#/additionalinfo/781/4. On the role of the U.S. invasion of Iraq and the formation of the Kurdish Regional Government in Iraq in reinvigorating the PKK and driving it back into Turkey, see Mustafa Gürbüz, *Rival Kurdish Movements in Turkey: Transforming Ethnic Conflict* (Amsterdam: Amsterdam University Press, 2016), 58–59. On the reformulation of the

PKK after 1999, see Ahmet H. Akkaya and Joost Jongerden, "The PKK in the 2000s: Continuity through Breaks?," in *Nationalism and Politics in Turkey: Political Islam, Kemalism, and the Kurdish Issue*, ed. Marlies Casier and Joost Jongerden (New York: Routledge, 2011), 143–162.

28. Barkey and Fuller, *Turkey's Kurdish Question*, 197; Joost Jongerden, "Village Evacuation and Reconstruction in Kurdistan (1993–2002)," *Etudes rural* 186 (February 2010): 77–100, 81, https://doi.org/10.4000/etudesrurales.9241.

29. Jongerden, "Village Evacuation," 80–81.

30. Henri J. Barkey and Graham E. Fuller, "Turkey's Kurdish Question: Critical Turning Points and Missed Opportunities," *Middle East Journal* 51, no. 1 (Winter 1997): 59–79, 77, https://www.jstor.org/stable/4329023. On the question of democratic regime type, the military issued strong recommendations to the government in 1997 but did not take control.

31. Human Rights Watch, *Weapons Transfers and Violations of the Laws of War in Turkey* (New York: Human Rights Watch, 1995), 35; Barkey and Fuller, *Turkey's Kurdish Question*, 122, 125, 131n67; Martin van Bruinessen, "Turkey's Death Squads," in "Turkey: Insolvent Ideologies, Fractured State," special issue, *Middle East Report* 199 (April–June 1996): 20–23, https://www.jstor.org/stable/3012887.

32. Hamdan, "Governmental Policies," 84.

33. Aliza Marcus, *Blood and Belief: The PKK and the Turkish Fight for Independence* (New York: New York University Press, 2007), 308–310.

34. U.S. Government Interagency Counterinsurgency Initiative, *U.S. Government Counterinsurgency Guide* (Washington, DC: U.S. Government Printing Office, 2009), 4.

35. Turkey, during this period keenly interested in joining the European Union, made promises of liberalization to external actors in trying to advance that goal.

36. Christopher Paul, Colin P. Clarke, and Beth Grill, *Victory Has a Thousand Fathers: Sources of Success in Counterinsurgency* (Santa Monica, CA: RAND, 2010), 16.

37. Tamar Gabelnick, William D. Hartung, and Jennifer Washburn, *Arming Repression: U.S. Arms Sales to Turkey during the Clinton Administration*, Joint Report of the World Policy Institute and the Federation of American Scientists (October 1999), https://fas.org/asmp/library/reports/turkeyrep.htm.

38. For example, an editorial in the *New York Times*, "America Arms Turkey's Repression," on October 17, 1995, condemned the "brutal" campaign that "betrays America's values." The U.S. Department of State condemned Turkey's "serious human rights abuses" in its *Turkey Country Report on Human Rights Practices for 1996* (Bureau of Democracy, Human Rights, and Labor, January 30, 1997), http://www.hri.org/docs/USSD-Rights/96/Turkey96.html.

39. Ted Galen Carpenter, "U.S. Policy toward Turkey: A Study in Double Standards," HR-Net Forum, January 1991, http://www.hri.org/forum/intpol/carpenter.html.

40. Özlem Kayhan Pusane, "Turkey's Military Victory over the PKK and Its Failure to End the PKK Insurgency," *Middle Eastern Studies* 51, no. 5 (2015): 727–741, 729, https://doi.org/10.1080/00263206.2014.979801.

41. Aysegul Aydin and Cem Emrence, *Zones of Rebellion: Kurdish Insurgents and the Turkish State* (Ithaca, NY: Cornell University Press, 2015), 8, 111.

42. Barkey and Fuller, *Turkey's Kurdish Question*, 140.

43. Bacik and Coskun, "PKK Problem," 251.

44. Hamdan, "Governmental Policies," 63.

45. White, *Primitive Rebels?*, 143, citing U.S. Department of State figures.

46. Barkey and Fuller, *Turkey's Kurdish Question*, 26.

47. Marcus, *Blood and Belief*, 240.

48. Ahmet S. Yayla and Samih Teymur, "How Did Change Help the Country of Turkey Deal with Terrorism More Effectively?," in *The Ethics of Terrorism: Innovative Approaches from an International Perspective*, ed. Thomas Albert Gilly, Yakov Gilinskiy, and Vladimir A. Sergevnin (Springfield, IL: Charles C. Thomas, 2009), 101–113, 105. The authors' figures are from the Turkish National Police and may include non-PKK violence. The PKK was the largest active violent nonstate group in Turkey at the time, making these figures illustrative if not precise.

49. White, *Primitive Rebels?*, 165.

50. Hamdan, "Governmental Policies," 185.
51. Human Rights Watch, *Weapons Transfers*, 128.
52. Hamdan, "Governmental Policies," 19–20.
53. Michael Radu, "The Rise and Fall of the PKK," *Orbis* 45, no. 1 (Winter 2001): 47–63, 57.
54. Barkey and Fuller, *Turkey's Kurdish Question*, 140.
55. Hamdan, "Governmental Policies," 169, 199–203.
56. Hamdan, 150. Turkish military accounts may not be precisely reliable, but they suggest that the PKK was paying high costs.
57. Kocher, "Decline of the PKK," 8.
58. Aydin and Emrence, *Zones of Rebellion*, 114.
59. Radu, "Rise and Fall of the PKK," 47.
60. Hamdan, "Governmental Policies," 213, 223.
61. White, *Primitive Rebels?*, 22.
62. Barkey and Fuller, *Turkey's Kurdish Question*, 71.
63. Hamdan, "Governmental Policies," 23.
64. Balta, "Causes and Consequences," 10–11.
65. The use of Kurds against Kurds ostensibly supports the argument that the use of coethnics is more effective in counterinsurgency, but the village guards were still widely hated in the southeast, and regular troops performed village clearance and destruction duties. Given the evidence available, it is difficult to argue that the use of village guards lessened popular resistance to the state. Jason Lyall makes the argument that the use of coethnics in counterinsurgency helps the government. See Jason Lyall, "Are Coethnics More Effective Counterinsurgents? Evidence from the Second Chechen War," *American Political Science Review* 104, no. 1 (February 2010): 1–20, https://doi.org/10.1017/S0003055409990323.
66. Hamdan, "Governmental Policies," 24.
67. Human Rights Watch/Helsinki, *Turkey: Forced Displacement of Ethnic Kurds from Southeastern Turkey*, vol. 6, no. 12 (October 1994): 13n34, 26.
68. Balta, "Causes and Consequences," 19.
69. Barkey and Fuller, *Turkey's Kurdish Question*, 148.
70. Human Rights Watch, *Forced Displacement*, 16.
71. Barkey and Fuller, *Turkey's Kurdish Question*, 148.
72. Bacik and Coskun, "PKK Problem," 254.
73. Barkey and Fuller, *Turkey's Kurdish Question*, 72.
74. Balta, "Causes and Consequences," 19.
75. Human Rights Watch, *Forced Displacement*, 26.
76. Human Rights Watch, *Weapons Transfers*, 18; Aydin and Emrence, *Zones of Rebellion*, 104.
77. The village guards date back to 1924–1925 as a tool for the central government to both accommodate local elements and repress local rebellions. Janet Klein, *The Margins of Empire: Kurdish Militias in the Ottoman Tribal Zone* (Stanford, CA: Stanford University Press, 2011), 178–179.
78. Human Rights Watch, *Forced Displacement*, 16–17.
79. Human Rights Watch, *Weapons Transfers*, 18, 35.
80. Klein, *Margins of Empire*, 180–181.
81. Cornell, "Kurdish Question in Turkish Politics," 39.
82. Balta, "Causes and Consequences," 11.
83. Henri J. Barkey and Graham E. Fuller, *Turkey's Kurdish Question* (New York: Rowman and Littlefield, 1998), 73.
84. Marcus, *Blood and Belief*, 262–264.
85. Bacik and Coskun, "PKK Problem," 253.
86. Barkey and Fuller, "Turkey's Kurdish Question," 68.
87. See Denise Natali, *The Kurds and the State: Evolving National Identity in Iraq, Turkey, and Iran* (Syracuse, NY: Syracuse University Press, 2005), 92–116, for a discussion of the lack of accommodation of Kurdish ethnic identity in Turkey.
88. White, *Primitive Rebels?*, 166.

89. Hamdan, "Governmental Policies," 20, 101, 104. The 360,000 figure includes 140,000–150,000 army, 10,000 air force, 40,000–50,000 gendarmerie, 40,000 police, and about 67,000 village guards, 20.

90. Bacik and Coskun, "PKK Problem," 255.

91. Jongerden, "Village Evacuation," 83.

92. Kocher, "Decline of the PKK," 14.

93. Barkey and Fuller, *Turkey's Kurdish Question*, 152–153n20.

94. Human Rights Watch, *Weapons Transfers*, 16, 15.

95. White, *Primitive Rebels?*, 167.

96. Jongerden, "Village Evacuation," 80.

97. Balta, "Causes and Consequences," 1n3.

98. White, *Primitive Rebels?*, 172; Hamdan, "Governmental Policies," 75.

99. Kocher, "Decline of the PKK," 7.

100. Human Rights Watch, *Weapons Transfers*, 16–17; Balta, "Causes and Consequences," 13.

101. Jongerden, "Village Evacuation," 89.

102. Aydin and Emrence, *Zones of Rebellion*, 84.

103. Joost Jongerden, Jacob van Etten, and Hugo de Vos, "Forest Burning as a Counterinsurgency Strategy in Eastern Turkey." Paper presented at the Kurdish Studies Conference, organized by the Kurdish Institute of Paris and Salahaddin University, Arbil, Iraqi Kurdistan, September 6 to September 9, 2006.

104. Hamdan, "Governmental Policies," 74.

105. Jongerden, "Village Evacuation," 89.

106. Aydin and Emrence, *Zones of Rebellion*, 112.

107. Human Rights Watch, *Weapons Transfers*, 32.

108. Barkey and Fuller, *Turkey's Kurdish Question*, 148.

109. Hamdan, "Governmental Policies," 21, 22.

110. Human Rights Watch, *Weapons Transfers*, 33.

111. Hamdan, "Governmental Policies," 23; Human Rights Watch, *Weapons Transfers*, 34.

112. Yayla and Teymur, "How Did Change?," 107–111.

113. Hamdan, "Governmental Policies," 21.

114. Human Rights Watch, *Weapons Transfers*, 31.

115. Cornell, "Kurdish Question in Turkish Politics," 45.

116. Barkey and Fuller, *Turkey's Kurdish Question*, 62–63.

117. Jongerden, "Village Evacuation," 91.

118. Aydin and Emrence, *Zones of Rebellion*, 101–102.

119. See, for example, Barkey and Fuller, *Turkey's Kurdish Question*, 113, 147–148, 107; Hamdan, "Governmental Policies," 136, 160; Barkey and Fuller, "Turkey's Kurdish Question"; and White, *Primitive Rebels?*, 40.

120. For example, Barkey and Fuller, *Turkey's Kurdish Question*, 135; Hamdan, "Governmental Policies," 54–57, 60–62, 69; Barkey and Fuller, "Turkey's Kurdish Question"; Michele Penner Angrist, "Turkey: Roots of the Turkish-Kurdish Conflict and Prospects for Constructive Reform," in *Federalism and Territorial Cleavages*, ed. Ugo M. Amoretti and Nancy Bermeo (Baltimore: Johns Hopkins University Press, 2004), 387–416, 387; and Veli Yadirgi, *The Political Economy of the Kurds of Turkey: From the Ottoman Empire to the Turkish Republic* (New York: Cambridge University Press, 2017), 221–223.

121. White, *Primitive Rebels?*, 170–171.

122. Pusane, "Turkey's Military Victory," 734.

123. Marcus, *Blood and Belief*, 251.

124. Pusane, "Turkey's Military Victory," 734; Marcus, *Blood and Belief*, 252.

125. Marcus, *Blood and Belief*, 245.

126. Human Rights Watch, *Weapons Transfers*, 19.

127. Barkey and Fuller, *Turkey's Kurdish Question*, 141.

128. David Romano, *The Kurdish National Movement: Opportunity, Mobilization, and Identity* (New York: Cambridge University Press, 2006), 255.

129. Barkey and Fuller, *Turkey's Kurdish Question*, 101–103.

130. Hamdan, "Governmental Policies," 105.
131. Barkey and Fuller, *Turkey's Kurdish Question*, 28, 47.
132. Barkey and Fuller, 40.
133. Barkey, "Turkey and the PKK," 356, 369; Barkey and Fuller, *Turkey's Kurdish Question*, 62–63.
134. Roth and Sever, "Kurdish Workers Party," 906.
135. Sozen, "Terrorism"; Cengîz Çandar, "The Kurdish Question: The Reasons and Fortunes of the 'Opening,'" *Insight Turkey* 11, no. 4 (2009): 13–19, 14; Barkey, "Turkey and the PKK,," 366.
136. Romano, "Iraqi Kurdistan and Turkey," 90.
137. Max Hoffman, "The State of the Turkish-Kurdish Conflict," Center for American Progress, August 12, 2019, https://www.americanprogress.org/issues/security/reports/2019/08/12/473508/state-turkish-kurdish-conflict/.
138. Kocher, "Decline of the PKK," 4.
139. Humeyra Pamuk, "A New Generation of Kurdish Militants Takes Fight to Turkey's Cities," Reuters, September 27, 2015, https://www.reuters.com/article/us-turkey-kurds-youth/a-new-generation-of-kurdish-militants-takes-fight-to-turkeys-cities-idUSKCN0RR0DS20150927.
140. Bacik and Coskun, "PKK Problem," 254.
141. Balta, "Causes and Consequences," 17.
142. Bacik and Coskun, "PKK Problem," 255.
143. Michiel Leezenberg, "The Ambiguities of Democratic Autonomy: The Kurdish Movement in Turkey and Rojava," *Southeast European and Black Sea Studies* 16, no. 4 (2016): 671–690, 679.
144. Ceylan Yeginsu, "Turkey's Campaign against Kurdish Militants Takes Toll on Civilians," *New York Times*, December 30, 2015, https://www.nytimes.com/2015/12/31/world/europe/turkey-kurds-pkk.html.

7. Counterinsurgency Success: Costs High and Rising

1. U.S. Government Interagency Counterinsurgency Initiative, *U.S. Government Counterinsurgency Guide* (Washington, DC: U.S. Government Printing Office, 2009), 4.
2. Jason Brownlee considers the record of U.S. intervention and state-building efforts and finds that local conditions preceding U.S. involvement play a significantly larger role in the outcome than do U.S. efforts. "It has done best where it has attempted less," he concludes in "Can America Nation-Build?," *World Politics* 59, no. 2 (January 2007): 340, https://doi.org/10.1353/wp.2007.0019.
3. The basic institutional responsibilities of the state include police, military, judiciary, education, and health. Andreas Wimmer and Conrad Schetter, "Putting State-Formation First: Some Recommendations for Reconstruction and Peace-Making in Afghanistan," *Journal of International Development* 15, no. 5 (2003): 525–539, https://doi.org/10.1002/jid.1002.
4. See Andrew Radin, *Institution Building in Weak States: The Primacy of Local Politics* (Washington, DC: Georgetown University Press, 2020).
5. Radin.
6. See Caitlin Talmadge, *The Dictator's Army* (Ithaca, NY: Cornell University Press, 2015).
7. Pierre Englebert and Denis M. Tull, "Postconflict Reconstruction in Africa: Flawed Ideas about Failed States," *International Security* 32, no. 4 (Spring 2008): 106–139, https://doi.org/10.1162/isec.2008.32.4.106.
8. See Douglas J. Macdonald, *Adventures in Chaos: American Intervention for Reform in the Third World* (Cambridge, MA: Harvard University Press, 1992); and D. Michael Shafer, *Deadly Paradigms: The Failure of U.S. Counterinsurgency Policy* (Princeton, NJ: Princeton University Press, 1988).
9. Brownlee, "Can America Nation-Build?"
10. This analysis does not consider the normative value of the governance approach or the wisdom of a decision to attempt to apply it in any specific conflict.

Index

INDEX

Hack, Karl, 31, 160n61
Hamilton, Mark, 108
Hernandez, Leopold Antonio, 116
High commissioner, Malaya, 36–38, 41,
    43–44
Hukbalahap, Huk, 7, 26, 29, 62–68, 71–80,
    90, 148, 150

institutions of government, 6, 8, 10, 12–13,
    15–16, 19, 27, 32, 40, 48–49, 53–58,
    63–70, 75–78, 80–81, 106–108, 109–125,
    128, 132–133, 138, 140–143, 150, 201n3

Komer, Robert, 39, 41–42, 46

land reform, 119, 122–123, 194n151,
    194n155. *See also* EDCOR
Lansdale, Edward, 74, 176n291
Lee, Henry S., 35
liberalism, 1–6, 8–10, 15, 19–20, 22, 24, 29,
    32–33, 38, 41–43, 46–48, 58–64, 74–78,
    83, 92, 97–104, 109, 112, 117–124,
    126–128, 134, 141–143, 145, 147–154

MacVeigh, Lincoln, 59
Magaña Borja, Álvaro Alfredo, 120–121
Magsaysay, Ramon, 64–65, 67–70, 72, 74–80,
    150
Malayan Emergency, 4, 7, 24, 25, 29–30,
    61–62, 80, 84, 105, 143–144, 148–150
    Alliance Party, 33, 44
    alternative explanations, 41–47
    background, 30–33
    elite accommodation, 35–38
    insurgency broken, 33–35
    Malayan Chinese Association (MCA),
        31–33, 35–38, 44–45
    New Villages, 32–33, 36–38, 40–42, 44–46
    popular support, 46–47
    reforms, 41–46
    United Malays National Organization
        (UMNO), 33, 35, 44
    use of force against civilians, 38–41
Malayan National Liberation Army
    (MNLA), 2, 30–34, 39–40, 42–47
Marshall, George C., 53, 59, 77
Marshall Plan, 48, 58
military, use of, 3–4, 6, 8–13, 15, 17–18,
    20–21, 23–24, 28, 148–154
    El Salvador, 27, 106–116, 118–126, 128–129
    Greece, 26, 48–51, 53–58, 61–62
    Malaya, 25, 32–35, 39–40, 42, 61
    Oman, 27, 83–99, 100–105
    Philippines, the, 26, 63–65, 68–75, 77,
        79–80
    Turkey, 28, 132–141, 142–146
military intervention, 2–4, 6, 10–12, 23, 106,
    148, 151–154

militias, 16, 21
    El Salvador, 110–112, 127
    Greece, 48–49, 51, 53–56
    Oman, firqats, 27, 84–90, 94, 102–104, 149
    Philippines, the, 65, 70–71
    Turkey, 28, 133, 135–138
Miller, Paul D., 10–12
modernization theory, 9, 12, 64, 83, 98, 130,
    157n18, 174n226
Mohammad Suhail, 89
Molina, Arturo Armondo, 107
Mussalam bin Tufl, 89

nationalism, 9, 11, 31, 46, 82
National Popular Liberation Army, 26,
    48–51, 62

Ocalan, Abdullah, 28, 131–133, 136, 141–142
Ochoa, Sigfried, 115
Oldman, Hugh, 87, 102
Onn Jaafar, 35, 38
Özal, Turgut, 133, 138, 140, 142

Paget, Julian, 41, 46
Papagos, Alexandros, 50, 53, 55
Partiya Karkeren Kurdistan (Kurdistan
    Workers' Party, PKK, Turkey), 7, 24,
    27–28, 130–146, 151
Perkins, Kenneth, 83, 92, 94, 103
the Philippines, 7, 11, 24–26, 28, 29–30,
    61–80, 84, 105, 117, 134, 144, 148, 150
    alternative explanations, 74–79
    background, 62–64
    elite accommodation, 68–69
    insurgency broken, 64–68
    popular support, 78–79
    reforms, 74–78
    uses of force against civilians, 69–73
Pickering, Thomas, 116
political order, 1–5, 10, 15, 20, 42–43, 47, 52,
    61, 78, 106, 121
political stability, 1, 15–16, 24, 26, 35, 47–48,
    59, 62, 64, 88, 90, 103, 148–149, 152,
    155n8
Pomeroy, William, 66
Ponce, René Emilio, 116–117, 125
public goods, 2, 8, 14, 17, 32, 92, 109, 123
Purdon, Corran, 85, 92–94, 101, 104

Qaboos bin Sa'id, 83, 85–92, 94–95, 97–104,
    150
Quirino, Elpidio, 67–68, 70, 74–77

Ramon Belloso Battalion, 116
Reagan, Ronald, 108–109, 121
reforms, 2, 5–6, 8–11, 13–15, 19–22, 24
    cases generally, 25, 84, 151–152
    El Salvador, 27, 106–113, 117–129